NEWTOWN PUBLIC LIBRARY
201 BISHOP HOLLOW ROAD
NEWTOWN SQUARE, PA 19073

COUSY

HIS LIFE, CAREER, AND THE
BIRTH OF BIG-TIME BASKETBALL

Bill Reynolds

Simon & Schuster
NEW YORK • LONDON • TORONTO • SYDNEY

SIMON & SCHUSTER
Rockefeller Center
1230 Avenue of the Americas
New York, NY 10020

Copyright © 2005 by Bill Reynolds
All rights reserved, including the right of reproduction
in whole or in part in any form.

SIMON & SCHUSTER and colophon are registered trademarks
of Simon & Schuster, Inc.

Designed by Paul Dippolito

Manufactured in the United States of America

1   3   5   7   9   10   8   6   4   2

Library of Congress Cataloging-in-Publication Data
Reynolds, Bill, 1945–
Cousy : his life, career, and the birth of big-time basketball / by Bill Reynolds
p. cm
ISBN 0-7432-5476-7
1. Cousy, Bob, 1928– 2. Basketball players—United States—Biography.
3. Boston Celtics (Basketball team)—History. I. Title.
GV884.C68R49 2005
796.323'092—dc22
[B]
2004052203

For information regarding special discounts for bulk purchases,
please contact Simon & Schuster Special Sales at 1-800-456-6798
or business@simonandschuster.com.

To my mother, Marion Coleman, who taught me about basketball, books, and everything else that was important.

And also to Donald "Dee" Rowe, friend to the Cooz, onetime coach to me. No one has ever loved the game more.

COUSY

Chapter One

You could buy a wool suit with two trousers for $49, and pork chops for 65 cents a pound. At the movies you could see *Lawrence of Arabia* and *To Kill a Mockingbird*. On television you could watch *Gunsmoke, Mission Impossible,* and *Peyton Place*. President John F. Kennedy was in Costa Rica to meet with leaders of Central American countries, and Willy Brandt, the mayor of West Berlin, was calling for the United States and the Soviet Union to meet in an attempt to lessen growing East-West tensions. A young singer named Barbra Streisand would end up with the album of the year.

It was March 17, 1963. St. Patrick's Day, in Boston, a city rich in history, but for all practical purposes a city as segregated as any in the country. It was a city where the travel brochures talked about Harvard, MIT, and the groves of academe, but the reality was strong ethnic neighborhoods that were almost like individual duchies, places where the values were all about turf and family, places where the Old World loomed heavy.

The fifties were over, the decade that ultimately would be remembered for its conformity and its repression, but in all the important ways the sixties hadn't started yet. No one had heard of the Beatles. Vietnam was off in the distance somewhere, some little place on the map few could locate. The Civil Rights Movement was still in its infancy, even though it had been nine years since Rosa Parks had refused to sit in the back of a Montgomery, Alabama, bus, and Martin Luther King's "I Have a Dream" speech in Washington was still five months away. The counterculture that would come to define the sixties was still a few years away. By its values, by its look, by its very texture, and in all the important ways, it was as if the fifties had never left.

It also was Bob Cousy's last home game in the Boston Garden.

Cousy had announced earlier in the year that this would be his last season. He was 34, and felt he had to position himself for the future, that it was time to get on with his life and make a living that had nothing to do with playing basketball. So even though he knew he was physically able to keep playing, he sensed it was better to leave while he was still near the top of his game, a time when fans would remember him as a great player, not someone on the downward slide, the rust all over his game, all about memories and yesterday's cheers. Maybe more important, he felt he could make money off his name if people remembered him fondly.

It was his 13th year in the National Basketball Association, and in the view of many, he was the reason there was still an NBA. He had been the most charismatic player in those early years, the first player to pass behind his back, throw no-look passes, the first to play with much of the flair that later would become so much a part of basketball. Through the first half of the fifties, particularly, he'd been almost universally hailed as professional basketball's greatest figure, a first-team All-NBA player 10 years in a row, the MVP of the 1957 season. He had led the NBA in assists for eight straight years, and played on six championship teams.

But it was more than just the stats.

Cousy was often called the Babe Ruth of basketball. In a sense, he was the first modern player, the flashy playmaker, the first improviser, the first player to look inside the boundaries of a basketball court and see endless possibilities, jazz musician as point guard. Watching him play was like watching a sneak preview of the game's future. During the fifties, before Bill Russell and Wilt Chamberlain came into the league, Cousy had been the biggest name in the NBA. Certainly, as the most charismatic player, and one of the few names that transcended basketball, he was known to the general public.

He was one of the first basketball players to do endorsements, one of the first to have his own basketball camp. He enjoyed the kind of celebrity that was unheard of for a basketball player in his era, often being called "Mr. Basketball."

But he had paid a price for that.

For years he had nightmares. Bill Sharman, who had roomed with him on the road for 10 years, used to say that it was not uncommon to wake up in the middle of the night and see Cousy walking around the hotel room speaking in French, although he hadn't spoken French since early childhood. As his career progressed these episodes had become more common. These nightmares eventually became so upsetting, so bizarre, complete with running out of his house one night and going down a road, that he'd gone to a psychiatrist, who told him he was having anxiety attacks and gave him medication for them. By the end of his career he had developed a nervous tic under his right eye, a physical manifestation of the pressure he felt.

His great fear was that he would somehow tarnish his reputation. He had worked a long time to establish it, 17 years if you counted his college career as well as his professional career, and he treated it as if it were a family heirloom.

"I always have been afraid that I would not be good enough," he would later say. "There was always the fear, before every game, that this would be the night it would all desert me, that this would be the game that everything would go bad and I would be out there, exposed and helpless."

For years he tried to analyze the apparent contradiction in his nature—fear, combined with confidence on the court. The trouble was he knew this only intellectually. Emotionally, the fear would grip him before every game, "The taste of fear comes back into my mouth and I have to suffer through it all over again."

Still, it's a contradiction that never left him.

"I'm 34 years old and I'm still a boy having to prove myself over again every time out," he said. "But if I've spent my life playing a boy's game, it's still what I do. And because it's what I do, I want to be the best. It's not enough to be good enough. It's not enough to be very good. I have to be the best because that's what it's all about."

This feeling had only intensified as his career wound down. He never had felt pressure when he'd been younger. He had had such confidence in his skills, was so sure of himself with the ball in his hands and the game on the line. But he had come to feel the pressure of trying to stay on top as new players, younger, kept coming at him, so now he felt like some old gunfighter standing in the middle of a dusty street in some Old West town taking on all the young guns. It had kept getting harder, and with that the pressure would envelop him, draining all the joy out of everything, for he knew he couldn't control his own destiny anymore, not the way he did when he was younger. His great, unspoken fear was that some father would be sitting in the Garden with his son saying, "There goes the best basketball player in the world," while he knew he no longer could perform at that level.

As he had grown older as a player, he also had come to resent the time he spent on the road. He hated the travel. He hated hotel rooms. He hated the endless waiting for the game to start. He hated his opponents. He hated the way he had to psych himself up for games, secluding himself, turning inward, eventually finding some dark place where he hated everything, including himself. He hated how depleted he felt when they were over, how completely drained. He hated the lifestyle of professional basketball. Most of all, he hated the time he spent away from his wife and their two young daughters. He had come to know that anything he missed could never be recaptured, that things you fail to do can never be made up.

He had come to realize that his daughters, now 11 and 12, were growing up and they were almost strangers to him, felt the guilt of knowing that his family's entire life always had revolved around his schedule, his games, his dreams, his life. He had come to know that life was all about priorities, and he was questioning his.

"My daughters would grow up and get married and what would I remember?" he once said. "A thousand hotel rooms?"

That month there had been an article in *Sport* magazine, called "Farewell to Bob Cousy," written by Al Hirshberg, who had written Cousy's autobiography, *Basketball Is My Life,* six years earlier. Cousy's picture had been on the cover of the magazine. It showed him peering off into the distance, his right hand on his chin, looking pensive. A green Celtics warmup jacket was over his left shoulder. There is a brooding quality to Cousy in the picture, with his dark hair, dark eyes, Gallic features, portrait of the artist as point guard.

Several other stories were touted on the cover: "Will Dissension Destroy the Dodgers?"; "Jimmy Brown: The Story Behind His Startling Revolt"; a story by Bill Veeck on how the big trading spree has shaken up baseball; and the *Sport* Special, "Life with Elgin Baylor."

On the 10th page of the magazine there was a double-page ad from the Columbia Record Club, billed as 79 albums from every field of music. You could buy any six albums for $1.99, and the list included *Andy Williams Sings Moon River, Doris Day's Greatest Hits,* a new album from Johnny Mathis, and another by Jimmy Dean, featuring "Big Bad John." There were love themes from Ferrante and Teicher, another album billed as a sing-along with Mitch Miller. There were few rock 'n' roll albums, save for *The Many Sides of Gene Pitney,* Bobby Vee singing *Hits of the Rockin' 50's,* and a twist party album with Chubby Checker.

There were ads for Charles Atlas, the most famous body-builder of the day, and one for the Mercury Comet, "the sportiest new hardtop you can buy." There was a "Sports Quiz," with Tom Harmon, who did a daily sports report on ABC radio. There also was a column called "Great Moments in Sports," written by a sports commentator on ABC radio named Howard Cosell.

There were two pictures of Cousy in Hirshberg's article. One was an action scene, Cousy at the top of the key, in the act of throwing a behind-the-back pass to a streaking Sam Jones. The other shows a smiling Cousy in a white shirt and dark tie, a black phone to his left ear.

The article was subtitled: "Behind-the-back razzle dazzle, five NBA titles, the Players' Association. They, and more, stand as monuments to the man now playing his final season of pro basketball, the small man who built a legend in the big man's game."

The article was a compilation of what several of his teammates thought of him, especially ones who had been very young when Cousy had been so instrumental in keeping the league afloat. Satch Sanders, a young Negro player in his third year, had probably said it best, saying that a man walks in his own shoes, and no one was ever going to fill Cousy's shoes, not ever. Frank Ramsey called him a natural leader, saying he always had looked up to him. Most of the thoughts had been obtained one night in the Celtics locker room before a game with the Warriors, and at one point, Hirshberg asked Red Auerbach about Cousy.

"What can you say when you know you're going to lose the greatest backcourt man who ever lived?" Auerbach said. "Nobody will ever take his place. There's only one Cousy."

Auerbach was going through some mail, and tossed the letter he was reading.

"He's the captain in name and the captain in action," he said. "He sets the pace out there. He never tells me he's tired. I've got to watch him myself, and pull him when he has to be pulled. He's an inspiration to the younger kids. He's their idol. He gives us all a morale lift."

Near the end of the article Hirshberg talked to Cousy. It was after the game. Cousy had played well, adding to the theory he shouldn't be retiring, that he wasn't yet finished as a player.

"How do you feel," Hirshberg asked.

"All right," Cousy said.

"You don't seem to have slowed up any?"

"I'm all right for 20–25 minutes," Cousy said. "I used to go 40–45."

"That's the only difference?" Hirshberg asked.

"The only physical difference. But I used to love it. Now it's a chore."

"Any chance of you changing your mind about quitting?"

"None whatever," Cousy said.

Now it was almost over, his last games starting to slip through the hourglass that had been his career, but there was a sense of regret, too, a life slipping away, this life that had come to define him. He had come so far from the tenement of his childhood on Manhattan's Upper East Side, from the dysfunction of his family and the kind of poverty that can deaden dreams. He had overcome so many obstacles, for what were the odds that someone who had been cut from his high-school team in the 10th grade would grow up to be "Mr. Basketball"? Were there odds that high?

On that St. Patrick's Day he was being honored in the most boisterous, gift-laden ceremony held for any athlete in the city's history.

This was no small thing, for Boston was one of the best sports towns in the country, had been the home address of several of the biggest stars in the history of American sport in Babe Ruth, Jimmie Foxx, and Ted Williams. Also Bill Russell, who had been Cousy's teammate for seven years now. Ruth had played for the Red Sox in the late teens, leading them to a world championship in 1918, but he'd been traded to the Yankees afterward, ostensibly because Sox owner Harry Frazee had blown much of his money financing a Broadway play, *No, No Nanette*. Foxx had had many of his best years with the Athletics, had come to Boston when Philadelphia no longer could afford to pay him, but was well liked and became a sort of mentor to the young Ted Williams.

Williams's presence towered over the Boston sports scene, but his tenure in Boston always had been complicated, layered with mixed emotions. He was mercurial at best, downright difficult at worst, a mixture of charm and self-absorption, charisma and boorishness. His career in Boston always had been somewhat tainted by his relationship with the Boston media. He derisively called them "the knights of the keyboard." They, in turn, largely considered him spoiled and arrogant, owner Tom Yawkey's pet. He had retired three years earlier, homering in his last at bat in Fenway Park, an event turned into literature in a John Updike magazine piece called "Hub Fans Bid Kid Adieu," but he never had been given a farewell day.

Cousy had always been loved by both the press and the fans in ways Williams never had been. Maybe that's because he had played in college at Holy Cross, just 40 miles to the west, had played many of his college games here in Boston, being regarded as the hometown boy. Maybe it was because he was flashy, an innovator, doing things with the ball people had never seen before. Maybe it's because the Celtics had now won five world titles, while the Red Sox never had won one during the Williams era. Or maybe it was as simple as what teammate Tommy Hein-sohn would later say, namely, that in those early years of the Celtics the Boston fans weren't necessarily pro basketball fans, they were Cousy fans.

But, even now, Cousy was the emotional link to the fans, adored in ways that Russell never was. No matter that it had been the arrival of Russell that had made the Celtics into the best team in the game's history. No matter that Russell had become the most valuable player in the game, the first man who used defense as a weapon, the one whose rebounding enabled the Celtics to run, their fast break eventually changing the way the game was played. Russell was aloof, distant, a six-foot-nine black man play-ing in a city with an unfortunate racial problem, one that would be on the national news a decade later when court-ordered school busing unraveled a city. Cousy, by contrast, was six-foot-one, white, looked like the majority of the fans looked, Everyman in sneakers.

His career also coincided with the rise in popularity of the NBA, the transformation from the dank arenas of the Northeast to the time when national television was starting to make the league an integral part of the American sports scene.

In its early years professional basketball had all the glamor of a smelly uniform stuck in some old gym bag. Founded in 1946, the NBA was overshadowed by college basketball, which had begun in Madison Square Garden in the mid-thirties. When Cousy joined the league in 1950 it was still in its infancy, and professional basketball was viewed in many quarters as comparable to professional wrestling, rodeo, and other events that came into arenas in the dark of night and disappeared almost as quickly. Certainly it was nothing that was taken too seriously by the American sporting public.

So by the time of "Bob Cousy Day" in the Boston Garden in March 1963, the NBA had significantly changed. While a variety of factors contributed to this, Cousy had been instrumental in changing the league's image. In a league that later learned very well how to market its stars, to the point of developing a cult of personality, Cousy was the first genuine superstar, even if the towering George Mikan had been the game's most dominant player in those early years.

But Cousy was the first whose name transcended his sport.

That had never been more apparent than two years earlier when he had been profiled in *The New Yorker*, the elite literary magazine that had become one of the unofficial arbiters of taste and culture in America. That Cousy had been so prominently featured in it was testimony to his stature, the perception that of all the basketball players on the planet he had become the most well known.

The article, by Robert Rice, had been written for an audience that probably didn't know the difference between a two-hand set shot and a moving screen, and it was a way of almost introducing this new sport that seemingly had snuck up on an unsuspecting country. At one point, the article proclaimed that one factor for the sport's growing popularity was "an affluent society's resourcefulness in creating new consumer needs," and that the "spectacle of ten tall, skinny young men running around in midwinter in costumes that look very much like summer underwear no longer appears quite as bizarre as it once did."

Throughout the article the NBA was referred to as the "Association," and Cousy was portrayed as the key performer, the best all-around player, someone who had scored, with the exception of the bigger Dolph Schayes, the most points in the league's history. He also was portrayed as driven and extremely focused, as someone who regarded his opponents as enemies and spent the few hours before a game brooding and working himself up into a quiet rage, a man whose outward stoicism belied the emotional storm he went through during every game. It talked about the time, in 1958, when the Celtics had lost to the St. Louis Hawks in the NBA Finals, and how Cousy had broken down and sobbed in the locker room, all the pent-up emotion dissolving as tears on a cement floor. Later, he would realize he hadn't cried because the Celtics had lost, or because he had played poorly. Rather it was because he felt he had failed to get himself into a proper mental state, thus had failed to be the type of leader he should have been.

In his view, his role was to make his teammates better. That was the way he'd been taught to play the game back in the school yards of New York City. That was the way he always played it, even if his own style of play pushed the envelope, Cousy becoming the basketball godfather of Larry Bird and Magic Johnson, men who instinctively knew that the great pass is the ultimate basketball expression. He called it "spreading the sugar," this conscious act of passing the ball, keeping everyone happy. He was the captain, and that wasn't just an empty title.

His Celtics' teams also had begun to change the face of American sport.

When Cousy joined the Celtics in 1950 they essentially had been an all-white team. Now four of their best players—Russell, Satch Sanders, Sam Jones, K. C. Jones—were Negroes. One of the main reasons the Celtics were a great team was the ability of both white and black players to get along, deal with one another, respect one another. This was no small thing in an America that was already in the nascent stages of the Civil Rights Movement, the time when race in America was about to be put under a national microscope.

But they all had come to the Celtics after Cousy. He already had played six years before Russell and Heinsohn had arrived. Sam Jones had been at a small Negro college in North Carolina when Cousy had first been on the cover of *Sports Illustrated,* K. C. Jones at the University of San Francisco. The guys he had come of age with on the Celtics were all gone now, Ed Macauley traded away seven years ago, his old roommate Sharman retiring two years ago. He was the one who had survived those early years, the one still standing. Him and Auerbach.

And now it was time even for him to leave.

The ceremony went on for almost an hour before the game with the Syracuse Nationals. Cousy was flanked by his wife, Missie, whom he had married 13 years earlier, his onetime hometown sweetheart. Also there were their two young daughters, Marie and Mary Patricia, in their identical green dresses with white bows; and his parents, who had come from St. Albans, New York. His parents sat on two folding chairs in the middle of the court. He was presented with numerous gifts, including a new Cadillac, as volley after volley of deafening cheers rolled down from the Garden's balconies.

Alternately, Cousy wiped his eyes, wrung his hands, fidgeted, bowed his head, shuffled his feet, and bowed to the crowd.

It was the biggest goodbye in the history of Boston sports, and afterward, Celtics' coach Red Auerbach, who earlier had read a proclamation from President Kennedy, would say, "In the history of my life I've never seen anything like this tribute to an athlete. You talk about Babe Ruth, Lou Gehrig, Ted Williams. This was second to none."

Also at the ceremony was Ned Irish, who ran the New York Knicks, the man credited with jump-starting college basketball 30 years earlier with his idea to stage doubleheaders in Madison Square Garden. There, too, was NBA commissioner Maurice Podoloff, called "Poodles" behind his back. He was a diminutive man who'd been chosen back in 1946 to be the ceremonial head of a new professional basketball league, even though he knew virtually nothing about the game, and resented Cousy for starting the Players' Association a decade later.

"There has been only one Bob Cousy," Podoloff told the crowd. "There never will be another and none will ever attain the heights you've reached."

If the NBA was different from when Cousy first had joined it in 1950, the Celtics were appreciably different, too. They were the best team in basketball, having won five NBA titles in the last six years. They had become perhaps the greatest dynasty in the history of American sport. They also had changed the way basketball was played, fast and free flow, the fast break as an art form, and they had the defensive brilliance of Russell, the first big man who was a great athlete, and not just some genetic freak rooted in the game's stationary past.

After the Celtics, professional basketball never would be seen the same way again.

The other key players were Heinsohn, Satch Sanders, Sam and K. C. Jones, and Frank Ramsey. They were white and black, city and country, all coached by a Jewish man who had come of age in a New York ghetto. In many ways, they were a precursor of a new America, a study in diversity before that concept became popular. They were different men of different backgrounds, all with their own hopes and ambitions, men who often went their different ways once the game was over. But together, within the insular world of the team, they were remarkably similar, shared both a vision and a pride that kept being reaffirmed the more they won, the more championship banners were raised to the rafters of the Boston Garden.

They were a team in the very best sense of the word, for they had come to that most simple, if often elusive, realization that they were better collectively than they were individually. That always had been the gospel according to Auerbach, and in this particular church there were no heretics. It was a message all the players bought into, whatever their reasons, the article of faith that was never questioned. Players came and went, the seasons kept changing, but the philosophy within the group never changed.

This was no insignificant thing.

America was changing, the tensions that later would erupt in the mid-sixties already beginning to run through the culture. Russell was the most obvious embodiment of that. From the time he arrived in Boston in December 1956, fresh from the Melbourne Olympics, he'd been a complicated personality, one of the first black sports stars who refused to be subservient and play by the white man's rules. He always was his own man, regardless of the consequences, but as part of the Celtics, within the group, he was also the ultimate teammate, someone who would subordinate his own interests for the betterment of the group.

He also brought to the team his obsession with winning, the feeling that he would do anything to win.

Years later, Heinsohn talked about this need to win. At one point he was talking about Cousy, Russell, and Auerbach, the three most dominant personalities on the Celtics, and how, beneath the surface, they were much more alike than anyone would realize: the point guard who had grown up the only son of French immigrants, the black center who had spent his early years in segregated Louisiana, and the Jewish coach who had hustled his way out of a Brooklyn ghetto.

It was Heinsohn's theory that while the rest of the Celtics certainly wanted to win, those three had to win, as though winning had become a form of validation. He called it the "love ache," thinking that their insatiable need to win again and again and again was a form of love deprivation, a hunger they could never satisfy, no matter how many cheers, how many victories.

Cousy and Russell never had been particularly close, though they had tremendous respect for each other as players, and perhaps more important, as teammates. But their relationship had seemed to grow more distant as the years went by. Cousy considered Russell almost impossible to get close to, as if he long ago had erected renewable barriers around himself, so that every time you got through one barrier another simply grew in its place. Heinsohn would later say that no one fully understood Russell, not even himself.

Not that Cousy and Russell were unfriendly to each other, or had problems. That certainly wasn't the case. But their wives were more friendly than they were. Cousy had come to believe that part of the reason the two weren't closer was that, at some level, Russell resented the fact that Cousy got endorsements and he didn't. In America in the late fifties that was probably inevitable.

A few years ago, during the filming of a television documentary, Cousy started crying when asked about the prejudice Russell suffered through as a player, essentially saying he wished he had done more at the time to help Russell, that he should have been more sensitive to Russell's plight. Afterward, Russell told Cousy he shouldn't feel guilty, that there was really nothing he could have done to make Russell's stay in Boston any easier.

Still, they always had been linked together, a fact of life they both understood.

"You want to know why Cousy was the greatest?" Russell once said. "Two reasons. First was his imagination. No matter what the situation was, he'd think of something new to try. He'd try anything. And he'd make it work for the second reason—his confidence. He just knew it was going to work."

Why not?

Hadn't Cousy's signature move—his behind-the-back dribble—been sheer instinct, a move he made to get around a Loyola of Chicago player in the dying seconds of a big college game in the Boston Garden in 1949? Hadn't he simply bounced the ball behind his back and then sunk a hook shot, with his left hand no

less, to win the game at the buzzer as the crowd became a hurricane of noise?

"That was from the president," Auerbach said to the crowd, after
reading a proclamation from Kennedy, "but I've got something to
add, too. I know you people are here to honor Bob, are sorry to
see him go. Well, how do you think I feel? I want to thank all you
people for seeing it, because that's Mr. Basketball."

There was a certain irony to that, too, though odds are that
most of the fans that had packed the Boston Garden that afternoon had long forgotten it. It had been Auerbach who had passed
over Cousy in the first round of the NBA draft in 1950, even
though Cousy had been the hometown star, the Holy Cross senior who had played many of his games in the Boston Garden, the
darling of the Boston sportswriters. Auerbach was newly hired
then, the brash young coach who had been hired to save professional basketball in Boston.

"Am I supposed to win, or please the local yokels?" Auerbach
had snapped that day, when pressed on why he didn't draft
Cousy.

So Auerbach and Cousy had grown together, like some
arranged marriage that turns out to flourish. They had shared a
success that would have seemed incomprehensible on that draft
day in 1950. Now on this day they hugged and cried together.

There were words from Mayor John Collins and Governor
John Volpe. Russell's wife spoke. Then Walter Brown spoke.

He was the Celtics' owner, and the Celtics were his baby, especially in the early years when he had paid a big personal price to
keep them afloat. He had been one of the founding fathers of the
entire NBA, not only the Celtics, even if he really knew very little
about basketball, his true sports love being hockey. No one loved
the Celtics, and its players, more than Walter Brown, a fleshy-
faced Irishman with a heart so big that the players always wanted
to negotiate with him instead of Auerbach, because they knew

that Brown would always take care of them. To Cousy, Brown was one of the world's good people.

"You feel bad?" he said to the crowd. "Think of how I must feel. I'm the guy who didn't want Bob Cousy."

He paused a beat.

"What a genius."

Then he paused again.

"Things weren't always so good for the Celtics," Brown said. "It was so bad one year I couldn't pay the players their playoff money for nearly a year. Cousy and [Ed] Macauley never asked me for it. Their generosity enabled the club to exist. That was the greatest tribute ever paid me. . . . For 13 years, Bob, you've been the Boston Celtics."

That was not hyperbole.

Cousy had been the Celtics, especially in those years in the early fifties when the NBA was new and professional basketball in Boston was viewed with skepticism at best, and was downright ignored at worst. The Celtics were trying to establish themselves in a city that had no basketball tradition, a city where the sport hadn't been played in the high schools from 1925 until after World War II, a place the fans had to be taught the game.

It hadn't been easy.

Cousy had been the show in those early years, a reason to see the Celtics. Maybe the only reason.

When Cousy entered professional basketball in the fall of 1950, the National Basketball Association was only a year old, a merger of different leagues, more of a curiosity than an attraction. Its eleven franchises included Syracuse, Fort Wayne, and something called the Tri-Cities, which played in three nondescript cities in Iowa. College basketball was far more popular, the NIT in Madison Square Garden every March commanding far more attention than the NBA playoffs. In many ways professional basketball was a regional game. The Northeast. The Midwest. Something to fill the time between football and baseball seasons.

More than anyone, Cousy changed all that.

And that transcended the fact that he was a small man in a big man's game, someone who was never blessed with obvious athleticism, couldn't even dunk.

He was called "The Houdini of the Hardwood," for his unique style of play, one that featured the fast break, the basketball philosophy that brought the game into the modern era. A corny nickname by today's standards, for sure. But it promised possibilities, the idea that to see Cousy play was to see something different, something you had never seen before. Cousy passed behind his back. He often dribbled behind his back. He threw no-look passes, as if he somehow had eyes in the back of his head.

But his influence had transcended his oncourt machinations.

Red Smith, the *New York Times* writer who was the most influential sports voice in the country, had written, "For him, basketball has a music of its own, but he also has powerful convictions about people and living, human rights, the rigging of games, and the recruiting of college athletes, officials and coaches, and the individuals he has played against."

He had been the leading force behind the birth of the NBA Players' Association, the group that later evolved into the players' union. For decades afterward, he was the standard-bearer for every flashy guard who came along, as if being billed as "the next Cousy" was the highest praise that could be bestowed on any young basketball player.

Now, on a rainy St. Patrick's Day afternoon in Boston, it was all about to end.

The spring before he had announced that he was only going to play one more year, that he was going to coach Boston College. That had set off the biggest farewell tour in NBA history, Cousy being honored in virtually every city as he went through the season: gifts at halftime, speeches, public thank-yous. The NBA was now major league, now stretched across the country— very different from its beginnings. Every year there seemed to be more and more young stars coming into the league, changing it, making it better. It was very, very different from what it had been only a decade ago, and more and more, as his career wound down, Cousy was being recognized for that transformation. There were some who even said he had saved the young league in those early years, that without Bob Cousy the NBA never would have survived.

After the game, Dolph Schayes, the Syracuse star, said, "I looked over and Cousy was crying before the fans were crying. When I looked over and saw the officials were crying I knew we were in trouble."

Schayes, who had been one of the NBA's best players for more than a decade, leading Syracuse to an NBA title in 1955, had first met Cousy 17 years earlier in the Catskills. He, too, was from New York, but he was two years older. He had been a big star at New York University in the forties, one of the last of the great Jewish stars who came out of the city, back when the city game had largely been Jewish.

The next day the headlines would scream out in big, black type: Cousy Weeps as 13,909 Roar Tumultuous Ovation . . . Hub's Tears Stir Cousy . . . Tearful Adieu to City's Beloved Star . . . Cousy Falters For First Time . . . Tears Not Out of Place at Farewell."

"It was just something I wanted to get through," Cousy would say years later. "It was a very stressful day."

No surprise there.

For all the public acclaim, Cousy was the most private of men. He never was comfortable with all the attention he received. He knew that it ultimately created more money, so he went along with it, saw it as part of his job. He always tried to exploit situations he thought could help him. But it wasn't something he necessarily enjoyed. He didn't go out of his way to promote himself, or particularly like being the center of attention.

Nor was he the easiest person to know. Heinsohn, who might have known him the best of all the Celtics, would later say Cousy could be difficult, that he was too much the perfectionist, too demanding, both of the people he played with and of himself. One of his favorite tactics was to throw the ball at the back of a teammate's head if he thought that particular teammate wasn't looking when he should have been.

But he was the perfect teammate, too. He often would come into a huddle during timeouts and ask what he could be doing better. He would find the open man rather than take the shot himself. And no one ever wanted to win more.

Heinsohn also knew how important it was for Cousy to go out the right way. For years he and Cousy had driven from Worcester to Boston together, had shared much time together, even if they were very different personalities, Cousy private and guarded with people he didn't know, Heinsohn open and easy and willing to talk to anybody. Heinsohn knew how driven Cousy was, how he always had had a fear of failure, and how he had used that fear to make himself such a fierce competitor. Heinsohn remembered how, after the Celtics had lost in the NBA Finals in 1958 (the year Russell had gotten hurt in the playoffs), Cousy had broken down in the locker room. It had been Heinsohn's second year in the league, and he had thought, okay, we lost, but there'll be more seasons, more titles. Sure, it had been important to him, but to Cousy it had been life and death, for he played every game as if it were his last.

After the game, Cousy would sit in the trainer's room, pale and drawn, and say that the upcoming playoffs would be easy compared to getting through this afternoon.

"How do you say goodbye?" he asked rhetorically.

But he had tried.

When it was his turn to speak to the crowd of 13,909 shoehorned into the Garden, the old Art Deco building in Boston's North End, he spoke haltingly, between sniffles and sobs, asking for forgiveness because he was using prepared notes.

"The biggest regret I have in leaving is no longer being able to share the camaraderie and esprit de corps and the common bond of competition and inspiration I have received by being the captain of this team," he said to the crowd, rolling his r's as he'd done all his life, a product of the Gallic speech characteristics that went back to his early childhood, the speech impediment that caused him to lisp slightly.

Those were not just words.

His sense of being on a team, of competing, had shaped his life in ways he didn't really understand at the time. It would be years before he would come to grips with his competitive nature, the way it had shaped his view of the world.

"I always hoped that my playing has, in a small way, seemed to repay you for your many kindnesses," he said to the crowd.

More applause tumbled down from the upper balcony.

"You know, in 17 years since I entered Holy Cross, I've had the occasion to stand so many times in front of an audience," he said, "but I'm afraid that the task has never quite been as difficult as it is today. It seems so difficult to find mere words that seem so inadequate in order to say these things."

He began to break down, didn't begin to speak for 15 seconds as applause engulfed him.

It was not the only time he would break down. Or have his remarks stopped by applause. Throughout his speech he would constantly be interrupted by waves of deafening applause.

At one point, he said he wouldn't have enjoyed playing anywhere but Boston, a remark that brought another 10 seconds of applause, but those words were redundant. He had become as much a part of Boston as the Old North Church and Paul Revere's Ride. For many years he had been the Celtics, from his number, 14, to his black sneakers, to the sense he'd been born into the Celtics' backcourt.

His eyes had filled with tears again, and his 12-year-old daughter Marie walked to the microphone and gave him a handkerchief. The Garden turned quiet as he wiped his eyes.

As he struggled to control his emotions, in the stillness of the old Garden that had been Cousy's field of dreams for so many years, a fan's loud voice came rolling down from the second balcony, cutting through the building.

"We love ya, Cooz," it said.

Chapter Two

Robert Joseph Cousy was born in a tenement block on East 83rd Street in Manhattan, near the corner of East End Avenue, even though he'd been conceived on a boat coming from France. It was 1928, a year before the stock market would crash and put America into the Great Depression. But the Cousys didn't need the onset of the Depression to tell them they were poor. The apartment didn't have any running water, the building was so tired and forlorn that it was condemned after the Cousys moved out of it five years later.

Cousy was an only child, although his maternal grandmother lived with them, too. Her name was Marie Corlet, and she took him everywhere. To church, To school. To the store. The neighborhood was called Yorkville, the German enclave in Manhattan, and there were several German-owned stores in the neighborhood, a distinct German presence.

His father, Joseph, had grown up in the Alsace-Lorraine region of France, near the German border. He had been conscripted into the German army as a young man and had fought in World War I. His first wife had died of pneumonia following the war, so by the time he had remarried and had come to America he had a daughter still living in France, Cousy's half-sister, although Cousy would be an adult before he met her. Cousy's mother had grown up Juliet Corlet near Dijon, in the wine country near the German border, even though she'd been born in New York. She had been taught by Catholic nuns as a schoolgirl and remained religious throughout her life. She was tall and dark-haired, with expressive brown eyes, her most distinctive feature. Before the marriage she had worked in both Dijon and Paris as a secretary and French teacher. She didn't speak much English, even after she came to America.

Cousy spoke only French for the first five years of his life. Once he started school he only wanted to speak English and become Americanized, no longer wanting to speak French at home, even though the kids he played with called him "Flenchy." He didn't necessarily see it as a pejorative, because the neighborhood was a little League of Nations. Trading ethnic insults, identifying people by their flaws, was all part of the street ethos. He also had a minor speech impediment, rolling his r's.

He played stickball, stoopball, boxball, the real city games then, games played in the narrow side streets that bisected the city's grand avenues. The street games were all variations of baseball, not surprising in a city that worshiped at the altar of the Yankees, the Dodgers, and the Giants. Baseball truly was the national pastime then, what people argued about on the street corners, what jumped out at you on the sports page every morning. Basketball might have been the city game, played in school yards, and starting to be showcased in college doubleheaders at Madison Square Garden, but Cousy never played it in those early years in Manhattan.

His parents had few friends. His father drove a cab, worked long hours, sometimes as many as 18 a day. He was only about five-foot-six, quiet, introverted, almost stoic in his demeanor. His mother spent most of her free time at St. Katherine's, a nearby Catholic church, where one of the nuns became her best friend. She was high-strung, emotional, the opposite of her husband. Cousy would later come to realize that he inherited both their personality types, the calm outward demeanor of his father, the churning internal volatility of his mother.

There were no newspapers in the house. The family didn't go to the movies. They didn't listen to music. Neither of his parents had any interest in sports, even though spectator sports had boomed in America in the twenties, the era of Babe Ruth, Jack Dempsey, Bobby Jones. In a sense there was a ghetto mentality that permeated the Cousy home, an impoverishment of the spirit. Both his parents spoke French at home, and when they spoke English at all it was heavily accented. Cousy was young when he first sensed the tension between his parents—how his mother would harp on his father, belittle him, constantly point out he had fought for the Germans in the First World War; how his father seemed to have withdrawn within himself, as if there was a moat around his feelings. He didn't relate easily to his son, to the point that Cousy grew up feeling as if he never knew his father, that they might have lived under the same roof, but they lived in two different universes.

He saw how his mother hated the Germans, had become almost obsessive about them, to the extent that if someone gave her a look on the street she would call him "a dirty German." She treated people nicely, and if that wasn't reciprocated she would storm out of stores if she felt the least slighted, make scenes, something that always embarrassed Cousy and made him not want to go out of the house with her.

More important, he learned early not to ask questions. How had his parents met? He didn't know. How difficult had it been for his father to walk away from the family farm in France, leaving behind his family and the familiar for some new land across the ocean, some strange place where he didn't even know the language? He never asked him. He learned not to fill in the silences that hung in the air between his parents with unwanted questions, already having intuitively sensed that in his family everyone lived in their own interior space.

"My father would never say 'boo,'" said Cousy. "His education was limited, but he was very good with his hands. He could fix anything. Mr. Fixit. He used to keep his car immaculate. He had an old Packard and he always was polishing it, working on it. But he never said a word.

"My mother was very strong-willed, very passionate and emotional about everything. They were exact opposites. They were always fighting and she would always be telling him, 'The house could be burning down and you would just sit there,' and he'd just shake his head."

Years later, he understood that his personality had been stunted growing up in that environment. Part of the reason was that he'd been an only child. But it was more than that, too. He was timid as a young kid, shy, growing up in a house where silences could hang heavy in the air. For the rest of his life he would dislike confrontations.

When he was 12 they moved to a small rented house on 112th Avenue in St. Albans, Queens. St. Albans was not far from Manhattan, but in many ways it was the country, with open space and green grass, full of promise, the sense that anything could happen. It had been his mother's dream, a life in the country, a home of her own, away from the grime and congestion of the Manhattan tenements.

"Breathe deep, Roby," she said proudly, as if she knew she was giving her only child an incredible gift.

He never saw the corner of 83rd Street and East End Avenue again.

Later, as an adult, he would drive by in a car on East River Drive feeling a certain recognition for the neighborhood, but no nostalgia. He was one of the most famous athletes in the country then, enjoying the kind of celebrity that would have been impossible to even fantasize about in those early years when there was no running water and the kids used to call him "Flenchy." But there was no emotional connection.

In the summer of 1940 they moved four blocks, to a house on 116th Avenue in St. Albans. It cost $4,500. His father had put $500 down for the payment. It had taken him 12 years to accumulate the money. He then divided the house into apartments so he could make the mortgage payments. The cellar was redone into a living room and kitchen, the place where the Cousys lived. They slept on the third floor. The first two floors were rented out.

"Roby, we are property owners," his mother said, the pride unmistakable in her voice.

St. Albans was what would later be known as a suburb, a place where people went into Manhattan during the day to work, returning by train at night, a place where people came to forget their small beginnings and dream of larger futures. It was full of cops and firemen, many of whom had fought in World War I. It was on the easternmost point of Queens, bordering Jamaica to the east and Nassau County and Long Island to the west.

The affluent part of St. Albans was called Addisleigh. It was near St. Albans' Naval Hospital, and was becoming known as a neighborhood full of show people, including the successful black entertainers Lena Horne and Fats Waller, and eventually Brooklyn Dodgers' ballplayers Roy Campanella and Jackie Robinson.

O'Connell Park was six blocks away from the Cousy house. It was there that one day he met a short, heavy man with curly black hair. His name was Morty Arkin, and he was one of those unsung heroes who help kids, not for any money, or recognition, or anything other than that that's what they do. Arkin was the new director of the playground, called a "parky," and for some inexplicable reason he took an interest in Cousy. He taught him how to shoot a basketball. How to hold it with his fingertips and not the palm of his hand. How to follow through. How to bend his knees when he took a set shot. How to learn to use his left hand, too, so he wouldn't be a one-dimensional player.

Cousy lapped it all up, excited that an adult would take the time to help him. Arkin was the early mentor, and whatever he suggested, Cousy would work on, as though he couldn't get enough instruction, enough of this new game. To a shy, introverted kid, the sense that an adult would actually care enough to pay attention to him, never mind teach him about basketball, was almost a revelation.

"Bob was soft-spoken, but he made friends," remembers Wes Field, who first met Cousy shortly after he moved to St. Albans, at a playground behind the Linden Lutheran Church off Linden

Boulevard, one of St. Albans' main streets. "It was the summer after fourth grade, and we had two groups of kids who played baseball and football together. I was the unofficial captain of one group, Angus Kennedy was the captain of the other. Well, one day Angus's team showed up with a new kid. Bob Cousy. He came to the plate in the first inning and hit a home run."

Baseball and football were the two big sports then for kids, but that would soon change for Cousy, Wes Field, and Angus Kennedy. The local high school didn't have a football team. The big sport was basketball, so basketball it became.

School-yard basketball was its own culture in New York, a Darwinian world where you were constantly being tested. It was improvisational, almost like a basketball laboratory, and every year it sent players to some of the best college programs in the country. At the most obvious level it was simple: Winners stayed on the court, losers had to wait to play again, the children of immigrants learning that America was all about winning, even in a pickup basketball game. It also was something more primal. You had to fight to survive, to keep proving yourself, the perfect metaphor for America in the Depression. Every day was another test, even if the kids didn't always know it at the time.

There also were unofficial rules. The younger kids had to wait their turn. If they actually did get in a game, they weren't supposed to shoot, simply run up and down the court and stay out of the older kids' way. This is how Cousy started to come of age in the game, hanging around the school yards at P.S. 36, waiting for a chance to get into the game with the older kids, then trying to emulate them.

Most of the games during the week were half-court, three-on-three. There was a lot of passing, a lot of cutting, the give-and-go style that was being played in the big college games over in Manhattan, in Madison Square Garden on Eighth Avenue and 49th Street. Players who shot every time they touched the ball were looked down upon, almost shunned. They were called ball hogs, gunners. The key was to play the right way. The idea was not so much to stand out as to blend in, be a good teammate, help your team win, because on weekends, anyway, at O'Connell Park, when the courts were crowded and the games were full court, to lose meant you might sit and wait to play for an hour.

The first time Field remembers Cousy making any kind of real impression as a basketball player was when they were in the seventh grade. It was their first time playing an organized game, complete with uniform shirts, and they were playing a game at St. Monica's Church in South Jamaica, the adjoining town.

"We all thought Angus was the best player," Field says, "so we just assumed he would be our high scorer. But Bob was. We were surprised."

Not that Cousy really was.

The basketball court already had become his sanctuary, the one place he felt comfortable, the little safe harbor in the swirling sea of his childhood. Within the boundaries of a court it didn't matter that his parents fought too much. Within the boundaries of a court it didn't matter that he was painfully shy, uncomfortable in many social situations. It didn't matter that he talked funny, or was only a mediocre student in school, often being too shy to ask questions in class.

On the court he was able to focus, even though he really didn't know he was doing it at the time. He was able to channel his emotions, make them work for him. Later, he would come to understand that this, too, was part of his ghetto background, this sense that doing well was vital, as much a part of who he was as his name. He didn't just want to win. He had to win.

Maybe more than anything, that was what the New York streets taught a young Bob Cousy, lessons he would carry with him always, like some movable feast, through all the years and all the games: The poor kid is more hungry. The kid who has to fight for everything in life will fight more in a game. Eventually, he would call it the killer instinct, believing that all the great athletes had it in one form or another, the notion that at their core they had to be successful, for not to be was a death of the spirit.

This intensity was what he brought to a basketball court, almost from the beginning. He would set little goals for himself. The first was to become a better player than Angus Kennedy, the first person who had befriended him in St. Albans, and who would remain a lifelong friend. Then it was to become better than Brother Higgins, the alpha wolf of O'Connell Park. He would set goals and tenaciously set out to reach them.

Cousy entered Andrew Jackson High School in the fall of 1942. The school, a three-story red-brick structure on Francis Lewis Boulevard, had opened three years earlier, having been built as part of Franklin Roosevelt's WPA project. Already it was huge, with nearly 5,000 students, and so overcrowded it had triple sessions. It had a new, spacious gym, even a swimming pool. Before that kids from St. Albans had gone to high school in Jamaica, but from the moment Andrew Jackson High School opened it had been successful in sports, especially basketball. It had won the city championship the winter before, something that had instilled almost a basketball mania in the town.

The coach was Lew Grummond, one of those no-nonsense guys who seemed to have stepped off the pages of adolescent fiction. He was even called "The Magician," for his ability to keep turning out great teams. He stressed fundamentals. He was in control, no questions asked. He believed in structure, to the extent that he numbered the positions from one to five, with each player having designated spots on the floor. His teams ran a play every time down the court. His players were not expected to deviate from the called play, and were certainly not allowed to freelance. Grummond was set in his ways, his ways had been successful, and he wasn't about to change now. And because he played a zone defense, he liked tall players.

Cousy wasn't particularly tall—not in the ninth grade, anyway. But he went out for the team, his hopes buoyed by his growing success in the school yard. But there were too many kids, as many as 250 trying out for both the varsity and the jayvee teams, as the new status symbol in town was to play basketball for Andrew Jackson High School. He was too small. The tryout was perfunctory at best, a couple of layups, and that was it. When he got cut he was crushed. He thought his budding basketball career was over before it had begun.

Instead, he got a second chance.

It was a basketball league sponsored by the *Long Island Press*. It was called the Press League and was played throughout the borough of Queens. Cousy played for a team called the St. Albans Lindens. It wasn't the high-school team, but it was competitive, and it gave Cousy a chance to be on a real team, play in real games, not just in pickup games in O'Connell Park.

What would have happened to Cousy without it? What would have happened to a kid with basketball dreams if there were no team to play on? Odds are they would have gone up in smoke, just another kid judged and found wanting, another kid deemed not good enough, who simply put basketball behind him and moved on to something else. He was fortunate, though. At a critical time in his basketball development the Press League gave him an opportunity.

"He and I were on the same team," said Wes Field, "and he was outstanding in that league. We didn't really have a coach, so he and I ran the team. It was a good situation."

His sophomore year at Andrew Jackson High School was some painful déjà vu. Again, the tryout was essentially a layup drill. Again, there were too many kids. But this time he didn't feel a crushing despair when he didn't make it. There still was the community league, there still was instruction from Morty Arkin in the park. He knew he was getting better as a player, still believed his time would come, still believed that one day Grummond would have to notice him, that basketball was his destiny, even if no one else seemed to recognize it.

As fate would have it, one of the two teams he was playing for in the Press League played in the gym at Andrew Jackson High School, which also functioned as a rec center at night. Grummond also ran the rec center. It was against the rules to play for more than one team, but what were rules when you had a burning desire to play, to get better? What were rules when basketball was really the only thing you had? Eventually, Cousy began playing for two teams.

"You can't be Bob Cousy twice," the manager of one of his teams told him.

So he played under a different last name.

One night he played a game that Grummond watched.

"Haven't I seen you over at school?" Grummond asked.

"Yes, sir," Cousy said.

"What's your name?"

"Cousy. Bob Cousy."

"What year are you?"

"Sophomore."

"You could use a little more height."

Cousy didn't say anything.

Grummond looked at him for a moment.

"Are you left-handed?"

"No, sir. I'm right-handed."

"Well, you were using your left a lot out there."

"I always do."

"Well," Grummond said, "I like a boy who can use both hands. Come to practice tomorrow. I want to see if you can make the junior varsity."

Cousy played the rest of the year on the jayvee team. He was extremely nervous, couldn't control his emotions. The jayvee team played four quarters of six minutes each, and sometimes less than that so the varsity game could start on time. Once, Cousy was the high scorer for his team with only four points.

Another alumnus of O'Connell Park was Frank Alagia, who was two years ahead of Cousy. He was one of the stars of the varsity, a team that went on to win the city championship, and he not only knew Cousy from the park, but also had coached a CYO team from St. Pascal's that Cousy had played on.

"Bob had very big hands for a young kid and they allowed him to be able to do things with the ball that other kids couldn't do," said Alagia, who was named All-City that year by both the *Journal-American* and the *World Telegram and Sun*. "We used to laugh at him because he couldn't say his r's, but even as a kid he would do things that made you shake your head, and say, 'Did you see that?' He was just a kid, but he was already special and you could see that."

Field remembers how driven Cousy was. There was an ice cream store called Wellbrooks on Linden Boulevard, a place where there always seemed to be kids hanging out, called "drugstore cowboys." Across the street was the school yard of P.S. 36, and often Cousy would stay and shoot after the other kids went to the ice cream store, sometimes even at night, using the light from a nearby used-car lot to illuminate the basket. He would watch older players, more accomplished players, look at their signature moves, then go into the school yard and try to copy them, adding them to his own repertoire.

Field remembers growing up in St. Albans as almost idyllic, a boyhood out of some old *Saturday Evening Post* magazine cover, a succession of sunny days seen through the prism of youth. Even though the war was going on, and even though some of the older kids they knew from O'Connell Park had gone overseas, for him and his friends life went on interrupted, as though they were somehow exempt from the world's grim realities, the ones that were on the front page of the newspapers every morning. They traveled around New York to play basketball games. They occasionally went to watch the Giants play at the Polo Grounds, the horseshoe-shaped stadium on 159th Street in Manhattan, between Coogan's Bluff and the Harlem River.

"We didn't think too much about the future," Field said. "We didn't even think about college."

Cousy remembers it as something less idyllic.

To him, his family was a constant source of tension. There was never enough money, never enough communication, never enough joy. Home was something to escape from. In many ways his world was very insular; there was basketball in the park, there was school, and there was hanging out with his friends. After that, the world didn't really exist for him.

Even World War II, the constant backdrop to the era, didn't really affect him. It was on the other side of the world, and neither Cousy nor his handful of friends had fathers or brothers fighting in it, so it was almost easy to ignore, outside of having to pull the shades down at night as part of the country's blackout plan, and having to wear resoled shoes, because shoes were rationed, as were meat and butter. Later, when he started to date Missie Ritterbusch, he realized her experience had been very different, even though she had grown up only about a mile from him. But she had two older brothers who were overseas and could not escape the war's realities. He could.

He listened to *The Shadow,* the serial about a crime-fighting hero, on the radio. He listened to Jack Armstrong, the All-American boy. He listened to Joe Louis fight on the radio, the only sporting events he had an interest in.

Sometimes he and his friends would sneak into the movie theater that was less than a block away, even though it only cost ten cents. They would chip in and buy one ticket, then wait until the kid with the ticket opened one of the side doors. Either that, or they would go up the fire escape on the side of the building, then go through an opening on the roof that led to the projectionist's booth. The big attraction was the serial before the actual feature. That, and the Movie Tone, a compilation of the world's news.

He went back for his junior year of high school, certain he was going to be a starter. Everyone in the park said so. He was finally going to see his dream of being a high-school basketball player realized. But he flunked "citizenship," of all things, courtesy of talking too much in homeroom, and was ruled ineligible for the first semester. He couldn't believe it. He asked Grummond to try to intervene for him. He wouldn't. He begged the teacher, told her how important it was to him to be eligible to play basketball. She wouldn't budge. Again, he was devastated. Once again, his summer dreams were put on hold. Once again, he had to sit and watch the Andrew Jackson High School team play, convinced he should be out there. Once again, he had to wait for his chance.

Cousy didn't play again until midway through his junior year. When he finally was eligible it was as though he had finally met his moment. He scored 28 points in his first game, complete with a banner headline in the *Long Island Press* the next day.

Bob Cousy's life had changed.

Not that he really knew it at the time.

If he had come of age today he would have started living in celebrity's glow, the way talented young basketball players do now. He no doubt would have gone to prestigious summer camps, where talented young players are paraded before college recruiters like show cattle. He undoubtedly would have played on an AAU team that traveled the country playing in national showcase tournaments. He would have started receiving letters from colleges by the trunkful, been courted by virtually every basketball school in the country, already living inside fame's bubble.

But there was none of that. Not then. Instead, Cousy's young life went on relatively unchanged. He went to school. He went to the school yard. He hung around with the same friends. In the summers he worked, one summer loading clothes at JC Penney in Manhattan, another at Loft's, a candy store in St. Albans, where his deadening job was to place candy in boxes that moved along the assembly line in front of him. Then again he had been working off and on since he was about 13, first delivering fish every Friday on his bicycle, then working in a grocery store one day a week.

"We expected to work and do what we had to do," he said. "We weren't looking for shortcuts."

In retrospect, he remembers himself as being without much of an ego then, remembers he was just happy to be playing. Becoming a high-school basketball star, even in a school where that was considered important, didn't change the fundamental aspects of his life. It didn't make his home life any less tense. It didn't give him confidence in social situations, or dramatically improve his self-esteem. It didn't make him any less shy. It didn't change the way he lived every day.

Except for one thing.

"You might be able to go to college," Morty Arkin told him one day.

Until then college might have been located on the far side of the moon as far as Cousy was concerned. College was where rich kids went. College was where smart kids went. College was some secret world that seemed light-years away from his life. In the days before the GI Bill began opening up college to the children of immigrants, college during World War II was, for kids like him, a place other kids went to.

But from the moment Arkin put the idea in his head, Cousy's new goal was to go to college, to play basketball in college. Almost instantly, he became a better student, no longer content to slide by getting C's. No longer did he just go through the motions in the classroom, just another kid on some assembly line to who knows where. His basketball success had given him a glimpse of a future.

So Cousy set out to go to college the same way he had set out to become a basketball player, by himself, without a whole lot of external support. Years later, he would realize he'd developed what he considered good common sense, one of the reasons probably being that from a young age he had to figure things out for himself. College was just one example. Grummond never gave him any advice, it simply wasn't the coach's style to take an interest in his players' lives off the court. Certainly his parents didn't, save for his grandmother, who always had wanted him to go to Catholic schools.

Years later, he would come to understand that in his own quiet way he had intuitively known how to go after things he really wanted, that he "always exploited opportunities well," whether it was courting Missie, acquiring his summer camp, or handling his own salary negotiations with the Celtics.

His senior year replicated the second half of his junior year. The team won the Queens division for the second straight year, and Cousy was scoring a lot of points. He was a forward then, not the point guard he would come to be, and maybe the best thing about his game as a high-school kid was that he could score. It was an era where most smaller players took two-hand set shots, but Cousy never did. From the beginning he shot a running one-hander, a shot he would use throughout his career.

It also was becoming obvious that even though Cousy was not particularly tall, he had other physical gifts for the game. He had long arms and big hands, two attributes that gave him the wingspan of a taller player. He was deceptively quick, and could change direction easily. He also had exceptional peripheral vision, able to see things in a virtual 180-degree arc. In his years as a Celtic, people would say that Cousy had eyes in the back of his head. Not quite. But he could see things most players were not able to.

He spent much of the season in a dogfight with a kid named Vic Hanson from Long Island City for the scoring title in New York City, a competition that got lot of attention in the local sports pages. Their battle went down to the last day of the season, and as fate would have it, Hanson played in the afternoon, so Cousy knew what he had to score that night. He came through with 28 points after a first half in which he'd been tense, to finish the season as the highest scorer in the city. So even though Andrew Jackson lost in the quarterfinals of the city championship, Cousy was named the captain of the *Journal-American*'s All-Scholastic team, the highest honor for any schoolboy basketball player in the five boroughs of New York City, even though he only really played one and a half years of high-school basketball.

There is a black-and-white picture of that team. There are five
players, in a semicircle, the three in the middle bending at the
waist. All are wearing their high-school uniforms. All are wearing
black sneakers. The other four are Vic Hanson, George Feigen-
baum from New Utrecht High School, Zeke Sincola from Franklin
High School, and Abe Becker from Lincoln High School. The only
non-Caucasian is Hanson.

Cousy is on the left in the picture, thin and angular, his dark
hair pushed back. His uniform top is dark, with a large "Jackson"
across the front in white letters. He is very thin, and almost looks
emaciated.

After a successful season like that he figured the scholarship
offers would come streaming in. They didn't. Maybe that was
because he was only six feet tall, not small certainly, but not the
kind of size that got anyone's attention, either, even in 1946.
Whatever the reason, as the weeks of his senior year went by he
still didn't have anything lined up for the following year. This was
becoming all the more urgent because Wes Field, who had graduated at midyear, already had been accepted to Dartmouth.

Cousy essentially was looking for two things in a college: He
wanted a Catholic school, out of homage to his grandmother's
wishes, and he wanted to leave the city, get away from home,
even though local Catholic schools like St, John's, Manhattan,
and Fordham all had serious basketball programs.

"I knew I wanted out of the house," he said. "I was 17 and I
was going to get away."

Then one day he got a call from Al McClellan, the coach at
Boston College, whom everyone called "Gen," short for General.

Boston College was a football school at the time, the place
where Frank Leahy had coached before he went to Notre Dame,
but the Gen was telling Cousy that BC had big basketball dreams.
Cousy went to visit and was much impressed. The school is on a
hill in suburban Newton, complete with Gothic towers and a
campus that looked like an English boarding school's. BC seemed
to have everything he wanted, and it was obvious McClellan

wanted him, offering a full scholarship. There was only one problem. There were no dorms. BC was mostly a commuter school then, and if Cousy were to go there he would have to live in a nearby rooming house. Even at 17, he knew he couldn't handle that.

So he went home and found a letter he'd gotten from Doggie Julian, the coach of Holy Cross, who had heard about him from Ken Haggerty, a Holy Cross player from St. Albans.

Haggerty had starred at Andrew Jackson High School four years earlier. He had hit a key shot from the corner in Madison Square Garden to win the city championship over Erasmus Hall from Brooklyn in triple overtime. In the locker room after that game he'd been offered a scholarship to Fordham. But after a year there he went into the service, stationed first at Cornell in upstate New York, where he played another year of college basketball, and then at the San Diego Naval Hospital. By the time he returned home there was a Holy Cross alumnus in New York City who was rounding up players for his alma mater. In the fall of '45 he had gone there.

During the war he had stayed in contact with one of the sportswriters from the *Long Island Press,* so he knew all about Cousy. During the season, Holy Cross came to nearby Jamaica to play Kings Point. Cousy was invited to sit on the Holy Cross bench. He met Julian, watched the game, liked what he saw, and in the end picked Holy Cross over Boston College because Holy Cross had dormitories. But not before Haggerty went to Cousy's house one night to speak to him and his mother, all the while touting Holy Cross.

"I notice that we have to go to mass every morning at seven," Cousy said, looking at the Holy Cross catalogue.

"Roby," his mother said. "You're going to Holy Cross."

Before he got there, though, he went to work in the Catskills, at a place called Tamarack Lodge, a few miles from Ellenville and about a dozen miles from the town of Monticello. Tamarack Lodge looked like a Bavarian lodge, complete with a playtorium, a pool area, and a large dining room. To the 17-year-old Cousy it all looked as "fancy as hell."

He and Wes Field had been given jobs by a man named Artie Musicant, who coached at Brooklyn College but lived in St. Albans and knew all about the stars of Andrew Jackson High School. In the summer he was the athletic director at Tamarack Lodge, and he sold Cousy and Field on the fact that not only could they save about $100 a week, they would also be exposed to great competition. The Catskills were the middle of a basketball culture, kind of like a New York City North, for basketball in the mountains had been going since the thirties when hotel owners first figured out that a lot of the guests liked watching basketball games at night.

Cousy and Field lived with six other guys in a large room in an oversized Quonset hut about 50 yards from the lodge. The big guys got the single beds. Cousy was not a big guy, so he slept in a bunk bed. On Sundays they would go into Ellenville, for mass at the Catholic church.

There were outdoor courts, and basketball games between the various hotels was part of the entertainment, right there with cards and dancing in the lounge, mah-jongg, and shuffleboard. Two nights a week they played against teams from the other hotels, one game at home and one game at another hotel. There were roughly 15 hotels that had teams, including the big ones like Kutscher's, Grossinger's, and the Concord. The basketball was highly competitive, full of some of the better college players in the country, including George Mikan, then at DePaul, Dolph Schayes, who would go on to be an NBA star with Syracuse, and St. Louis University star Ed Macauley, who would later become Cousy's teammate with the Celtics.

Surprisingly, not only did Cousy hold his own against some of the top college stars, he surpassed many of them. To Field, it was just another indication that Cousy was a college star in the making, that he had the ability to keep getting better as the competition kept getting better.

"With Bob, you always felt you were going to win," said Field, "and when I played with other great players I didn't have that same feeling."

Five years later, the Catskills would be blamed for spawning the college basketball scandals of '51, the theory being that gambling on games was such an inherent part of summer basketball in the mountains, and that gamblers were such a presence, that they struck up friendships with players, creating the environment that spilled back into the city. Cousy and Field were never approached by gamblers, but there was no mistaking the gambling culture that permeated everything.

Before every game tickets to a betting pool were sold for a dollar, and the one who came closest to the combined score won a cash prize, with the balance going to a players' pool that was split up at the end of the summer.

"The games were very competitive," Field said. "The first game we played was against Nevele Country Club with Schayes, who already was a big star at NYU, and the team from Klein's Hillside had practically the entire team from CCNY. There also were a few pros. But Bob clearly could play with anyone."

Field also said that one time they lost a game to Klein's Hillside at Tamarack Lodge, after which one of the busboys said that two of their teammates and one of the assistant dining hall managers had bet $700 on Klein's Hillside.

"There was probably a lot of that going on," he said, "but we didn't pay too much attention to it."

Tamarack Lodge was called a five-and-three house, which in the parlance of the Borscht Belt meant that waiters were to be tipped five dollars a week, busboys three. That first summer Cousy was a busboy, his job being to clean the tables and make sure the water glasses were full.

That and dance with the girls after dinner.

But only the ugly ones.

"That was the rule," Cousy said. "We were supposed to dance with the ugly girls so they would keep coming back to the lodge."

In a sense, it was his sexual awakening. Before that, his only real interaction with girls was at skate-alongs, sponsored by the local parish, St. Catherine's. Skate-alongs cost a nickel, and if you were really cool you got a chance to skate with a girl, maybe even hold her hand. Somehow this was less intimidating than school dances, where Cousy and his friends mostly stood on the fringes, shy around girls, not being comfortable dancing. They were the jocks, a little unofficial fraternity, and they mainly stuck to themselves.

That first summer in the Catskills was the first time he had been away from home for any significant time, and he loved it. The Catskills were only about an hour north of the city, but they could have been on the other side of the world as far as he was concerned. There were girls, there was competitive basketball, there were a handful of friends, and there was the sense that he was growing up, that there was a big world out there that had nothing to do with the little house on 116th Avenue in St. Albans and the tensions inside it.

He returned from the mountains with a large paper bag full of money, all in one-dollar and two-dollar bills. He dumped the bag on the kitchen table. It was roughly $1,200. His parents couldn't believe it. Twelve hundred dollars? Hadn't his father saved for 12 years to get the $500 for the down payment on the house?

At the end of the summer Bob Cousy left his parents' house and went off to college.

For all practical purposes he never went home again.

Chapter Three

He had taken a late-night train out of New York's Penn Station headed for Holy Cross and his future, arriving at an old, bleak, cavernous train station in the middle of a strange city shortly after dawn. It was raining, and as he came out of the train station all he could see were forlorn buildings in an old industrial city. Nobody paid any attention to him. Nor did he see any other kids his age who might be Holy Cross students. He felt as lost as lost could be, instantly wishing he could be back in St. Albans, back somewhere where life was familiar.

He found a taxi and headed off for his first look at Holy Cross.

Worcester, Massachusetts, was an old factory city 40 miles west of Boston, halfway between Boston and Springfield, the city where James Naismith had first invented basketball in 1891, ostensibly to give his gym classes something to do in the winter. Its main feature was the seven hills that surrounded the city, while downtown was in the valley.

Its history dated back to the 17th century, but it wasn't until 1848 that Worcester became a city, and that was primarily because the railroads had come, as many as 24 trains a day. After that came the Industrial Revolution, with scores of people moving in to work in the new factories and plants that seemed to be springing up everywhere, people called "mechanics." By the time a young Bob Cousy got off the train on that early morning in September of 1946, Worcester was the second-largest city in Massachusetts, with a huge manufacturing base. Four years later the population would top 200,000 people, the all-time city high.

Worcester was its own entity then, an hour from Boston. Providence, Rhode Island, was an hour to the south. Springfield was an hour to the west. Worcester was still surrounded by a lot of farmland and small towns, but the city itself, at least the part he saw that first morning, looked old, grimy, unwelcoming. Not surprising. It was blue-collar, an ethnic stew, full of people who had come from somewhere else to work in the mills, the kind of place where people were identified by what parish they belonged to, what neighborhood they were from, the kind of city that had been built by hard work and sweat, by long hours and lives dictated by factory whistles.

But when he first saw the campus from the taxi, saw it sitting up there on the side of a hill in its red-brick splendor, saw Fitton Field at the foot of the hill, saw the green-lined road that went up the hill leading to the main buildings, he instantly felt better.

The College of the Holy Cross, the oldest Catholic college in New England, had opened in 1843. Every Holy Cross student wore a jacket and tie every day. There was mandatory mass every morning at seven. There were mandatory mealtimes. Everyone went to class on Saturday morning, and everyone had to take Latin. There were no women allowed in rooms, no alcohol on campus, and lights went out at 10:30 during the week.

It was the fall of 1946, and Holy Cross was a small Jesuit school on Mount Saint James in the southern part of the city. But even if the game's roots were in New England, basketball had never really caught on, not like it had in New York and parts of the Midwest. Even though there'd been a semiprofessional league dating as far back as the early days of the 20th century, by 1946 basketball wasn't even played in the Boston public schools anymore.

New England was hockey country in the winter, and Red Sox country all year round. They were both well-established, particularly the Red Sox, whose history dated back to the 19th century.

College basketball? Outside of Rhode Island State, which played in the tiny hamlet of Kingston and was coached by Frank Keaney, the man credited with inventing fast-break basketball, and some decent teams at Dartmouth up in the New Hampshire woods, there were no good teams—at least none with any national success. College basketball in New England rarely transcended the campuses it was played on.

Holy Cross didn't even have its own gymnasium. Practices were held in a wooden barn, which once had housed cows that had produced milk for the school's dining halls. The court was so narrow that players could lean against the walls and still be in bounds. The coach was Alvin "Doggie" Julian, who also doubled as the backfield coach for the Boston Yanks of the National Football League. He had been hired in 1945, primarily to be the backfield coach for the Holy Cross football team, then had been given another $500 to coach the basketball team.

Doggie had grown up in Pennsylvania, and had earned 11 letters at Bucknell, graduating in 1923. He had been a catcher in the Baltimore organization, and then played professional football for the Pottstown Maroons, a team that beat the Chicago Bears for the 1925 NFL title, in a game they later forfeited. He was called Doggie because, as his high-school yearbook explained, he was walking with a group of friends when he stepped aside to help a couple of elderly ladies pass by. "Come, come, doggie," one of his friends said, snapping his fingers. The appellation stuck.

By the time he arrived at Holy Cross he had coached a state championship football team in Pennsylvania and semipro football. He had also been a basketball referee, known for wearing a necktie while officiating, and had been a successful basketball coach at Muhlenberg, a small Pennsylvania college. But he was primarily a football coach, to the point that after a brief, cursory meeting his first day on campus, Cousy didn't see Julian again for weeks.

Nor did Holy Cross have any basketball tradition.

Three years before Julian became the coach, Holy Cross had

only played six games, winning one. The year before he got there the record was 4–9. Until then, no more than 1,500 people had ever watched Holy Cross play a basketball game. In Doggie's first year, though, the Crusaders went 12–3, upsetting vaunted City College of New York and Bowling Green, then the second-ranked team in the country. More important, they began selling the sport. They had played several of their home games in the Boston Garden and had become very popular, drawing big crowds. Basketball in New England was about to change.

It has become revisionist history that Cousy led the Crusaders of Holy Cross to the national championship in 1947. It's often included as part of his glittering basketball résumé.

That's not the case.

The year before Cousy arrived, the starting five was Joe Mullaney, George Kaftan, Dermie O'Connell, Bobby Curran, and Ken Haggerty, the one who had first told Cousy about Holy Cross. Four of them were from New York City, bringing the city game with them to central Massachusetts, as if the give-and-go and cutting to the basket had been packed in their suitcases with their clothes and family pictures. Several of them had been in the service during the war.

The star was Kaftan. He was six-foot-four, athletic, the only guy on the team who could dunk. He could hit the foul-line jumper and score inside. He was from Brooklyn, so he also had a certain savvy, and he didn't get rattled. He was the only one on the team confident enough to tease Julian. One of Julian's idiosyncrasies was to rub the foreheads of his players before games.

And Doggie was nothing if not idiosyncratic.

"Not too much French pastry on that ball," Doggie once told Cousy, an expression that became part of basketball lexicon decades later, courtesy of Marquette coach and television broadcaster Al McGuire, who had worked with Julian at Dartmouth in the early fifties.

Kaftan was the only player who would rub Doggie's forehead in return. Sometimes, he would walk into the locker room and say, "Don't worry, Kaftan is here."

Mullaney, thin and sandy-haired, was from Queens, and had gone to Chaminade High School on Long Island. He was very clever with the ball, innovative. He was a basketball purist, already knew he wanted to be a coach. He was forever moving salt shakers around on the table, plotting strategy, devising defenses, infatuated with the intricacies of the game. He loved talking basketball. He even had been the player/coach of his high-school team as a senior, when the coach had gone off to the war. He had been in the Army Air Corps for three years, and had come to Holy Cross only because he had gotten out of the service after the school year had started and his brother Dave was already enrolled. Later in his life, as he thought back on his Holy Cross teammates, Cousy believed no one loved the game more than Mullaney did.

Curran, from Worcester, was a rugged six-foot-four. He was tough defensively, hard-nosed, but not much of a scorer. O'Connell was a bit of a loose cannon. He was streaky offensively, but also took some bad shots. Yet he played with high energy, the kind of player that made things happen. Haggerty was another smart New Yorker. He played guard, shot two-hand set shots, and possessed the toughness gleaned from a thousand playground games back in St. Albans.

They were all back. So the roster was an odd mix of service veterans and young kids from metropolitan New York. There were eight New Yorkers on the team, and some had never even heard of Holy Cross until about a year before they enrolled.

To even the most casual observer, the idea of a hotshot young freshman breaking into a lineup that had been so successful the year before was sheer folly, but Cousy didn't know that. Hadn't he been All-City the year before, the symbolic captain of the team? Hadn't he spent the summer playing in the Catskills against some of the top college players in the country? So even though Julian told his six incoming freshmen he was going to use a two-platoon system in order to get everyone playing time, Cousy didn't really understand that. He felt he was being snubbed. When practice started and he was not on the first team he often sulked. He was upset and made no attempt to disguise it. It so affected his mood the first semester of his freshman year that he sometimes went to the campus chapel after practice and prayed Doggie would give him his chance. It was an attitude that colored not only his freshman year, but also his relationship with Julian.

Even so, Cousy got his time on the floor.

It usually went like this: The first team, the five that had been there the year before, started the games. After nine and a half minutes Cousy and the other freshmen would come in as a group to spell them, usually led by Curran, who had become the unofficial captain of the second team. Sometimes, Curran wouldn't even wait for Julian to summon him. He would simply get off the bench after nine and a half minutes and start walking to the scorer's table, Cousy and three other freshmen following him.

Sometimes they would play half the game, sometimes only a third. Julian was the antithesis of Lew Grummond as a basketball coach, essentially letting the players use their creativity. Cousy played enough to score 227 points for the season, third highest on the team.

But he was only part of the ensemble, not the star.

Cousy was one of six freshmen.

Andy Laska, one of two Worcester kids on the team, was another.

"Bob was very adept at handling the ball," Laska said. "That was apparent right away, stood out from the beginning."

Laska had played at North High School in Worcester, had been overseas for two and a half years as an Army Air Force gunner, both in Guam and off the Japanese coast. By the time he got to

Holy Cross he was 21, on the GI Bill. He had all but grown up in the Boys Club, one of those kids who had been guided and shaped by sports, and going to a school as prestigious as Holy Cross was a dream come true.

The Crusaders captured New England's imagination. They were flashy, playing a wide-open, give-and-go style. A Boston sportswriter dubbed them "The Fancy Pants A.C." in homage to their showy style. They played some games in the Boston Garden and others at the smaller Boston Arena, which was across the city, near Huntington Avenue. They even played some games at South High School in Worcester. They often played the first game of doubleheaders in the Boston Garden because they had to get back to Worcester afterward, traveling back and forth in limousines. The crowd would invariably be big for their games, sometimes even selling out the Garden. Then the overwhelming majority of the crowd would leave before the second game started, usually one featuring either Boston College or Harvard.

College basketball had been big in New York City since the early thirties, most of the city schools having teams that generated a lot of interest. The problem was they all had small gyms, to the point that many of their more important games were played in nearby armories.

Enter Ned Irish.

Irish was a young New York City sportswriter in the early thirties who became convinced—after a tripleheader for the Unemployment Relief Fund had sold out Madison Square Garden—that college basketball could be promoted. He quickly realized doubleheaders made more sense than single games, both because four teams translated into more fans and because two games were a better entertainment value to the paying customer. So starting with St. John's versus Westminster, and NYU against Notre Dame in 1934, the Garden soon began hosting doubleheaders that were an immediate hit.

There's no underestimating the impact of this on the college game. It created intersectional rivalries. It created stars. It increased interest. It created a spiritual center for the game, doing things Irish never could have envisioned—all this in the country's media center. In a sense, it made the college game as we've come to know it. Many schools quickly realized the public-relations benefit that went with having a good team, not to mention the revenue it could generate, and began recruiting good high-school players. Both star players and coaches became known to the sporting public. The National Invitational Tournament, first played in the Garden in 1938, was an instant hit, so much so that the National Collegiate Athletic Association began its own post-season tournament the following year.

The college game grew.

It grew even more quickly during the war, for the simple reason that professional sports were decimated. Some players in the service even were allowed to play college basketball if they were fortunate enough to be stationed on a college campus. And as the Garden doubleheaders continued to attract huge crowds, other arenas in the Northeast tried to capitalize, too, all wanting their piece of the action.

One was the Boston Garden, the building that became Holy Cross's de facto home court.

After a slow 4-3 start, the Crusaders ran off 20 straight games, as the excitement of the season kept building through the winter of '47. The combined scores of many of those games reflect the basketball of the era, most being under 70 points. That was basketball in the late forties. To shoot 40 percent from the field was considered good.

Holy Cross entered the NCAA Tournament, playing at Madison Square Garden, with a 24-3 record. The Garden was on Eighth Avenue and 50th Street on Manhattan's West Side. It had an upper balcony that always seemed to be enshrouded in haze, courtesy of innumerable cigarettes and men who sat in the front rows and smoked cigars. The side balcony extended so far out over the arena that part of the court was obscured.

To anyone familiar with today's NCAA Tournament, and the

"March Madness" that dominates the sports world for three weeks, complete with its 64 teams and media saturation, the NCAA Tournament of 1947 would seem as if it were played on the dark side of the moon. There was no "Selection Sunday," no television, no early rounds at different sites. It wasn't even the most prestigious postseason college basketball tournament, the NIT having that distinction. There were only eight teams in the tournament, and the entire tournament was played over five days. There was a cartoon in the *Boston Herald,* though, essentially wishing the Holy Cross team good luck. It showed Julian, billed as a basketball tutor and phrenologist, rubbing the head of Bobby Curran, as Haggerty, Kaftan, Mullaney, and O'Connell stood and watched.

Holy Cross was the eighth seed, and entered the tournament with few expectations. In fact, they had even struggled in a tuneup game against New Britain Teachers College, a small Connecticut school. But they upset Navy in the first round in a sold-out Garden. Few teams scouted then, but Navy did, and it backfired on Navy coach Ben Carnevale. He had instructed his players to back off from Mullaney, the Holy Cross playmaker with the reputation of being a nonshooter. Mullaney responded with 18 points.

"I ended up with nine baskets because the guy didn't play me," Mullaney said afterward. "I never shot that much before."

The next year Carnevale told Mullaney's brother, Dave, who had transferred to Annapolis, that Navy never would have lost except "your brother had the luckiest day of his life."

The next opponent was CCNY, the school that had been synonymous with the best of college basketball in the late thirties and forties. They were coached by Nat Holman, one of the giants of the sport, whose roots went back to the old Original Celtics in New York City. In many ways, Holman had come to define eastern basketball, both in his stature and in the way his teams played. Three years later Holman and his team would win both the NCAA title and the NIT title, an incredible accomplishment, but after getting off to a quick lead, they let Holy Cross come storming back to win 60–45 behind Kaftan's 30 points.

The day of the 1947 NCAA championship game was highlighted on the Madison Square Garden marquee that hung out over Eighth Avenue. The marquee was small, with letters that said Madison Sq. Garden on the top, then TONIGHT and BASKETBALL over Texas vs. CCNY, and Oklahoma vs. Holy Cross. Underneath it said FRIDAY BOXING.

The Garden was sold out that night, as 18,445 people sat in the smoky haze and watched Holy Cross became the first New England school to win a national basketball title, this team that seemed to have risen out of the ashes of sports irrelevancy. Holy Cross, the team that just four years earlier had only played six games all year, the sport being so insignificant. Holy Cross, which didn't even have its own gym. This was the best team in the country? It seemed almost impossible to believe.

The final score was 58–47, as Kaftan scored 18 points and was named the tournament's most valuable player. He was carried off the court by his jubilant teammates in some age-old storybook scene, pictures of which went out across the country.

Cousy had been 2–13 from the floor, didn't really feel as if he'd been a part of it. Still, he was on a national championship team just three years removed from being cut from his high-school team, and after essentially playing only a year and a half of high-school basketball.

The team returned next day by train to a hero's welcome. There were 10,000 people standing in the cold at Union Station in downtown Worcester, the same place Cousy had arrived at just six months earlier. A number of the station doors were snapped off their hinges as the crowd pushed to see the players being carried to their cars. A huge sign from the Boys Club congratulated Andy Laska, the hometown boy. A victory parade brought the players to a ceremony at City Hall where the school's purple banner was hoisted between the U.S. and state of Massachusetts flags.

The players were given keys to the city and $200 gift certificates, treated like royalty in ways that would have been unimaginable just a year before.

"The whole thing was a fluke," Mullaney would later say. "Not that we didn't have talent, but in the way we had all gotten to the school. In many ways the team came together by accident. Nobody knew us."

That team also left a remarkable legacy.

And it was more than the fact that immediately afterward you couldn't ride around Worcester without seeing baskets on street poles, in backyards. The city had fallen in love with this team that had come out of nowhere, one that had given it an incredible, unexpected gift. Worcester was the home of the national basketball champions, and who could have ever believed that could happen to Worcester, the gritty mill town in central Massachusetts, the place you went through on the way to someplace else?

It was the sense that the 1947 Holy Cross team became the unofficial godfathers of basketball in New England, the head of an extended coaching tree whose branches have dominated the college game in the area ever since. Julian coached one more year at Holy Cross, then coached the Celtics for two years before being succeeded by Auerbach. Julian later coached at Dartmouth for 17 years before dying in 1967. One of his players was Dave Gavitt, who went on to coach the 1980 Olympic team and start the Big East Conference, the league that changed college basketball in the East, in the late seventies.

Six of the players from that '47 team went on to be college coaches, including Mullaney, who transformed tiny Providence College from a small, mostly commuter school that no one ever heard of into a basketball name, winning two NIT titles in the early sixties, the architect of a basketball tradition that exists to this day. He later coached in the NBA.

Frank Oftring and Bobby Curran both eventually coached at Holy Cross, and Laska coached 17 years at Assumption College in

Worcester, turning that school into a small college power in the sixties.

In 1997, a half-century after that dream season, the '47 team was honored at Holy Cross. The eight surviving members were honored at halftime of the Holy Cross–Navy game in the school's 2,800 seat Hart Center, located at the top of Mount Saint James. The college basketball world was a far different place that afternoon than it had been 50 years earlier, and maybe nowhere was this more evident than at Holy Cross, which had turned its back on big-time basketball when it spurned an invitation to join the Big East in the late seventies. Now it played in the Patriot League, a low-level Division I league.

Cousy, Mullaney, Kaftan, Laska, Haggerty, and a little-used player named Jim Riley all returned for the reunion. So did Julian's widow, Lee, and several of the spouses of the players who had passed away.

Two of the eight at the ceremony were Charlie Bollinger, who at six-foot-seven had been the tallest player. He had played at St. Cecelia's in Englewood, New Jersey, a team that had been coached by Vince Lombardi. Charlie Graver, a 27-year-old freshman, had come from a Pennsylvania coal mining town.

"A Jewish guy who knew Doggie recruited me," he said. "I was 27 and just out of the service. I got a telegram from Doggie which simply said he had a scholarship and an open spot for me. I was born a Lutheran, but I didn't hesitate."

There also was a blind student named William Gallagher, whom everyone called "Rocks." He first sat on the end of the bench, because he shared a philosophy class with Haggerty, but after the team won that night Julian called him a good luck charm and he sat there the rest of the season. He, too, returned for the reunion, and was featured in a column by John Gearan of the *Worcester Telegram,* along with a picture of him in his wheelchair holding the championship trophy at center court.

Gallagher had lost his sight while in high school, but had been an athlete before that. At Holy Cross he never used either a cane or a Seeing Eye dog, getting around by himself by memorizing the hundreds of steep steps on the campus instead.

"Rocks was down at the end of the bench and I didn't get a lot of playing time," Graver told Gearan. "That's when the Good Lord asked me, 'Why don't you go down there and be his eyes.' That's how it began."

"In a strange way how they treated him was representative of what those guys were all about," Gearan said. "They took care of him. They made him a part of it. They took care of each other."

Gearan came away from that reunion with a respect for those men who once had been young in 1947, their faces freeze-framed in youth in the commemorative program, as if—if you closed your eyes, a half-century of time could be wiped away, and it would be right after the war, when they used to practice in an old barn and then take limos to the Boston Garden, in the season that they achieved their slice of immortality.

"There were no shitheads," Gearan said. "They were quality people. They didn't expect the world to take care of them. That day of the reunion they were all self-deprecating. They knew that what they had done 50 years earlier hadn't been all that big a deal, but history had made it so. But they were proud of it, too, and of the fact that people still remembered."

They were also proud of one another. As happens with men who have been to war together, that year had linked them together, a bond that had endured all these years, all through their lives, as if they knew that once upon a time they had shared something significant, something that seemed only to grow in importance as the years went by.

"This team passed on its unique style of play to the game of basketball," said Dee Rowe, one of the speakers. "Doggie Julian threw the first stone in the water and the ripples of that team continue today."

Rowe, the former coach at the University of Connecticut, had been in high school in Worcester in 1947. He had listened to the Holy Cross games on the radio, falling in love with a game that would come to define his life, and he spoke lovingly of the team, and the effect it had on the city of Worcester, "in a way no other team has ever been, or ever will.

"These players were my heroes," Rowe said. "Fifty years ago we put you on a pedestal. And 50 years later, you're still there."

Winning the national title did not resolve Cousy's feelings about Julian. If anything, it only intensified them. He had only played about a third of the Navy game, even less in the finals against Oklahoma. And this was in the Garden, no less, back in New York, where he figured he was going to be returning home to cheers and accolades. Again, he felt Julian had slighted him, and this time he had had enough. Julian didn't like him, and he had spent the entire year feeling as if there had been reins on him. Well, now he was going to do something about it.

So he wrote a letter to Joe Lapchick, then the coach of St. John's in Brooklyn, saying he wanted to transfer. At the time Lapchick was one of the biggest names in the sport, one of the Original Celtics, and St. John's was one of the glamor basketball schools in the city.

Lapchick answered back in a letter.

"Doggie Julian is one of the finest basketball coaches in America, and some day you'll be proud you played for him. He doesn't want to hurt you and isn't doing it deliberately. I know he is depending heavily on you in future years and would be very much upset if he knew how you felt.

"Aside from everything else, transferring from one college to another is at best a very risky move. You don't know if you're going from the frying pan into the fire. And college rules dictate that you must wait a year before being eligible for varsity competition. This would hardly make it worthwhile for you. Be patient. You're only a freshman. Your turn will come. Stay at Holy Cross. You'll never regret it."

If life was, indeed, a Hollywood script, Cousy and Julian would have reconciled in some dramatic, defining moment, complete with violins playing in the background. That never happened. Just as it seemed their relationship was going to get better, something would invariably happen. In short, they simply didn't like each other very much. So they rarely communicated in practice in anything but a perfunctory way in Cousy's sophomore year, although on the surface things were better than the year before— until the day Doggie thought Cousy missed practice because he was playing in an outside game on a Sunday afternoon.

It was a fairly common practice then. College players would play in some town league on a Sunday afternoon under an assumed name, picking up a few bucks, even though it was against the rules. So when Cousy failed to show for a Sunday afternoon practice two days before Holy Cross was to play a big game against Loyola in the Boston Arena, Julian erupted in a rage. No matter that Cousy and a couple of students had been in a minor traffic accident that morning while returning from a dance at a girls' school about two hours from Worcester. No matter that he tried to explain to Julian what had happened. Doggie didn't want to hear it, and wouldn't even listen to Cousy's explanation.

When the starting lineup was announced shortly before the game, Cousy wasn't in it. He couldn't believe it. Once again, it summoned up all of last year's feelings. Once again, he felt as if it was always going to be his fate to have his dreams snubbed by some coach. The longer he sat on the bench the more upset he became. Then, without looking at him, Julian called his name.

There were 30 seconds left in the half. To Cousy, this was the height of humiliation. The second half began the same way. The game was close. Julian didn't call his name. Eventually, there were only five minutes left, Loyola up by seven. The game appeared over.

Then it started.

"We Want Cousy. . . . We Want Cousy."

At first it was just a brushfire of noise. It quickly escalated. Until the chant swept across the Boston Arena.

"WE WANT COUSY. . . . WE WANT COUSY."

Suddenly, there was a timeout and Julian was motioning for him to go into the game.

He took seven shots in the last few minutes and made six of them, as Holy Cross pulled the game out. He had been the hero. But when the game ended Cousy ran into the locker room, his emotions raw, feeling equal parts grief and relief. By the time he got his uniform off he was crying. He went into the shower room and didn't want to come out. By the time he returned to the locker room he was under control, as if all the emotion had been drained out of him. On the ride back to Worcester he watched the lights go by on Route 9, talking to no one. He didn't say another word to Julian the rest of the year. Julian spoke to him only when he absolutely had to, and the two finished the rest of the season in an uneasy truce.

Cousy went on to have a breakout sophomore year, establishing himself as one of the top players in all of college basketball. He set the all-time Holy Cross single-game scoring record, he and Kaftan were the New England college players of the year, and the Associated Press had him on their All-America team.

More important, he was starting to get recognition for the unique way he played, for the show he had become, as if he were some preview of the future, even if no one could have possibly envisioned what that future was going to be. The first to see it, at least publicly, was a sportswriter from the *Chicago Sun* named Bill Siler. He covered the Sugar Bowl Tournament in New Orleans in December 1947.

"Cousy is a court magician," Siler wrote. "You see better shots than Cousy's, but you've never seen anyone as good at passing and retrieving the ball. He gets rid of the ball underhand, overhand, sidearmed, with two hands, one hand, deflects it, bounces it, and, as often as not, bewilders his own teammates."

The only bad moment came in his last game of the season, in the second game of the NCAA Tournament against Kentucky. All 12 players had returned from the national championship, and the team had had a great year, drawing huge crowds in the Boston Garden, and huge interest in Worcester, finishing 26-4. But they couldn't replicate the magic of the year before, losing to eventual champion Kentucky and their stars Ralph Beard and Alex Groza in the semifinals. Cousy was awful, missing 13 of his 14 shots, and Holy Cross got beat.

The season was over, and still Cousy had not spoken to Julian—until one day in the spring when Cousy was shooting around by himself in the gym and Julian approached him.

"I'd like to talk to you for a couple of minutes," Julian said.

"Sure," Cousy said.

"Cooz," he said. "I've just accepted an offer to coach the Boston Celtics next year."

Cousy took a long breath.

"I want you to know that I'm sorry for anything that might have prevented us from getting along better," he said. "It's too bad that there seemed to be a personality clash between us, but now I'd like to shake hands and part friends."

He held out his hand, and Cousy took it.

"That's fine with me, Doggie," Cousy said. "I know there was never anything personal involved, and I guess I did plenty of things I shouldn't have done. I'm sorry about those. But it's all over now."

They looked at each other for a minute.

Then Cousy said, "Best of luck with the Celtics, Doggie."

"Thanks," Julian said.

The new coach was Lester "Buster" Sheary, and to Cousy, he was everything Julian had not been.

He was one of those larger-than-life Damon Runyon characters, old school before there was old school. He was short and stocky with a brush haircut, and he seemed to exude both strength and authority. Later in his life, he achieved a certain local notoriety as a lecturer at kids' basketball camps, where he would start out by rubbing the ball in his hands, caressing it, even kissing it.

"You have to love the ball," Buster would say.

Eventually, he would be on the ground with the ball, rolling over and over with it, him and the ball, as if off in some private world.

He would go on to win the NIT in 1954. He always was idio-syncratic, telling players that if they urinated on their feet while taking showers the skin on their feet would get tougher, less prone to blisters. He believed in his ability to motivate, and often said that if you gave him five red-blooded American boys and let him motivate them anything was possible. But he was also a father fig-ure to many of the players, and that affection was reciprocated.

It was said that when Buster lost he hid in the alleys, and when he won he paraded down Main Street.

In 2001 Sheary was near death. He was 93, an invalid. In his final days, Cousy, Dee Rowe, Andy Laska, and a couple of others who had once played for him paid a last visit. As the story goes, they were sitting in the backyard.

"Robert," he said to Cousy in his old, raspy voice. "Run over and touch the fence and run back."

"Coach, I'm too old, and my knees hurt," Cousy said.

"Robert," commanded Buster. "Run over and touch the fence."

Cousy did.

On the day Sheary died there was a funeral service for him in Worcester. Cousy was one of the pallbearers, along with several other men who once had played for Sheary. Going to the ceme-tery, the funeral procession went down Main Street.

"Is this the quickest way to St. John's Cemetery?" Cousy asked.

It wasn't.

It was Buster Sheary going down Main Street one last time.

Sheary turned Cousy loose. The frustration he had felt with Julian disappeared. In fall 1949, in a Dell magazine called *Basket-ball—1950,* he was called the best college player in the country, "perhaps the finest shooter in the game today."

The magazine stated Cousy should have been a first-team All-American the year before, and the fact that Tony Lavelli of Yale, Alex Groza and Ralph Beard of Kentucky, Vince Boryla of Denver, and Ed Macauley of St. Louis had been chosen ahead of him didn't necessarily mean they were better players, they just got more votes. Inside the magazine he was featured in a photo spread. All of the pictures were shot at Holy Cross, in what was meant to be a smorgasbord of campus life. There were pictures of Cousy in the library, Cousy in the trainer's room, Cousy talking to one of the school's deans, Cousy in a shirt and tie seated at a desk studying, Cousy getting a letter from the mailroom, Cousy in a shirt and tie packing a suitcase to go on a road trip, Cousy on his way back from mass. It was all meant to convey the impression that Cousy was not simply some jock who lived in the gym, but was a well-rounded student immersed in campus life, the prototype for what the NCAA, years later, would start referring to as "student-athletes."

And one picture showed Cousy with his hometown girlfriend, Marie Ritterbusch, whom everyone called Missie. They are pictured outside against a railing in front of the brick library, Cousy in a suit and tie, Missie in a dark skirt, high heels, and white jacket, her dark hair shoulder length. There is a certain quiet elegance to the picture, as though they are both ready to go out to some expensive restaurant in some chic city, not on some campus date.

The text said, "It's not every girl who's got the country's best basketball player for a boyfriend. Pretty Marie Ritterbusch usually comes to Worcester when HC plays a home game."

He had known about her while in high school, even though she went to Bishop McDonald, a parochial school in Brooklyn. Her brother Ed had been one of the older guys who used to hang around O'Connell Park. Missie was part of a different circle than the one Cousy traveled with, for she was eight months older and two years ahead of him in school, even though she had also grown up in St. Albans, only 8 to 10 blocks away.

She was the youngest of four children, and was nicknamed

Missie by one of her older brothers who used to refer to her as the "little missie." Her father had died when she was 12, and her mother worked two jobs, at Merrill Lynch in New York during the day and for a beauty salon three nights a week. So Missie had been the one who did most of the cooking. She also had to travel by bus, and by train, to get to high school every morning. While in high school she had worked at the Gertz department store in nearby Jamaica. She liked working with the buyers, being in the center of things. She was attractive, outgoing, had been raised in a warm, loving family. Years later she would listen to Cousy talk about his family, how he and his parents never went anywhere together, how holidays had been something to endure, not enjoy, and it had all seemed so foreign to her, her experience being so different.

She had seen Cousy play a couple of times at Andrew Jackson, had heard people say he was a good player, but she really didn't meet him until Cousy was a freshman at Holy Cross and she was still working at Gertz. The place was some bar on nearby Long Island, a German place that had entertainment. A group of kids had gone out, pooled their resources for a pitcher of beer and a platter of cold cuts. After a few similar nights she realized things were changing between them, even if she hadn't necessarily been aware of it.

"We used to go out in groups," she said, "and he always seemed to be sitting next to me. One night he asked me if I would write to him because he was lonely."

That was the beginning. Their first date was to see *Brigadoon* on Broadway, taking the train from Jamaica into the city.

Eventually, it became steadier. She went to the Holy Cross dances, and to some of the Holy Cross games with her brother. Yet when she saw her picture in the basketball yearbook she couldn't believe it. Nor could her friends, or the people in the neighborhood. Missie Ritterbusch in a national basketball magazine?

"I wasn't happy," she said years later, "because then nobody from home would ask me out."

She would again realize the price of fame when she and Cousy were engaged, the item appearing in Ed Sullivan's *Talk of the Town* section in one of the New York papers, noting that Robert Cousy of Holy Cross, one of the best college basketball players in the country, was engaged to marry Marie Ritterbusch of St. Albans, New York.

Most of the time, though, his life revolved around the quiet, sequestered world of the Holy Cross campus. A big night out was to go downtown and have a few beers at the French Club, a working-class place where the Holy Cross players could belly up to the bar. In his mind, he was a jock, and this is what jocks did.

By the beginning of his senior year Cousy was being called the best player in the country. Kaftan was gone, as were many of the players he'd started out with at Holy Cross. It was his team, and he'd become a national figure, his picture in basketball magazines, his name known inside the world of the college game.

He also had become known for his flashy style of play, most of which was never planned. It's difficult to understand now, in this era when self-expression has become as much a part of basketball as dunks and expensive sneakers, but in the basketball world of the late forties, to stand out, to draw attention to yourself, to do anything outside the established norm, was almost frowned upon. That Cousy would come to be known as the originator of this style is not without a certain irony, given both his personality and the basketball culture he'd come out of.

The beginnings had been the Holy Cross team itself. Joe Mullaney could pass. Andy Laska could pass. Even Kaftan, the team's high scorer and big man, could pass. Many of the other players were from New York, and had grown up playing pass-and-cut basketball, with its emphasis on making your teammates better. Julian also employed a "figure eight" offense, classic city school-yard basketball, with its heavy emphasis on speed, ball-handling, and cutting.

Often, in practice, some of the players fooled around with behind-the-back and over-the-shoulder passes, or looking one way and throwing the other, things perceived as tricks back then, certainly things they never would do in an actual game. Cousy loved this kind of stuff, had in fact thrown the ball behind his back a couple of times while in high school, not in any desire to showboat, but out of desperation, because the situation in the game required it. He also used to occasionally throw over-the-shoulder passes in games. Still, it was not something he often did, at least not in an actual game. So even he was surprised during his junior year when he dribbled behind his back in a game in a sold-out Boston Garden, a move that would not only become one of his basketball signatures, but would be a sneak preview of basket-ball's future, even if he had never practiced it before, never had even thought about it before.

It happened against Loyola, with the game tied in the final seconds. Cousy had been held scoreless in the second half, toughly guarded by Ralph Klaerich, who had been sitting on his right hand throughout the half.

"We were in a timeout," Cousy recalled. "We decided to hold the ball for one shot, and I was going to take the shot. After pass-ing the ball around, until the clock went down to about eight sec-onds left, I started driving to the basket. I was on the left side of the court, going to my right. But when I got down to the right side of the basket my opponent was on my right side and I had no room to shoot. I had no choice."

So without changing direction he bounced the ball behind his back with his right hand, picked it up with his left, and then drove in and made the winning shot with a sweeping left-handed hook shot. The Garden erupted in a hurricane of noise, people realizing they had just seen something they never had seen before.

That was the beginning.

Showtime had been born.

Only no one knew it yet.

In the winter of 1950 Cousy was the most celebrated college player in the country, getting accolades from virtually every

opposing coach, some of the biggest coaching names in basketball, for his unique style of play, the growing sense that no one
played the game quite like he played it.

- "You know something," said Nat Holman, the famous CCNY
  coach, "that Cousy is going to be the greatest pro player."
- Kansas coach Phog Allen, who once had played for James Naismith, the man who had invented basketball, said, "I think
  that Cousy can watch both corners and the basket, too."
- "I see him pull this stuff right in front of me, but I still don't
  believe it," said St. Louis coach Ed Hickey.
- "Cousy is simply out of this world," said Harold Anderson of
  Bowling Green.
- "He is a basketball quarterback," said famed Kentucky basketball coach Adolph Rupp, who also said Cousy was the trickiest
  player he'd ever seen. "He has a quick change of pace that
  makes him very dangerous. He has every shot in the book and
  will go down in history as one of the greatest basketball players of all time."

Yet even all this didn't really change his life.

There were still classes to go to, curfews to meet. There was still
mass every morning at seven. You still had to be in your room
when you were supposed to be. There was still the daily structure
of Holy Cross, and the Jesuits, who were not going to let any student feel too self-important, even one who was doing things on a
basketball court that few people had ever done before, someone
who seemed to be reinventing the game, showing a glimpse of its
myriad possibilities, even if, to him, it was simply playing the
same game he always had played.

"I was naive about publicity," Cousy says. "Every once in a
while a sportswriter would show up, but I was in Worcester, Massachusetts. At Holy Cross. With a Jesuit on every floor. I was pretty
much unaffected by it."

But the drum rolls were beating.

In February 1950 there was a two-page story in the *Boston Sunday Advertiser* by Murray Kramer, complete with nine pictures, under the headline, "Magic Bob Cousy—Pass-Master of Basketball."

The pictures show him in a white Holy Cross uniform with number 17 on the front. He is wearing a white T-shirt underneath his uniform top because Buster Sheary thought a T-shirt absorbed sweat.

"The 21-year-old basketball marvel is what Babe Ruth was to baseball and Red Grange to football," Kramer wrote. "Even staid old Boston goes berserk when Cousy comes to town."

Holy Cross again went to the NCAA Tournament, the third time in Cousy's four years. This time the Crusaders lost to North Carolina State in the first round at Madison Square Garden. Cousy's college career was over, and it seemed as if it had come right out of a storybook.

And now he was ready for the highest level of all.

He wanted to play for the Celtics, but it wasn't as if it were some consuming passion, the culmination of some childhood dream. He hadn't gone to college to become a professional basketball player. He hadn't even seen the Celtics play during his time at Holy Cross.

"I just wanted to earn a living and exploit my notoriety," says Cousy. "I wasn't even thinking of the NBA, first because it seemed so Mickey Mouse, and no one from any team had spoken to me. I don't think I had ever even seen a professional game."

He and some of his teammates had organized a mini–barnstorming tour around central Massachusetts and throughout New England, games against local town teams, after which they would split the gate. It was called the "Bob Cousy All-Stars" and it had been a huge success, with Cousy making nearly $10,000. Virtually everywhere they went people came out to see them, packing the small gyms. They even played a couple of games in the Worcester Auditorium against a semipro team named after a construction company, games that were sold out. So Cousy figured he could keep doing that as long as people kept coming to watch him and his ex-teammates play, as long as he could keep his name in front of the public. He and teammate Frank Oftring had also decided to start both a driving school and a gas station, another way to use their local reputations to make money.

He just assumed that if he were going to play in the NBA it would be for the Celtics. But one day in the spring of 1950, a few days after Auerbach had been named the new coach, a sportswriter called him to tell him the Celtics had passed him over in the first round, choosing a near seven-footer from Bowling Green named Chuck Share. From a public-relations standpoint it was a strange decision, considering that the Celtics were having difficulty drawing fans and building any significant interest in the team.

"Who picked me?" he asked the sportswriter.

"Tri-Cities," he was told.

Tri-Cities?

Where oh where was Tri-Cities?

He quickly decided that if he had to go to some place in Iowa to play professional basketball then the hell with it. If the Celtics didn't want him then so be it. He would do something else with his life. Tri-Cities? No way.

The reason given for snubbing Cousy certainly made basketball sense. He was only a shade under six-foot-two, a small man in a game that was becoming increasingly big. There had been a recent *Sport* magazine story written by Eddie Gottlieb, the owner of the Philadelphia Warriors, that said the little man was through in basketball, that bigger players now had the same skills the smaller players had. Plus, the most dominant player in the professional game was 6-foot-10 George Mikan, who would plant himself in the middle of the lane and was almost impossible to stop. Cousy had mostly played as a forward in college, but he knew he was too small to be a forward in the NBA.

There also was the fact that three of his former teammates—Kaftan, Mullaney, and O'Connell—all had failed to make it with the Celtics, as had Tony Lavelli, a local kid who had played at

Yale. All had been given a chance by the Celtics to capitalize on their local fame. None of them had worked out. Why was Cousy going to be any different?

That theme was elaborated on a few days later in a press conference, when Auerbach was asked why he hadn't taken Cousy, already a fan favorite in the Boston Garden, already the darling of the sportswriters who had covered Holy Cross.

Auerbach, never known for his tact, turned to Celtics' owner Walter Brown and asked in a line that would become part of Boston sports lore, "Am I supposed to win, or worry about the local yokels?"

"Just win," Brown said.

By this time Cousy had calmed down and had gone to Buffalo where Tri-Cities owner Ben Kerner had one of his businesses. He didn't go with an agent. He didn't go with an advisor. He didn't go with anyone. He simply flew up there one afternoon by himself after classes at Holy Cross. He told Kerner he wanted $10,000. Kerner countered with $6,500. That was the end of the meeting.

Kerner's next offer was $7,500. The Tri-Cities were in Iowa, Moline, Rock Island, and Davenport, and try as he might Cousy couldn't see himself living in any one of them, especially since he and Missie were making wedding plans. What he didn't know, though, was that Kerner was trying to unload him. Eventually he did, to the Chicago Stags.

Not that Cousy was overly concerned. He never thought basketball was going to be his life's work. Then he heard he'd been traded to Chicago. So what, he thought. He wasn't going to play in Chicago, either. He was going to get married in the fall, and if he wasn't going to be able to play in Boston, he figured his basketball days were over, and it was time to get on with his real life. Either way, he was going to be successful. He had no doubt about that.

But the Stags folded before the season started, its players distributed among the other teams. Eventually, only three were left: Max Zaslofsky, a proven star whom the Knicks coveted because he was Jewish and might be able to sell some tickets, and whom Cousy knew from the Catskills; Andy Phillip, a veteran guard and proven playmaker; and Cousy, the hotshot kid who had yet to prove he could play in the league. The three players were going to go to the Knicks, the Warriors, and the Celtics. And no one wanted Cousy.

The rest is basketball history, one of those curious twists of fate that changed everything.

No one could decide where each player should go. After much bickering, and a meeting that kept dragging on interminably, Podoloff finally decided to drop the names into a hat, putting a $15,000 price tag on Zaslofsky, $10,000 on Phillip, and $8,500 on Cousy. Ned Irish of the Knicks picked first and ended up with Zaslofsky. Eddie Gottlieb, the Philadelphia owner, picked next and got Phillip. That left Walter Brown.

The "local yokel" was coming to Boston.

Chapter Four

Bob Cousy was graduating from Andrew Jackson High School when the Celtics were being born.

It was June 1946, and the birthplace was the Commodore Hotel in New York City, a building next to Grand Central Station. It was the second anniversary of D-Day, the day the Allies landed in Normandy and changed the war. A handful of men, most of whom owned arenas in which hockey was played, wanted a basketball league to fill up some of those long winter nights when their buildings were empty. They named it the Basketball Association of America, and by the time they left the Commodore Hotel there were 11 teams, 6 in the East, 5 in the Midwest.

The Celtics' owner was Walter Brown, who owned the Boston Garden. He had inherited it from his father, and by the mid-forties he was concerned he didn't have enough events to put into it.

The Boston Garden was located in the city's North End, over North Station, complete with a hotel on one side and an office building on the other. Across the street, on the other side of the green elevated train tracks, was a scene out of some film noir. The streets were narrow and congested. There was a cafeteria that seemed to come right out of an Edward Hopper painting. There were small shot-and-beer bars. There were pawn shops and shoeshine parlors, barber shops and Sullivan's Tap, which had a bar as long as a city block, a neighborhood where Leigh Montville once wrote in *Sports Illustrated*, "Jimmy Cagney could have very easily tipped his hat to George Raft."

Inside was more of the same. Downstairs was the hustle and bustle of North Station. There was a bar called the Iron Horse, all dark and smoky. There were newsstands. You got to the Garden by walking up cement ramps, and the smoke always seemed to be hanging over the court, the residue of innumerable Red Auerbach cigars. The locker room was out of some lost era, a homage to every old YMCA. Each player had only one hook for his clothes. There were two showers. There was one toilet, two steps up from the floor, and often water would flow onto the locker-room floor.

Originally, the Garden had been the idea of Tex Rickard, a New York boxing promoter who owned Madison Square Garden. In 1928 he decided to replicate the Garden in six other cities. Boston had been the first, but then Rickard died and the plan died with him.

As soon as the Boston Garden opened in 1929 the Boston Bruins, who had been playing hockey since the late twenties, moved in. Brown tried just about everything to make the cavernous building work, everything from the circus to midget auto races to indoor softball. He even once staged a Notre Dame football game there. Still, by the mid-forties the two biggest tenants were the Bruins and the Ice Capades, both of which Brown owned. He was looking for something else.

Professional basketball had been around since the early 1900s, many teams playing as warmup acts in local dance halls. Some teams even played inside steel cages to protect themselves from unruly fans, wore pads, and played a game that often resembled football scrimmages. Little wonder that, in those days, basketball players came to be called "cagers."

Perhaps the most famous team of the twenties had been the Original Celtics, based in New York City. They were the descendants of the New York Celtics, which had disbanded when America entered World War I. They played Sunday nights at the 71st Regiment Armory in Manhattan, signed players for the season and not just individual games, and instituted the kind of teamwork that came to revolutionize the sport. They had a pivot man, played zone defense, and used an offense that put a premium on passing. Two of their stars were Joe Lapchick, who would go on to coach both the Knicks and St. John's, and Nat Holman, whose City College of New York teams came to dominate college basketball in the forties.

The other significant professional basketball area of the country was the Midwest, the teams mostly connected to companies. They were called the Cleveland Rosenblums, the Indianapolis Krautskys, the Fort Wayne Zollner Pistons, the Oshkosh All-Stars, the Toledo Jim White Chevrolets. But it was all on the far side of glamor. Teams came and went. Players switched teams. There was no stability. It was all decidedly minor league, especially in light of the fact that college basketball was booming, doubleheaders routinely filling Madison Square Garden.

But the war was over and attendance at sporting events was soaring. Baseball. Golf. Tennis. Auto racing. Horse racing. It didn't seem to matter. In 1945 Major League Baseball had set a record with 11 million people attending games, as the sport rebounded from the war years, when it often seemed as if all the real players were overseas, there was no spring training because of gas rationing, and the only reason Major League Baseball hadn't closed down was that President Franklin D. Roosevelt didn't want it to, convinced that baseball was one of the few things that gave people a brief respite from the realities of the war.

The new basketball league's premise was simple: Try to capitalize on the popularity of college basketball, and use hockey as the blueprint, the National Hockey League having already been in existence for 19 years. The founding fathers set the length of the games at 48 minutes rather than the 40 minutes of the college game, because they wanted two hours of entertainment. They outlawed zone defenses because zones tended to slow the game down, and each player was to be allowed six fouls instead of five.

When Brown left New York that June day in 1946 his new basketball franchise didn't even have a name. Several were tossed around until Brown came up with the name Celtics. Didn't the name have a certain history in the game, what with the Original Celtics in New York in the twenties? Didn't Boston have a lot of people of Irish descent? So Celtics it became. Walter Brown would put his new team in green uniforms and call them the Boston Celtics.

Brown's first choice to be the coach was Frank Keaney, then the coach at Rhode Island State College, the man credited with being the granddaddy of fast-break basketball. The season before, Keaney's college team had gone to the finals of the National Invitational Tournament, the most prestigious college basketball showcase in the country. But in August of '46 Keaney backed out due to health reasons, and at the last minute Brown chose John "Honey" Russell, a basketball name who had been a highly successful coach at Seton Hall.

It hadn't worked out.

The team was bad. The interest in it was worse.

The team practiced at the Boston Arena Annex, a building Brown owned that was on the other side of town from the Boston Garden. The players worked out on the second floor and slept on cots downstairs. Honey Russell once said that the first time he saw the practice site the building was cold, the lighting was bad, and the baskets had been put up upside down. That might be apocryphal, but there was no question the Celtics' first training camp was taking place in virtual obscurity, for in the world of Boston sports they barely existed. Making them even more irrelevant was the fact that the Red Sox were in the World Series against the St. Louis Cardinals.

The Celtics' first game was played in Rhode Island before 4,406 people, the Celtics losing to the Providence Steamrollers, a game that received one paragraph in the *Boston Globe*. The story was wedged between a schedule for Boston Park football and Watertown's high-school football victory over Framingham. But it was better than coverage in the *Boston Post,* which didn't cover the team for its first two seasons.

"The papers wouldn't put box scores in because they didn't know how to type them in," Auerbach said.

It is part of Celtics lore that they played their home opener in the Boston Arena because Gene Autry's rodeo was in the Boston Garden, and that it was the night that hometown boy John F. Kennedy first got elected to Congress. And that while the Celtics were warming up, Chuck Connors, who later would go on to become television's Rifleman, broke a backboard with a long two-hand set shot. And that Walter Brown was not pleased, considering that he had to send a truck across the city to the Boston Garden where a replacement backboard was found behind the Brahman bull pens. Or by the time the game began most of the people had already left.

Cousy knew none of these things, even though they were happening only 40 miles away. Not that there was any reason for him to know them. Not only were the Celtics little more than an irrelevancy, but Cousy wasn't at Holy Cross thinking of one day being a professional basketball player.

But the Celtics bizarre beginnings were a harbinger of things to come.

The team finished 22-38, averaging about 4,000 people a game, less than a third of the Garden's capacity of 13,909 for basketball. About the only thing worthwhile that came out of that season was the parquet floor in the Boston Arena, made by left-over scraps of wood, due to the shortage of wood from the war. The parquet floor would be moved to the Boston Garden a few years later, and eventually would become the most famous floor in basketball, the Celtics' signature. But all that was a long way off in that winter of 1947. At the end of the dismal year Honey Russell was let go, replaced by Doggie Julian, as Walter Brown kept seeing Holy Cross fill up the Garden and wanted to capture some of that magic for his struggling new team.

That didn't happen, either.

George Kaftan, Joe Mullaney, and Dermie O'Connell were

added to the Celtics, all without a lot of success, either on the court or at the box office—at least not anything that endured. Kaftan's first game in February '49 was a sellout, unheard of for the Celtics back then, but after the curiosity ended it was back to relative obscurity. There were rumors the new league already was in trouble, since the league was plagued with too many weak franchises, the legacy of its dance hall past. One game in 1949, a home game the Celtics played in Providence against the Philadelphia Warriors, drew 216 people.

The Celtics even had rookie Tony Lavelli, a true local hero, play the accordion at halftime. Lavelli was from nearby Somerville and had been so popular in high school that his team had played the state finals in the Boston Garden. He had then gone on to Yale, where he'd been an All-American, his game marked by an unbelievable hook shot he seemed to be able to make from just about anywhere. He also played the accordion, well enough to have considered skipping pro ball to go to prestigious Juilliard in New York City after Yale. By the 13th game of the season Walter Brown was so desperate to put more people in the seats that he not only begged Lavelli to sign with the Celtics, but also agreed to pay him another $125 a night to perform at halftime.

The first time he played, he played "Lady of Spain" and selections from the *William Tell* Overture, all the while wearing his Celtics' shiny green warmup jacket.

Lavelli's deal was to perform 25 halftime concerts, at least one in every city, but Lavelli's Celtics' career was short-lived when Julian was fired at the end of the year and replaced by new coach Red Auerbach.

"He's gone," barked Auerbach about Lavelli. "He's not tough enough to play pro ball, and I have no time for sentiment."

It was vintage Auerbach.

He was 33, had been born in the Williamsburg section of Brooklyn in 1917. His father had fled Russia when he was 13 and ran a small dry-cleaning business. Auerbach was one of four children, nicknamed "Red" for his red hair.

Even in the thirties basketball was the city game in Brooklyn, and Auerbach eventually made second-team All-Brooklyn, even though he was only five-foot-nine. But he was always tough and gritty, always a hustler, and he parlayed that into a spot at a local junior college. A year later the school folded, and he transferred to George Washington University in the District of Columbia. Auerbach went on to play three years at GW, the heady point guard, the so-called coach on the floor. More important, he fell under the tutelage of Bill Reinhart, a veteran coach who believed in fast-break basketball. Auerbach quickly became a disciple.

It's a style he took with him as a high-school coach in D.C., before he went into the Navy in 1943. When he came out three years later and the Basketball Association of America had just been born, he tried convincing Mike Uline, the owner of the new Washington team, to hire him, primarily because he had made extensive contacts while in the Navy and was familiar with players all over the country. Uline knew nothing about basketball, but he liked Auerbach's enthusiasm. Yet when Uline offered him the job it was a big decision. Auerbach already had a young family, and being a teacher-coach at a high school had a certain stability—certainly more than being the coach of a professional basketball team.

But he was 29, had big ambitions, and was able to convince Uline he could stock the team with guys he had seen play in the Navy.

His Washington team was an instant success. He was feisty, he was aggressive, he was brash, and from the beginning he showed many of the traits that would mark his coaching career with the Celtics. Two years later he jumped to Tri-Cities, but quit after getting into an argument with owner Ben Kerner. But Walter Brown, stuck with a losing team in a city that seemed to have little interest in it, was talked into hiring Auerbach, primarily because of Lou Pieri, the former owner of the now-defunct Providence Steamrollers who had become one of Brown's financial backers.

And then the first thing Auerbach did was alienate both the Boston sportswriters and the few fans the Celtics had by dismissing Cousy, the local star who had been thrilling fans with his ball-handling wizardry.

"I don't give a damn for sentiment," he told the press, "and that goes for Cousy and everybody else. The only thing that counts for me is ability and Cousy hasn't proven to me he's got that ability. I'm not interested in bringing someone in just because he's a local yokel. That won't bring more than a dozen people into the building on a regular basis. What will bring fans in is a winning team, and that's what I want to have."

That wasn't Auerbach's only public swipe at Cousy.

On the day Cousy was going to meet Auerbach for the first time, Auerbach said, "Cousy is going to have to make the ball-club."

There's been a lot of revisionist history concerning the relationship between Cousy and Auerbach in those early years, a smoothing over of some of the rough edges, but there's little question there was some uncertainty, a testing of the waters. Cousy knew Auerbach hadn't wanted him. Auerbach was too proud to admit he'd made a mistake in dismissing Cousy, at least in the beginning. Even later, Auerbach's public stance was he was well aware of Cousy, knew all about his ability, but he simply needed a big man instead.

On that first day, Cousy believed that being Bob Cousy might do him more harm than good, as though Auerbach had some bias against him, even if he had no idea what it could be.

"You're not a big man," Auerbach said as he greeted him. "I hope you make the team, but if you don't, don't blame me. It's a big man's game."

So began their strange dance.

If a sportswriter complimented Cousy's productivity, Auerbach would counter, "Yeah, he scored plenty of points, but he gave away more with his lousy defensive tactics."

If some writer said Cousy certainly was shooting well, Auerbach would counter with, "Sure, and he's passing like a clown." Or else it would be reversed, Auerbach saying, yeah, his passing was all right, but his shooting was off. It was always something, some little dig, some little slight that Cousy would either read or hear about.

Eventually, Cousy would come to understand that, in a sense, it was Red being Red, his way of motivating him. Or else it was Auerbach's way of always being the contrarian, a role he never seemed to get enough of. Since he knew the Boston sportswriters loved Cousy, he seemed to take delight in puncturing their perceptions.

But he also thought it was more than that, too. As if at some level, Auerbach could never get over the fact that he initially had bypassed Cousy, virtually dismissing him, as if that was forever some blight on his résumé and he resented Cousy for it. From the beginning, Cousy respected Auerbach. In time, he came to like him. Eventually, they would spend a lot of time together, traveling around the world to do clinics, and in many important ways they were forever linked. But they were never close, not in the way Cousy had been with Buster Sheary, for Cousy believed Auerbach wouldn't allow anyone to get truly close to him.

They were only a decade apart in age, both had grown up in New York to immigrant parents, and they shared a similar worldview, namely that you had to fight for everything. Cousy also always called Auerbach "Arnold," his given name, although virtually everyone else on the planet called him Red. Later, Cousy would say that was because he used to hear Auerbach's wife, Dorothy, call him Arnold, but whatever the reason, it gave the impression Cousy had a different relationship with Auerbach than the others had.

In a sense he did. It would be too simplistic to say it was father-son, and that wouldn't be accurate, either. But to a young Cousy, who had a nonrelationship with his own father, a cursory relationship at best with his high-school coach, and downright troubles with Doggie Julian, it's not far-fetched to realize Cousy was looking

for reaffirmation in the older authority figures in his life. That's
what he had found with Buster Sheary, and what he was looking for
with Auerbach.

He didn't get it.

Not in the beginning, anyway. No matter what he did, Auerbach always qualified his praise, pointed out Cousy's shortcom-
ings. After the first couple of years Auerbach was publicly saying
Cousy was the best playmaker in the league, after he first led the
league in assists. Then it was the greatest little man in the league.
Cousy wanted him to say he was the best player in the league, but
that wouldn't be for a while, years, in fact.

At his first practice Cousy came onto the court with a white
T-shirt underneath his uniform top, as he had done at Holy
Cross.

"What are you doing, Rook?" Auerbach growled. "Get your ass
downstairs and take that damn thing off."

From the beginning, though, Cousy had no doubt he could
play in the league, even if he had to make the adjustment to
guard. He started off in training camp playing behind the veteran Sonny Hertzberg, the man Auerbach told Cousy to learn
from, but that didn't last long. In the first game of the season,
the Celtics losing to the Pistons in Fort Wayne, Indiana, Cousy
had 16 points. He was off and running, with a now-you-see-it,
now-you-don't style that hadn't been seen in the NBA before. He
threw the ball behind his back. He dribbled it around his back.
He threw it over his shoulder. In short, he did all the things he'd
been doing at Holy Cross, even against older players and better
competition.

And Auerbach let him do it. Would Cousy have been able to
play in the league with a different coach, someone who wanted
his guards to walk the ball up the court and run a patterned
offense? Maybe. Maybe not. But Auerbach's philosophy was perfect for Cousy's game, and Auerbach certainly was astute enough
to quickly realize that. He was also secure enough as a coach not
to harness Cousy's style, his only real message being that a pass is

not a good pass unless someone catches it, no matter how creative it might be.

"Give me credit for this much," Auerbach said later. "I'm not dumb. Okay? I could see Cousy had great talent, but I had to control him. If I hadn't been able to harness this great, great talent we'd have wound up with a wild-ass, sulking athlete who never would have utilized his great talent. . . .

"Cousy went out there on the first day of practice and threw the ball all over the place. What the hell good is that? I had to get the message through to him. He was getting 90 percent of the publicity as it was, and unless I stepped in right away and put my foot down, he'd keep getting fancier and fancier without any appreciable results. So one day I took him aside and had a talk with him.

"'Bob,' I said, 'will you agree with me that guys like Macauley and Cooper are pretty good athletes with good, quick hands?'

"'Sure.'

"'Well, then, would you please tell me why they can't catch their passes? How come they're hitting these guys in the head, or bouncing off their chests, or just missing their fingertips?'

"He could very easily have told me to go to hell, or complained to the writers, or blamed all his problems on the other guys. We both knew that everyone in Boston, including the press, would have taken his side. He could have made my job unbearable and disrupted the team at the same time. But he didn't. He looked at me and asked, 'What am I doing wrong?' Right then I knew I had a superstar on my hands. I wasn't about to tell him that, of course. His head was big enough, thanks to the writers. But he still had a champion's attitude, a champion's heart."

The myriad sides of Auerbach's personality are evident in the above statement, both the resentment toward the writers who questioned his assessment of Cousy, and his ability to change his original opinion, too.

Auerbach believed that, even though he had definite ideas on how basketball should be played, Cousy could bounce the ball off his head for all he cared, just as long as his teammates could catch it. That was vintage Auerbach, too. He was into results, not giving lessons.

That first year, especially in the first couple of months, Auerbach was forever taking Cousy out of games when he thought his young guard was out of control, and every time he did it he would get harpooned again by the Boston press. But Auerbach was nothing if not stubborn.

"Down deep inside, though, I was just as excited as the writers were," he said. "Cooz would go out there and pick the whole team up by its bootstraps. You couldn't always see what he was doing to make it happen, but you sure could feel it. No, he wasn't the greatest damned thing I'd ever seen in my life when he came out of college, and some people never forgave me for that. The truth is, Cousy didn't really become great until his third season with the Celtics. After that, he was the best I ever saw for our type of game."

Jim Loscutoff, who would join the Celtics in 1956, liked to say Auerbach treated players badly, especially in the beginning, and could be obnoxious to people, especially to those he didn't know.

One time he took a player out of the game.

"What did I do?" the player asked Red.

"Nothing," said Auerbach. "That's why you're out."

Cousy had few problems with Auerbach, though. One reason was that Auerbach quickly learned Cousy was not one to be bullied, something that grew out of an incident in a New York hotel when Auerbach yelled at him across the lobby and Cousy yelled back. After that, Auerbach didn't yell at him.

The other was Cousy quickly realized Auerbach's bark was always worse than his bite.

"About every two weeks Arnold would scream at us," Cousy said, "but he also had a very good understanding of human nature. He knew what guys he could yell at, and what guys he couldn't. He didn't treat all the players the same way. He knew what buttons to push."

Auerbach's big thing was to try to intimidate the referees. He would be on them from the opening minute, on the theory that if he kept verbally abusing them he might get a big call down the stretch. It was part of his coaching personality. He always was aggressive, downright hostile at times, and he would never, ever, back down. He and Rochester Royals owner Lester Harrison always seemed on the verge of a fight.

Later, he would adopt his trademark of lighting up a cigar on the bench, after he had determined the outcome was no longer in doubt, and there was no way the Celtics could lose. It soon became his trademark, this victory cigar, to the extent that the sight of Auerbach on the bench puffing on his cigar while the game was still going on, seemingly without a care in the world, came to infuriate opponents.

"I think it started as a habit," said Cousy, "but he began to get attention for it, and it became a trademark. He even used to have people send him free cigars. We didn't like it, because it only got the other team angry and made it tougher on us. Paul Seymour of the Syracuse Nationals once said that the only thing he wanted out of basketball, even more than winning a championship, was to see Arnold light it up and then to shove that cigar in his face."

To Auerbach, it was his way of getting back at the NBA hierarchy, whom he always thought were out to get him. So when he got a note from the NBA office telling him to stop smoking cigars on the bench, he said he would stop smoking cigars when the other coaches stopped smoking cigarettes. He didn't stop. And the fact that it incited opposition players, coaches, and fans only made it better.

Not that Cousy or any of the other players were ever going to say anything to Auerbach about it. Although Red was only 11 years older than Cousy, Cousy never considered him a contemporary, at least not in the beginning. Part of the reason was that Red was already balding and looked older. Part of it was that he was more mature, seemed to be doing everything, whether it was coaching the team, making the travel arrangements, running all the practices, doing all the things that later took maybe a dozen people to do.

He was so consumed by trying to make the Celtics work, make them a winner, that he lived in a Boston hotel while his wife, Dorothy, and their two daughters lived in Washington, a practice that went on for 40 years. In the beginning no one knew, or much cared. But as Auerbach's reputation grew through the years there were a couple of reasons given for his untraditional marriage, everything from the fact that one of his daughters had asthma, to his wife realizing her husband's obsession, and intuitively sensing the marriage worked better if she stayed in Washington and raised their two daughters, while he eventually lived in a suite at the Hotel Lenox in Boston's Copley Square and coached his team.

Years later, when Cousy and Auerbach had traveled several times to Europe together, and Cousy had gotten to know Auerbach's wife, he said to her, "Dorothy, we have him eight months a year. Then I take him to Europe for another month. That leaves you only three months. Can you handle it?"

She had just laughed.

In many ways Auerbach was an overgrown adolescent, eating junk food all day, then Chinese food at night, smoking his cigars, all the while trying to create an extended family around him, his group of players that he tried to turn into his surrogate sons, all of them living in a world that, in his mind anyway, went from game to game, year to year, one big season that never ended, just went round and round, like one big boys club.

Missie Cousy, who had married Bob in December 1950, eventually realized that beneath the gruff exterior Auerbach did indeed have a soft side, but she thought he probably wasn't going to let anyone see that. Then again, she had learned all about Auerbach and the realities of the NBA. She had spent her wedding night in the Boston Garden, courtesy of a late scheduling change, something that happened all too frequently in those days. So there was her new husband out on the Garden floor, there was the wedding party watching him, and there she was getting a crash course on life in the NBA. Her consolation? The organist played "Here Comes the Bride."

She believed all the wives were afraid of Auerbach. Heinsohn told about the time his first wife, Diane, and Missie Cousy came to the end of a practice one day to pick up their husbands, only to have Auerbach scream, "For Chrissakes, who let the broads in. No broads at practice." Another time, he saw Diane Heinsohn in a hat and said, "You got another new hat? What are you doing? Spending all of Tommy's money?"

But one of Auerbach's greatest strengths was that he knew himself as well as he knew his players' games. For all of his occasional bluster, and the perception that he was brutal with referees and a dictator with a cigar and a rolled-up program in his hand, he was more multifaceted than that. He was forever telling his players he wasn't married to them, his way of telling them that he could get rid of them at any time, but he was loyal to them, too, creating an "us versus them" world. He often sought the advice of his veterans, something he would do throughout his coaching career. He had learned two important things about coaching from Bill Reinhart, and they became articles of his coaching faith: Be honest with people, and don't be afraid to admit you made a mistake. Reinhart had believed it was not a sign of weakness to say you had screwed up, and Auerbach's ego was strong enough, even from the beginning of his career, to allow him to walk into a losing locker room and confess he'd done a poor coaching job. It also was another form of being a contrarian, of doing something his players didn't expect. They expected him to come in and rant and rave, jump all over them. Instead, he did just the opposite.

Auerbach understood people: what motivated them, what pushed them, what they wanted. To him, that was more important than all the x's and o's scribbled on some blackboard, all the dissertations on the intricacies of the game. Most important of all was the ability to lead his players, to deal with their individual vagaries.

"It's a dictatorship with compassion," he said at the end of his career. "I don't think I'm a dictator to the extent I'm never wrong. The thing I've got to watch is being carried away with my own importance. . . . A man thinks he's infallible, he's ridiculous. I admit it if I had a bad day on the bench."

This, too, was another glimpse into Auerbach's personality, and some of the tactics he believed made someone a better player, most of which came from the playgrounds of his youth, tactics he later compiled into an instructional book. There is a list of questionable ethical tactics in that book, maybe the best being, "Grabbing or pulling the pants or shirt of an opponent can be very aggravating," and, "Wait until the other team has started warming up and then request their basket. This request must be honored away from home."

Then again, Auerbach had many idiosyncrasies. He made his players wear jackets and ties on the road. He wouldn't allow them to eat pancakes, or have mixed drinks on the road. He seemed to have an opinion on everything.

Cousy would come to realize later that Auerbach was a chameleon, functioning in any milieu. He could be gruff and caustic, yet shrewd and amazingly well-informed, too. He could be arrogant and rude, yet loyal to those around him. Starting in the mid-fifties they took several trips around the world together in the summer, doing basketball clinics sponsored by the State Department. Cousy thought Auerbach was auditioning for the lead in *The Ugly American,* smoking his cigars in no-smoking areas, being rude to waiters, going through Europe as if he expected the Europeans to genuflect. Yet he also could go to a flea market in Turkey and seemed to know what items would cost in New York.

Most of all, Cousy came to learn that Auerbach was a survivor, that he would do whatever it took to accomplish his goals.

"Arnold was such a businessman," he said. "He looked at basketball as a business, not as a labor of love. He always had people in the locker room, people he was in business with, giving gifts to purchasing agents, things like that. He was in the cellophane business with Sid Luckman, and he used to say that he made more money in the cellophane business than he ever did coaching the Celtics."

In the beginning, though, Cousy was simply glad Auerbach let him alone, let him play his game. Cousy would end his first professional season as the NBA's rookie of the year, finishing ninth in the league in scoring at 15.6 points a game. He also had established much of the playing style that would mark his career. Certainly, there were the physical characteristics, the poker face, the lack of obvious emotion, the ability to look calm in moments of stress. These traits were apparent that first year, even if his game was raw, a little wild, his talent like some big wind that had yet to be controlled.

Cousy wasn't the only Celtics rookie that year and, historically, wasn't even the most important. That distinction fell to Chuck Cooper, whom Brown selected on the first pick of the second round.

"Walter, don't you know he's a colored boy?" one of the other owners asked.

"I don't give a damn if he's striped, or polka dot, or plaid," Brown shot back. "Boston takes Charles Cooper of Duquesne."

Cooper thus became the first black player in the NBA.

Sort of.

Soon after the Celtics chose Cooper, the Knicks' boss Ned Irish signed Nat "Sweetwater" Clifton of the Globetrotters, so named because he liked to drink soda, what he called that "sweet water." But neither Cooper nor Clifton would be the first black player to participate in an NBA game, that distinction going to Earl Lloyd, a forward from West Virginia State, who had been selected in the ninth round but whose Washington Capitals opened their season on the night before the Celtics and Knicks began theirs.

While these were the three men who broke the color barrier in the NBA, blacks had already been playing professionally against whites for decades. The New York Rens began in 1923, named after the Renaissance Casino Ballroom in Harlem, which attracted the likes of Count Basie and Duke Ellington. People danced before games, at halftime, and after games.

The Globetrotters began in 1927, the brainchild of Abe Saperstein, a white immigrant who had been born in London but had moved to Chicago as a child. He started out coaching youth teams, and that eventually led to an all-black team that he named after a local dance hall. He called them the Savoy Big Five.

But dance halls died during the Depression, and the Rens went on the road, even touring through the South in the early thirties in a bus they called the Grey Goose. They endured innumerable incidents of racial prejudice and discrimination, and in their barnstorming tours through the Midwest would use Chicago and Indianapolis as home base, riding hours after games in the little Podunk towns to get back to cities where they could get hotel rooms. Yet they were well paid, for that period. Their road secretary carried a pistol, telling his players not to go on the court until he had the money.

They were a serious team, a talented team. They eventually joined the National Basketball League, but by 1949 they were done.

Saperstein's team also went on the road, beginning in the small Illinois towns outside Chicago in 1927. For a while they were called Saperstein's New York, until eventually the name got changed to the Harlem Globetrotters, Harlem being the symbolic home of Negroes in the United States at the time. He dressed them in red, white, and blue uniforms that had been made in his father's tailor shop. The first game they played was in Hinckley, Illinois, for the princely sum of $75, although no one was calling them the "Clown Princes of Basketball" then.

The Globetrotters would play anybody, anywhere. They played in dance halls, livestock barns, warehouses, ole opry houses, and

"Bob Cousy Day" in the Boston Garden, March 1963.

Cousy during "Bob Cousy Day," with his daughter Ticia.

NAISMITH MEMORIAL BASKETBALL HALL OF FAME

NAISMITH MEMORIAL BASKETBALL HALL OF FAME

THE PROVIDENCE JOURNAL

Lou Pieri and Walter Brown presenting Cousy with a silver set during "Bob Cousy Day" in the Boston Garden, March 1963.

NAISMITH MEMORIAL BASKETBALL HALL OF FAME

Bob Cousy and Bill Russell, after Cousy's last game in April 1963.

NAISMITH MEMORIAL BASKETBALL HALL OF FAME

The 1946 All–New York City high-school team, with Cousy on the left.

COLLEGE OF THE HOLY CROSS

Cousy as a college player for Holy Cross.

COLLEGE OF THE HOLY CROSS

The 1947 Holy Cross team that won the national title. Cousy is third from the left in the second row.

NAISMITH MEMORIAL BASKETBALL HALL OF FAME

Cousy against the Knicks in Madison Square Garden.

NAISMITH MEMORIAL BASKETBALL HALL OF FAME

Bob Cousy and his wife, Missie, reading *Parade* magazine, whose cover had Cousy and his two daughters—Ticia and Marie—holding on to his legs.

THE 1956-57 BOSTON CELTICS---WORLD'S CHAMPIONS

Front row, left to right: Lou Tsioropoulos, Andy Phillip, Frank Ramsey, Coach Red Auerbach, Bob Cousy, Bill Sharman, Jim Loscutoff. Standing, left to right: President Walter A. Brown, Dick Hemric, Jack Nichols, Bill Russell, Arnie Risen, Tommy Heinsohn, Harvey Cohn and Vice President Lou Pieri.

© DICK RAPHAEL

The Celtics' first world championship team.

Cousy in the Boston Garden, with teammate Jim Loscutoff in the background and Bill Russell in the foreground.

Red Auerbach lighting one of his infamous victory cigars.

Cousy, Russell, Auerbach, Walter Brown.

© DICK RAPHAEL

Tom Heinsohn at the foul line in the Boston Garden.

© DICK RAPHAEL

Jim Loscutoff taking a hook shot, with teammate
Sam Jones alongside.

© DICK RAPHAEL

Tom "Satch" Sanders shooting over the Lakers'
Jerry West in the Boston Garden.

THE PROVIDENCE JOURNAL

Cousy being guarded by the Knicks' Dave Budd in a 1961
game in the Rhode Island Auditorium. Teammate Tom
Heinsohn is on the left and Bill Sharman is on Cousy's right.
The Knicks' Richie Guerin completes the picture.

Tom Heinsohn firing a jumper in the Boston
Garden against Philadelphia.

Bill Russell blocks Wilt Chamberlain's shot in
the Boston Garden.

© DICK RAPHAEL

Elgin Baylor.

© DICK RAPHAEL

Oscar Robertson.

© DICK RAPHAEL

Cousy against the Cincinnati Royals in the Boston Garden. The Royals' Oscar Robertson is at the far left.

Frank Ramsey being guarded by the Lakers' Don Nelson in the 1963–64 season.

The Lakers' Jerry West being guarded by John Havlicek.

© DICK RAPHAEL

K. C. Jones driving against Wilt Chamberlain in the Boston Garden in a game in the late sixties.

© DICK RAPHAEL

Sam Jones against the Knicks in the Boston Garden.

© DICK RAPHAEL

Auerbach and Russell in the Boston Garden.

JAMES J. MOLLOY

Cousy coaching Boston College in the sixties.

BOB GREENE

Bob Cousy in a 1994 publicity
shot for the movie *Blue Chips*.

© DICK RAPHAEL

The Boston Garden in the eighties, with the Boston Bruins and
Celtics banners hanging from the rafters.

even once in an old drained swimming pool. All for a percentage of the gate, which sometimes wasn't much.

"We earned just enough to get to the next town but never enough to get back home," Saperstein once said. "So we just kept going until we reached the Pacific Ocean."

Their legendary clowning happened almost by accident, beginning as a way to get invited back. They began to spin the ball on their fingers, bouncing it off their heads into the basket, even drop-kicking it in. Crowds loved it.

But they were also a serious team, and would win most of the games they played. In 1935 they had been tied with the Original Celtics with two minutes left, when the Celtics called a timeout and simply left the court. By the late forties the Globetrotters were the most famous basketball team in the world, touring Canada, Europe, and North Africa, in addition to the United States, and grossing more than three million dollars. They even played in Olympic Stadium in Berlin in front of 75,000 people, getting a huge reception. The highlight was a halftime appearance by Jesse Owens, who circled the stadium in a track suit as the crowd applauded. It was 15 years after Adolf Hitler had snubbed Owens at the '36 Olympics.

In 1948, two years after Walter Brown's new league began, the 'Trotters beat George Mikan and his Minneapolis Lakers before nearly 18,000 people in Chicago Stadium, the Lakers being the NBA champions at the time.

This was not insignificant, considering that the towering Mikan was being called the "Paul Bunyan of Basketball," part mythic figure, part circus freak. Mikan was 6-foot-10, nearly 250 pounds, had played his college ball at DePaul for Ray Meyer in the war years. His story was emblematic of the early days of basketball in that he hadn't even played high-school basketball. He had grown up in Joliet, Illinois, of Eastern European stock, and had wanted to go to Notre Dame, but was deemed too clumsy after a tryout. He blossomed at DePaul, though, thanks to an arduous program of skipping rope, squeezing a rubber ball, and 400 hook shots a day, 200 with each hand. He led the country in scoring for two years, and after college he signed with the Chicago Gears of the National Basketball League for $60,000 over five years, remarkable money at the time.

By the fall of '48 he was playing for the new team in Minneapolis, called the Lakers, and they quickly became a phenomenon, with Mikan a draw everywhere he played. The next year the Lakers came into the Basketball Association of America, and Mikan instantly became the most dominating player in the pro game.

There was nothing very pretty about Mikan's game. He wore glasses, he didn't move particularly well, and compared to the big players who would follow him he was all but rooted to the floor. But he was very big, and very strong, and he could score in the low post, being able to hook with either hand. Or else he would receive the ball with his back to the basket, lower his left shoulder, and turn around and score with his right hand.

But the times were changing, and Saperstein was shrewd enough to figure that out. In the beginning of the NBA he had used his clout to keep owners from signing Negro ballplayers, because he wanted them for himself, the owners acquiescing to this because the Globetrotters routinely sold out their arenas when they made appearances there. In fact, as the story goes, Saperstein was so upset that Walter Brown drafted Cooper that he threatened never to bring his Globetrotters into the Boston Garden again

"So what?" said Brown.

It had been three years since Jackie Robinson integrated baseball, but two black players had played for owner Lester Harrison with the Rochester Royals in 1946 in the old National Basketball League. Unlike baseball, which had white players who didn't want to play against black players, basketball didn't seem to have this problem, one theory being that professional basketball had few players who were from the South.

Or as Earl Lloyd said, "I never had any problems with other

NBA players, and neither did Chuck or any of the other blacks . . . basketball people were college people. If they did harbor any racial prejudice, they were smart enough to keep it to themselves."

Cousy would later come to believe the NBA seemed to integrate more easily than baseball for the simple reason that no one cared about the NBA, to the extent that anything that was happening in it was almost, by definition, irrelevant, at least on any kind of national level.

But Cooper's presence was also a seminal moment in Cousy's evolution.

Cousy had never had a colored teammate before, but became friendly with Cooper, who was from Pittsburgh. One year the Celtics played an exhibition game in Raleigh, North Carolina. It was the first time Cooper had been in the South, and he was both apprehensive and uncomfortable. He couldn't stay in the same hotel with his teammates, eat in the same restaurants, even go to the same movie theater. After the game, the plan was to fly to New York the next morning, but Cousy was concerned about Cooper, especially about where he was going to spend the night.

"He's taking a train out tonight," Auerbach said.

"Can I go with him?" Cousy asked.

Auerbach said yes.

The train was due to come through Raleigh at three in the morning. Cousy and Cooper walked around, killing time. They decided to go into a package store near the train station to get a few beers for the long ride. Eventually, they had to use the men's room. There were two entrances. One was marked, "White," the other "Colored."

Cousy didn't know what to say. He felt embarrassed. For the first time in his life he felt ashamed to be white, his eyes beginning to fill with tears. On an intellectual level he always had known racism was wrong, but this was the first time he had personally experienced its effects. Yet he also lacked both the maturity and wherewithal to know what to say to Cooper. So instead of going into the respective bathrooms they both urinated off the platform into the darkness. To Cousy, it was somehow symbolic, the fact that this was the only thing they could do together.

They waited for the train in silence.

"All night we'd studiously avoided the subject," Cousy said. "I felt as though I was at a wake. Finally I spoke up. 'The colored aren't the only ones who are persecuted,' I said. 'Hitler persecuted the Jews and so did a lot of others. And I was reading in the papers where they threw bombs at Catholic churches somewhere in Louisiana not long ago.'

"Chuck looked at me for a minute. Then he said quietly, 'That's all right, but you can't always tell a Jew or a Catholic by looking at him.' I changed the subject quickly. And when the train arrived I couldn't get on it fast enough to shake the dust of Raleigh from my feet."

But the experience had a profound effect on him.

Part of that, certainly, was that as a child of immigrants Cousy had grown up being an outsider of sorts, going back to those early years in Manhattan when he was called "Flenchy." He had known what it was like to be different, to have to battle for acceptance. His thesis at Holy Cross had been on the persecution of minorities, but the focus of that paper had been on Jews.

For a while, realizing there were segregated churches in the South, he seriously thought about leaving the Catholic church, as he couldn't understand how such an obvious injustice could go on in the church. Years after, Cousy became active in Big Brothers, and was honored by Lyndon Johnson in the White House as the "Big Brother of the Year." He thought bigotry was the biggest problem in the world, and that if he had been born black he probably would have ended up throwing bombs. But there's little question his experience with Cooper that night in the Raleigh train station was more than just him reaching out to help a friend. It was also a defining moment.

———————

The star of the Celtics team was Ed Macauley, then in his second year in professional basketball.

He had been the college player of the year in 1948, as a junior for the St. Louis Billikens, his hometown team. His father had been a successful attorney until an automobile accident had left him in a wheelchair. In January of '49 Macauley had been profiled in *Sport* magazine. It had been typical of many of the sports articles of the time, and Macauley had come across as the boy next door who just happened to be six-foot-eight. He was well-liked by his teammates, had a steady girlfriend, someone who hadn't let his growing celebrity change him. In fact, while in New York City the previous spring for the NIT, he had passed up an opportunity to go to Toots Shor's, the noted celebrity hangout for athletes and theater people, because he needed his rest.

He had played for a year for the St. Louis Bombers, before that team disbanded and Auerbach acquired him in a dispersal draft. From his first days as a pro Macauley could score, as skilled a big man as there was then. But he was less than 200 pounds and simply didn't have either the frame or the strength to be an effective rebounder or good interior defensive player, not in a league that was rough and physical, certainly more so than the college game was.

The only other name player on the team was Kenny Sailors, a sort of journeyman pro who had been an All-American in 1943 after leading Wyoming to the NCAA championship. What gave him his sliver of basketball fame, though, was that he was one of the handful of players credited with creating the jump shot. That happened almost by accident, something that first took place on a Wyoming farm when Sailors, battling his older brother on a netless rim next to a windmill, started jumping before he shot, anything to get the ball over his bigger brother.

Sailors began calling it "my shot," and it was the future. Now, many years later, Sailors is widely considered to be one of three men who created the jump shot, the other two being Joe Fulks, a star with Philadelphia in the early years of the NBA, and Hank

Luisetti, a Stanford All-American in the thirties, who was shooting a running one-hander in the days when just about everyone else was shooting two-hand set shots.

The combination of Cousy and Macauley made the Celtics better, and the addition the next year of Bill Sharman gave Auerbach his third star.

Sharman would prove to be the ultimate backcourt complement to Cousy. If Cousy was the product of the New York school yards, his game based on instincts he had honed there, Sharman was the personification of the little kid shooting in his backyard by himself, lost in his own dreams, and the constant solitary repetitions. They were yin and yang, at least in basketball terms, representative of the game's two dominant strains, the city kid and the kid shooting by himself in the dying twilight.

Sharman was from a small town called Porterville, on the edge of California's Central Valley, and he was right out of a script for Jack Armstrong, All-American Boy. He was the captain of the football team, a great baseball player, and a great shooter in basketball. He won 15 letters at Porterville High, was also a boxer, a weight lifter, and a good enough tennis player to have played in a national tournament in Michigan as a high-school senior. According to legend, he once won two events in a morning track meet, won a tennis tournament in the afternoon, and then pitched the baseball team to victory at night.

When he was 18 he graduated from high school, married his high-school sweetheart, and enlisted in the Navy. When the war ended he went to Southern Cal, where he played basketball, baseball, and tennis. But he was already a father, and needed money. Even though he had broken the great Hank Luisetti's scoring record in the Pacific Coast Conference, he left school to sign a professional baseball contract.

By 1950, after bouncing through the minor leagues for several years, he joined the NBA's Washington Capitals, and was now playing two sports professionally. But the Caps were coached by Bones McKinney, an angular man who had played for the Celtics

in the late forties. McKinney wouldn't fly, so they were forever
taking endless train rides around the eastern part of the country,
or driving four guys in a car. To Sharman, it was all very minor
league, and when the Caps folded in the winter of '51 he went to
spring training with the Dodgers.

At the end of the year he was brought to Brooklyn, ostensibly
to back up outfielders Duke Snider and Carl Furillo, but never got
into a game. That was also the year the Dodgers and Giants played
in a playoff game to get to the World Series, the year of Bobby
Thomson's classic home run against Dodger pitcher Ralph Branca,
"the shot heard round the world." Sharman had been in the
dugout.

But in the fall of '51 Sharman belonged to the Fort Wayne Pistons, and its colorful owner Fred Zollner.

The Fort Wayne Pistons were one of the remnants from the
days in the Midwest when teams were named after their owner's
company. Zollner was considered a playboy of sorts, and his team
traveled in Zollner's private plane, called "The Flying Z," which
had a luxurious compartment for Zollner and his succession of
girlfriends.

Auerbach had heard about Sharman from McKinney, who
would later alert Auerbach to a little-known kid named Sam
Jones, who was playing at a small black school in North Carolina.
McKinney told Auerbach that Sharman was a great shooter. Zoll-
ner owed Auerbach a couple of players. One of them became
Sharman.

"I really knew little about Bob when I joined the Celtics," said
Sharman. "I had read about him in basketball magazines, but I
didn't really know how he played."

Sharman, a forward at Southern Cal, considered ball-handling
the weakest part of his game. So from the beginning Sharman
blossomed playing with Cousy. Auerbach wanted to run, to fast
break, to constantly look to push the ball, and Cousy was the
ideal quarterback, with his ball-handling ability and his love of
the pass. Time and time again Cousy would find Sharman in the

open court, and when Sharman got an open shot you could almost turn around and head back the other way to play defense, because he rarely missed. Or Cousy would push the ball up the court, approach the circle as if he were about to drive to the basket, a tactic that sucked in the defense, only to flip the ball back over his shoulder to Sharman, who invariably would be open for a shot. People would think Cousy had eyes in the back of his head. What he really had was a keen sense for where his teammates were on the floor and what they wanted to do.

The first night Sharman played with Cousy in a regular-season game the two combined for 44 points.

"Bob really invented the point guard position," Sharman said. "He was the best I ever saw at running a team, guiding a team."

Sharman was six-foot-two and not the quickest of foot, but he was a phenomenal midrange shooter, plus being the best free throw shooter in the game. He studied shooting, breaking down its facets, constantly refining his stroke, his release. While most players relied on their physical skills, or their basketball instincts, Sharman was like some apprentice in a basketball workshop. He studied the game, worked at it.

"He never would lose a H-O-R-S-E game," said Cousy. "He would just never miss. The rest of us would start taking trick shots. Not Billy. He would never take a bad shot."

In many ways Sharman was ahead of his time. He stretched before games in an era when no one else did. The other players would be sitting in front of their lockers before a game, just killing time before going out for the pregame warmups, and Sharman would be lying on the floor in front of them, stretching and doing situps and pushups. He was an ardent believer in conditioning and good nutrition, in an era when some players smoked cigarettes and wolfed down cheeseburgers as pregame meals. He ran every morning, often behind a car driven by his wife.

Midway through his career he used to go to a high-school gym in Framingham, the town between Boston and Worcester where he lived, on the morning of games so he could shoot some baskets and get loose. He believed that made him play better that evening. This became a practice he implemented years later when he became a pro coach. He called these morning sessions "shootarounds." Shortly after he became the coach of the Lakers, the team won 33 straight and "shootarounds" soon became part of NBA culture. Now every NBA and college team in the country does them.

This attention to even the smallest detail was part of Sharman's personality. He made lists for himself. He kept notes on opponents. He had tea with honey before every game because he thought it gave him more energy. He believed in details, believed that they allowed him to be successful against people more physically gifted than he was.

In that sense of drive and determination, he and Cousy were very similar, as if they both had the same aching need to succeed. Cousy considered Sharman the most disciplined player he'd ever seen. Cousy also sensed they were alike in another way, too: Their oncourt personalities were different from their offcourt personalities. On the court they were killers.

They became very close, roommates for 10 years. They socialized together, played tennis and golf together. Years later Sharman would say he couldn't remember an argument or serious disagreement they had ever had.

The Celtics now had three of the best players in the league. They were an entertaining team, one that ran and scored a lot of points, and Cousy had already established himself as the game's most charismatic figure, the one fans wanted to see. Because of him the Celtics were popular on the road. More important, because of him the Celtics were able to survive, even if it was never easy.

"This isn't a basketball town," Walter Brown told Curt Gowdy in 1951. "It's a hockey town."

In his first four years Brown had lost a half-million dollars on the Celtics, huge money then. He had mortgaged his house, sold some of his Ice Capades stock, but still the Celtics were often drawing only a few thousand people a night. In truth, they were

existing week-to-week, as Brown searched for some way to survive.

He tried everything. In February 1952 he even tried something
he advertised as a "Milkman's Special," a game starting at the
stroke of midnight because the more popular Ice Capades had
been in the Boston Garden earlier in the evening. It wasn't
exactly a rousing success, drawing less than 2,500 fans.

"So many of our friends were telling Walter to give it up,"
Brown's wife, Marjorie, said, "and I wanted him to give it up, too.
We had just finished paying off our house when the Celtics came
along. We owned stock in the Ice Capades, and we had used the
dividends to pay off the mortgage. By 1950 we had sold most of
the stock and remortgaged the house. Almost everything we
owned was locked up in the Celtics. All I could think of was,
'What will happen to us if it's all lost?' I was worried.

"But Walter loved that team. I've heard people say that he
hung on because he was stubborn, or because he was too proud
to admit failure. That wasn't it at all. The Celtics were Walter's
idea from the beginning, and he just never stopped believing in
them."

He also was the ultimate fan, living and dying with every
game. Although he'd been to the manor born, having gone to
prestigious Exeter Academy in southern New Hampshire, he had
an infamous temper, one with a short fuse.

One time, as the story goes, Brown became upset at Auerbach
after a game on the road in which he only played eight players.

"What am I paying 10 men for, if you're going to lose with 8?"
he asked.

You would think Brown and Auerbach would have clashed,
given Brown's temper and Auerbach's ego, but they didn't. Brown
understood that he knew nothing about basketball, thus he let
Auerbach run the team, something Auerbach deeply appreciated.
In turn, Auerbach knew Brown was completely committed to the
Celtics, to trying to make them work. They needed each other.
Even when Brown owed Auerbach $6,000 Auerbach downplayed

it. He understood Brown's predicament, and often publicly called him the finest man he had ever met.

In the first couple of years people in Boston thought so little of the Celtics that they believed Holy Cross could beat them, a claim that always infuriated Auerbach, further lending credence to his belief that people in Boston had no clue about basketball. Several sportswriters also espoused this belief in Holy Cross's superiority, most notably Cliff Keane of the *Boston Globe*. Eventually, Auerbach scrimmaged Holy Cross and made sure several sportswriters witnessed the fact that the Celtics, as insignificant as many local sportswriters thought they were, were far superior to any college team.

That was why Auerbach was always taking the Celtics on pre-season tours throughout New England, scrimmaging against town teams. Unlike the barnstorming tradition of the Globetrotters, who used to toy with the local teams, Auerbach wanted to crush them. It was his way of educating the fan base, trying to convince them that, contrary to what they often read in the press, professional basketball was the best basketball in the world.

Educating the public to professional basketball was one of the key things Curt Gowdy was trying to do when he started broadcasting Celtics' games, even going so far as to give a basketball lesson to fans when the Celtics first started to televise some games. Gowdy's main job was doing Red Sox games on the radio, but he had been a college basketball star at Wyoming, and Brown had virtually begged him to do the Celtics games, too.

Before television, though, Gowdy would even do some road games on radio, even if he never actually traveled to the site of the game. Instead, he would try to "re-create" the game, listening to a Western Union ticker tape, a picture of a basketball court in front of him, and something that sounded like crowd noise playing in the background.

But getting some games on television was considered essential in spreading the game, even if Brown was initially opposed. The Celtics lived by the gate, and the last thing Brown wanted was to give the fans a reason to stay home. But Auerbach was in favor of it, so Brown reconsidered.

Yet there were only about 3,000 in the Boston Garden for a Sunday afternoon game against the Knicks, the first televised game, a paltry crowd Brown blamed on Gowdy and Auerbach.

"You're ruining me," said Brown. "Look at this crowd today."

"Walter," Gowdy pleaded. "We're on the air."

"I'm going to kill you when this game is over," said an oblivious Brown. "I should never have listened to you and Auerbach. I'm going to go broke."

Gowdy tried to placate him, to no avail.

"I'll see you after the game," continued Brown. "You're fired. I never want to see you again around a basketball."

It had been an exciting game, though, Cousy, Sharman, and Macauley all having big games, and television had brought it to people who would never have gone to the Boston Garden to see a professional basketball game. The next Sunday the Celtics nearly filled the Garden. Walter Brown started to like television.

But those early years were never easy for him. The Celtics had a small office on the mezzanine of the Boston Garden. There was an old metal-and-glass door covered by green drapes. Above the handle was a leprechaun spinning a basketball, the team's logo.

It wasn't exactly the Old North Church and the Freedom Trail on Boston's list of tourist attractions. You almost had to be a detective to find it. But it seemed almost fitting: the perfect office for a team struggling to survive in a league struggling to survive.

Chapter Five

Even though he was quickly establishing himself as one of the best players in the world of professional basketball, Cousy was still looking for ways to make money in his first years in the NBA. No one was sure if the new league was going to survive, and even if it did it wasn't real life. This was men playing a child's game. Real life was what was going to happen after basketball ended.

Which might have been one of the reasons Cousy decided to live in Worcester, even though the commute to Boston down Route 9, through the towns of Framingham, Natick, Wellesley, and Newton, was a good hour, and not always the easiest of rides, full of endless stoplights and congestion. But Worcester had become home ever since he had first gotten off that train in the early morning in the rain in the fall of 1946. He felt comfortable there, had good friends there. In Worcester, he felt he and Missie could have a normal life, could escape the demands that would have come if he lived in Boston, as if the city were the buffer between his private life and his public life. Years later, he would say he'd always loved living in Worcester because people left him alone there.

He was married with two small daughters, Marie born in August '51, Mary Patricia in October of the following year. They lived in an apartment off Main Street, in the city's south end. In all that mattered, he was an adult.

"I don't know if I was prepared to be a husband and a father," he said, "but I was prepared to be a breadwinner."

He had seen his father work long hours, first driving a cab, then as a maintenance man at Idlewild, the airport in Queens that one day would come to be known as Kennedy. He was very cognizant of the need to make money, to be successful. He believed that if basketball hadn't been the means to that end, something else would have.

In the fall of '51 he and former Holy Cross teammate Frank Oftring opened a Texaco gas station in Worcester, on the corner of Main and Piedmont Streets, about a mile from the center of town. It was called Cousy and Oftring. Initially, they saw it as the flagship in what was to become many similar stations, using their names for something that could be profitable long after Cousy's basketball days were over. The first day was an incredible success. There were flags and a band and hundreds of cars standing in line as he and Oftring handled the pumps. A local radio station was there, doing some gas station version of play-by-play, and the next day the *Worcester Gazette* gave them great coverage, complete with a picture of Cousy pumping gas in a Texaco hat.

They did great business for two days, until the novelty wore off and, in Cousy words, "We quickly became just a couple of local guys running a gas station, and not a very good one at that." It was soon apparent they knew next to nothing about running a gas station. So they decided to run a driving school instead, the idea he'd had a year earlier if pro basketball hadn't worked out.

The next venture was going to be summer basketball on Cape Cod, specifically Cousy and some friends doing a barnstorming tour. He was billed as the "Houdini of the Hardwood," a new sobriquet he'd acquired, and the plan was to sell basketball to the tourists that flocked to the Cape every summer.

"The Cape will be electrified," one of his friends told him.

Not quite.

He and Joe Sharry, a friend from Worcester who later came to serve as Cousy's unofficial agent, leased some land in Hyannis across the street from the police station, installed a court, and added some lights. The idea was to play the Bob Cousy All-Stars against all comers, basketball at night. He and Sharry distributed circulars outside a movie theater, passing them out all around Hyannis, even outside two Catholic churches on Sunday morning. On the day of the game he and Sharry drove a convertible through all the beach areas from Falmouth to Hyannis, the car festooned with posters advertising the "Houdini of the Hardwoods," with Sharry announcing the upcoming game through a rented loudspeaker.

The plan was to charge $1.80 a ticket. The hope was to sell 3,000 tickets. The problem was he and Sharry had to sweep the court, set up the ticket booths, and get everything ready. The other problem? Fewer than a hundred people showed up, and the shower room in the police station across the street flooded and he and Sharry had to mop up about a foot of water. The next night it was even worse. The opposing team refused to get out of their cars until they were paid up front, and minutes before the game began there were no fans. Sharry called the game off.

"It was a pretty horrible beginning, and if I'd had any brains it would have been the end," Cousy said. "But we kept going all summer and were even daffy enough to do it the next summer. Once Joe even hired an airplane and rode with the pilot while he tried to skywrite "See the Houdini of the Hardwoods at Hyannis Tonight." But it was a windy day, and the message was blown out to sea. It cost us fifty bucks, but I got that much in laughs."

But a summer camp was another story.

Cousy had always loved camps, ever since he had first gone to one on Long Island when he was in high school, and he thought it would make a wonderful investment, something he could continue to do when he was through playing.

It was common practice for visiting NBA players to go on local radio to tout the upcoming game, and virtually everywhere they went Cousy, Sharman, and Macauley would end up sitting in some studio on the air. Cousy would invariably ask the host if he could mention his summer camp, adding that if anyone had an interest they could send him a postcard in care of the Boston Garden. By the end of the year he had a bagful of postcards.

One day he found a camp in southern New Hampshire, outside the town of Pittsfield. It was owned by Jacob Geib, and it had fallen on hard times. Cousy essentially said he wanted to be partners with Geib, but he didn't have any money.

"Why would I want to do that?" Geib asked.

Cousy went out to the car and came back with a bag of postcards.

He had his summer camp, as a part-owner.

Every summer he and his family lived at Camp Graylag. He was hands-on, giving clinics, playing pickup games with the kids. It became a certain sanctuary, away from people, away from his growing celebrity, an environment he felt completely comfortable in, one he could control.

John Gearan, who grew up about 45 minutes north of Worcester in Fitchburg, Massachusetts, and went on to be a sports columnist for the *Worcester Telegram,* went to Camp Graylag for two summers in the late fifties.

"My father was a lawyer and active in Holy Cross sports as an alumnus, so he knew Cousy," Gearan said. "In fact, Cousy and Sharman had come up to a clinic at my parish, St. Bernard's, when I had been in the eighth grade. The Celtics players used to do a lot of that kind of stuff in those days, probably made $50. So that's how I got to Camp Graylag.

"But he had everybody there. Red. Johnny Egan, the great Providence College star who went on to play in the NBA. One summer Sam Jones was my cabin master. They'd go up there, do clinics, play tennis, play golf. And Cooz was always around. He had a very good memory, used to know everybody's name. He genuinely liked kids. You could see that. Everything was always real low-key, informal. At night we used to sit up on a hill and watch some of the counselors play three-on-three. That was phenomenal. They really went at each other. Those games were like Tong Wars. One night George Blaney, who was at Holy Cross then, stole the ball from Cousy to win a game and Cousy was so mad he must have drop-kicked the ball 75 yards into the lake."

By the beginning of the 1953–54 season Cousy was on top of the world he had created for himself. He was now living in a tan stucco house on Worcester's west side, a leafy, mostly Jewish neighborhood on the other side of the city from Holy Cross. He had spent the past two years finishing third in the league in scoring. He had starred in All-Star games, Walter Brown's idea to showcase the league and its stars. And in the '53 Eastern Division semifinals Cousy made an emphatic statement that he'd become one of the elite players in the game, the NBA's next star.

The game was against the Syracuse Nationals, the second in the best-of-three series. It was the first round of the playoffs, in the Boston Garden, and the Celtics had never advanced beyond the first round before. More than 11,000 fans were there.

It was a typical Celtics-Syracuse playoff game of the era, rough, physical, ill-tempered. The two teams didn't like each other, nor did Syracuse owner Danny Biasone like Auerbach, feeling that he was always trying to manipulate the referees, and would do anything to get an edge. Dolph Schayes and Celtics strongman Bob Brannum got into a fight, and when several security guards came onto the court to break it up the Nats' Paul Seymour and Billy Gabin started fighting them. Even now, many years later, Cousy's game in spring 1953 still ranks as one of the greatest individual accomplishments in the Celtics' storied history.

He started his run at brilliance at the end of regulation play when his two free throws with just two seconds left tied the score. In the first overtime he scored six of the Celtics eight points, including a free throw with one second left to tie the game again. In the second overtime his driving layup in the final seconds tied the game yet again. All this before a frenzied crowd.

And he was only just beginning.

With just 13 seconds left to play in the third overtime the

Celtics were down by five points, an almost impossible situation. All Cousy did was score a basket and a free throw to cut the Nats' lead to three, then come up with a long pass that had been batted around by several different players and sink a running one-hander from midcourt to send the game into still another over-time. Then he ended the game by scoring 9 of the Celtics' 12 points in the final overtime.

It had been a bizarre game, to say the least, so many players fouling out that Syracuse finished with just four men on the court, one of them being Seymour, who had hurt his leg and couldn't move.

Cousy had played 64 of the game's 68 minutes, playing him-self to near exhaustion. He had scored an amazing 50 points, including 30 out of 32 shots from the free throw line, and 25 points in the four overtimes. More important, he had scored six of the Celtics' nine points in the first overtime, eight out of nine in the third overtime. In the second overtime he had hit a run-ning hook shot in the dying seconds to keep the game going. Time and time again he had bailed the Celtics out, constantly reaching into a grab bag of heroics and coming out with another beauty. He had dominated a postseason game as no guard had ever done before. He was 24 years old.

"There was a prayer going with every shot, and I certainly needed them," he said afterward, hunched over in his seat in front of his locker, fighting back tears. "I don't want to have to play another game like that again. Boy, it's too much. I was lucky."

He also had been cleared that year of any involvement in the scandals that had rocked college basketball in the winter of 1951, and eventually ruined the careers of some promising young pros, including Alex Groza and Ralph Beard, the two for-mer Kentucky All-Americans whom Cousy had played against in college. They had played for the famed Adolph Rupp, who once had said, "Gamblers couldn't touch one of my kids with a 10-foot pole."

The scandals began when Junius Kellogg, a Manhattan College player, said he'd been offered $1,000 to "shave points," a euphemism for the practice of trying not to lose the game, but to win by less than the point spread established by gamblers.

At first this was seen as an isolated incident, but it wasn't long before Frank Hogan, the New York district attorney, uncovered the fact that many college basketball games had been fixed, and that many college players had been involved, including the entire starting five of the City College of New York's great team of the year before, which had been coached by the venerable Nat Holman and had won both the NCAA and the NIT titles, one of the great sports stories in New York City history. Soon after, some players from Long Island University were implicated, as well as some from New York University.

"Basketball is through as a big time sport," wrote Irving March of the *New York Herald Tribune*.

He was not the only one to report that the sky was falling. The story exploded across the world of sports like a bomb, the biggest sports scandal in the country since members of the Chicago White Sox had conspired to throw the 1919 World Series. Newspapers around the country editorialized about the evils of gambling and the shame of college athletes being involved in illegal activity. The mood was one of outrage, as if the very thought of college athletes taking money from gamblers was an affront to the new postwar sensibility. How could this have happened? And who was to blame?

Ultimately, the feeling was that the practice of point-shaving had been going on for years, part of the game's culture, and had certainly been going on before the scandals broke. Phog Allen, the famed coach of Kansas, had supposedly warned, as early as 1944, of a scandal that "would stink to high heaven." Later, there would be rumors of schools whose players had been fooling around with point spreads for years, the thinking being that the scandals of '51 were almost inevitable, a product of the blatant commercialism that had come to hang over the game like fog over a summer resort.

The scandal's legacy?

It ruined Madison Square Garden as the citadel of college basketball, the predominant thinking being that the games had gotten too big there, that that the atmosphere had corrupted college kids. Ned Irish was blamed for making the games too commercial, for creating the environment that had allowed both gamblers and gambling to flourish. The Garden was seen as some corrupted Eden, poisoned by point spreads and the perception that gamblers lurked in the shadows.

It dramatically changed the basketball programs at CCNY and Long Island University, two city schools that had used the game both as a moneymaker and an incredible public-relations vehicle. Never again would they be big-time programs. It also ostensibly ended the glittering coaching careers of Nat Holman of CCNY and Clair Bee at Long Island University, although Bee would go on to coach Baltimore in the NBA for a few years and also write the Chip Hilton novels, a sports series for young adults, something for which he's remembered more now than he is for his coaching.

The scandals also cast suspicion on virtually anyone who had either been a star college player or played summers in the Catskills, the supposed breeding ground of relationships between players and gamblers. Ultimately, it ended summer basketball in the Catskills, with players being banned from playing in resort summer leagues in 1951.

In the end, 33 players from seven schools had been arrested, and 49 games in 19 states were believed to have been fixed. A few of the players even went to jail, though most were given suspended sentences. CCNY and Long Island University suspended their basketball programs, and the University of Kentucky was given a one-year suspension. There was also the sense that this was merely the surface, that the integrity of the college game had been compromised, not only by recruiting abuses and the use of marginal students, but by the patina of commerce.

But the biggest legacy of the scandals of '51?

They indirectly helped the fledgling NBA. With the college doubleheaders dead in the Garden, the college game enshrouded in shame, the climate improved for professional basketball. For the first time ever, the pro game had become more respectable than college basketball, as if the NBA were seen as somehow pure, not like the tainted amateurism of the college game.

There were also rumors that the players from the Catholic colleges in New York had been spared due to Cardinal Spellman's influence on Frank Hogan. But in the winter of 1953 Cousy was stopped by two detectives while leaving Madison Square Garden after a game against the Knicks. He had heard the rumors that he'd been one of those players involved in dumping games while at Holy Cross. It was almost impossible to be a college star in the late forties and not have your name part of the rumor mill once the scandals broke. Guys on the Celtics were always asking who was next, the rumors everywhere. But that night as Cousy came out of Madison Square Garden, the two detectives said they wanted to talk to Cousy the next time the Celtics came to New York. After that, the rumors about him only intensified.

Soon afterward, Walter Brown called Cousy into his office, wanting to know if there was any truth to what he'd been hearing. Brown knew that if anything happened to Cousy he might as well put all the basketballs away, burn the uniforms, and put a padlock on the Boston Garden.

"Walter," Cousy said. "I have never done a dishonest thing on or off the basketball court."

Brown said that was good enough for him.

Cousy eventually met with the New York City district attorney in February '53. He sat in the waiting room for nearly three hours before he was brought in to the district attorney's office. There were several men present, and almost as soon as he sat down the district attorney said he was sure Cousy had been involved with gamblers when he'd been at Holy Cross, that his name had been on the list of the bookie who had died the previous summer.

"Your name is on that list," the district attorney said, "so you might as well tell us about it."

"I don't know the guy," Cousy said. "I never heard of him."

That set the tone.

A couple more hours went by, Cousy sensing he could proclaim his innocence all he wanted, but no one really believed him. He was allowed to go to dinner, after which he told one of the detectives he wanted a lawyer. The detective told him to wait and went back inside the main office to talk to the district attorney. Cousy waited for four hours.

When he went back inside the tone had changed.

One of the things they'd asked him about during the afternoon was if he knew two men from St. Albans. He had told them yes, but had never heard their names mentioned in the scandals. As it turned out, while he'd been waiting outside, the district attorney had brought the two men in.

It seems Cousy had met them before a game in New Haven, Connecticut, against Yale when he was in college, but it was to give them tickets to the game. What he didn't know was that the two men had been telling the dead bookie they had Cousy in their pocket, thus receiving money from the bookie. Paying Cousy for the tickets in New Haven was to show the bookie evidence of this. So the district attorney told him he could go, that the two men had corroborated his story.

Cousy was doing well; the league wasn't.

It was now called the National Basketball Association, thanks to the addition of several National League teams from the Midwest.

In the beginning of the 1953–54 season there were nine teams, down eight from 1950, when there had been teams in such nondescript places as Sheboygan, Wisconsin, and Anderson, Indiana.

The remaining teams were located in Boston, New York, Philadelphia, Syracuse, and Baltimore in the East; Minneapolis, Rochester, Fort Wayne, and Milwaukee in the West. There was also talk of NBC showing some games. The year before, the DuMont Television Network had done 14 Saturday afternoon games, but this promised to be more games, a national showcase. On the surface, this seemed like a wonderful breakthrough, a chance to take this new league to a national audience, as television had surfaced in the late forties, and by 1949 was on the verge of overtaking radio as the country's dominant form of entertainment. But the owners squabbled over home games, squabbled over TV rights, squabbled over just about everything, another indication that the NBA was little more than a bunch of individual duchies whose allegiance to each other was ephemeral at best.

The NBA was now seven years old, and several truths had become evident. The most important was that it still had all the cachet of an old sweatsock. The Celtics had training camp in Ellsworth, Maine, then, a small town several hours north of Portland. Why some outpost like Ellsworth, Maine? No one really knew, save for the fact that Auerbach must have arranged a good deal. No one wanted to ride to Maine with him, as Auerbach always drove as if he were escaping a fire. Stories of Auerbach's driving became part of early Celtics lore, and Cousy even had it written into his contract that he didn't have to ride with Red.

"Quite frankly, he scared the shit out of us," Cousy said.

It's part of the Celtics' legend how Auerbach drove like a madman, and how the players were always trying to play little practical jokes on him. Like the time Cousy and Macauley stole his red fedora and, much to Auerbach's dismay, cut it up in front of him, Auerbach not realizing they had already bought him another. Or the time they pretended they were out of gas on the way to Maine, causing Auerbach to stop his car in the middle of nowhere, bawl them out for being so stupid, then go off to fetch them gas, only to have Cousy and several of his teammates blow by him as he was stopped in some tiny gas station.

Sophomoric?

No doubt. In many ways Auerbach was the father, and the players were his adolescent children, equal parts obedient and yearning to be rebellious. But it was also a testimony to the fact that training camp too often resembled a boys camp.

Auerbach believed in conditioning, felt that too many NBA teams simply went through the motions in training camp and used the first few weeks of the regular season to play themselves into shape, so that if his team was in great condition they had a big advantage when the regular season began. So training camp was difficult, running, running, and more running. He liked nothing better than to bring new players into camp and see them wilt before his eyes.

Auerbach also believed in the fast break, and much of training camp was spent honing it. The Celtics ran very few set plays, in fact all through Auerbach's 16-year tenure as coach the team only had about six or seven plays, possibly the simplest playbook in the league, so few that all of the opposing teams eventually learned them. Everything else was a variation off those plays. Another of Auerbach's philosophies was that the team that got up the most shots usually won, so that became how the Celtics played. Auerbach wanted his team to run and take a lot of shots, believing that shooting percentage would take care of itself.

The Celtics spent much of training camp barnstorming around New England, sometimes playing as many as 20 preseason games. In Auerbach's first years, when he was trying to sell both the sport and his team to a public who seemed to look at both with a collective yawn, he often did clinics in the morning in some local gym, then scrimmaged some town team at night. To Auerbach, these were not just friendly little practice sessions, something to keep the customers satisfied. Instead, he wanted to bury them, one more message in his campaign to convince the locals that the NBA was, unquestionably, the best basketball there was.

Later, the Celtics would often scrimmage against other NBA

teams. One year they played the Rochester Royals over and over again, almost every night, with Cousy always matched up against Rochester's star guard Bobby Davies. Familiarity bred contempt, and by the end of all these exhibition games Cousy would be sick of playing against Davies, sick of seeing him, even though the two became very friendly after their careers were over. In those days, though, Davies was always pulling on Cousy's pants, doing something irritating, doing things Cousy found obnoxious, especially as Davies was known as a Bible reader.

Every night they would play a game in one of the small towns in northern New England. The next morning they would drive to another town and get ready to play another game. They would either drive their own cars, or three or four guys would pile into one car. The rookies would ride with Red. Cousy and Sharman would invariably get up early, play golf somewhere, and meet the team later, something Auerbach allowed them to do. But there was a lot of hanging around, killing time, training camp becoming its own reality, a world unto itself.

There was a boys-will-be-boys attitude toward training camp, one Auerbach fueled. He thought wives were the enemies of teams, potentially disruptive. He liked nothing more than training camp, just him and his team, away from the wives and the families, the distractions of real life.

It was an environment devoid of glamor. Small towns. Small gyms. Days of hanging around, waiting for another game. Often the players would end up in some diner someplace, some greasy spoon in the middle of nowhere, the Boston Celtics of the National Basketball Association, sitting there with the small-town burghers and farmers, who would look at them as if they had just parachuted in from Pluto.

Bob Brannum liked to go into some little diner and order a Porterhouse steak, saying "Okay, honey, go out and get a steer, knock off its horns, wipe its ass, and run it in here."

Brannum was the enforcer, a big, strong man of limited skills, whose job was to give the Celtics a physical presence. He had

gone to Michigan State, had played for Sheboygan in the late forties, had cut his teeth in professional basketball by riding in cars
to games through the Midwest. Later, the role of enforcer would
fall to Jim Loscutoff, who became a cult figure.

Brannum remembered the first time he met Auerbach:

"It happened in 1949,1950. I was playing for the Sheboygan
Redskins and Red was coaching at Tri-Cities. It was the year the
National League was merged into the BAA. There was a rivalry
between Sheboygan and Tri-Cities you just wouldn't believe. And
in those days in the NBA you won on your home court. Red used
to get thrown out of the games a lot, and he'd go up in the balcony and coach from there. The fans loved to yell and scream at
him. There was an old man, maybe 60 years old, who was our
biggest fan, and he hated Red, *hated* him. One night, Red went
racing down the court on a bad call, and this little old bald-
headed man runs up to him and belts him with a program, right
on top of the head. Red turns around and starts hitting him, and
I grabbed Red and held him off."

One of Brannum's jobs was to protect Cousy, who was forever
being manhandled, especially at the end of games when the
Celtics were ahead and he was killing the clock before there was a
24-second clock. Cousy would start dribbling around, using his
quickness and adroit ball-handling ability to maneuver around
slower guards. Eventually, they would have to foul him to stop
the clock, fouls that often resembled tackles. One opponent who
fouled Cousy that way was Paul Hoffman, a guard for the Baltimore Bullets, a burly ex–college football player who went by the
nickname of "Bear."

As the story goes, Bear Hoffman tackled Cousy in the last seconds of a game in Baltimore on a Saturday night. Due to the
vagaries of NBA scheduling, the two teams were scheduled to play
the next afternoon in the Boston Garden, riding in a train all night
from Baltimore to Boston. In Sunday's game, Cousy was guarding
Hoffman when the Bear decided to make one of his barrel drives to
the hoop.

"Let him go," Cousy head Brannum whisper. "Let him go."

Cousy stepped aside, like a matador escaping a charging bull, only to see Brannum move up and hit Hoffman in the throat with his forearm. Hoffman fell to the floor. Brannum stood over him, as if waiting for him to get up so he could hit him again. But when Hoffman finally got up he went past Brannum and ran the length of the court to attack Auerbach.

"You son of a bitch, you told him to do that," Hoffman yelled at Auerbach.

"You're damn right I did," Auerbach replied.

The league suffered because it was in too many small cities, as if it couldn't escape its past. Ben Kerner had taken his Tri-Cities franchise and moved to Milwaukee and a new 11,000-seat downtown arena, but there were still visible reminders of what professional basketball had once been. The Fort Wayne Pistons played in a high-school gym that resembled a pit, capacity under 4,000. The Syracuse Nationals played outside the city in something called the fairgrounds, and its two stars, Paul Seymour and Al Cervi, played to a fanatical crowd that wanted blood. In a sense, both franchises performed in front of fans who thought professional basketball games were contemporary versions of Christians versus the lions. The word was that one of the veteran referees used to tell the younger refs in Syracuse to watch the clock, and when it got down to 10 seconds they were to run to the locker room no matter what the score was. There was the sense that visiting teams in both Syracuse and Fort Wayne had little chance of winning there, giving credence to the growing feeling that the home teams always won in the NBA, as if the overriding theme was to keep the customer satisfied.

The game was rough and physical, with too many fights. Knicks coach Joe Lapchick used to say that everyone in the NBA was tested as soon as they entered the league, and if you couldn't handle the physical aspect of the game you couldn't play in the league. In November of '53 Cousy and the Warriors Neil Johnston started a fight that required the police to stop. Later on, in that same season, a wild brawl interrupted the Celtics-Nats playoff game for a half-hour.

The officiating was inconsistent at best, downright atrocious at worst, referees coming and going, constant turnover. The coaches and referees always seemed to be yelling at each other. No one was making a whole lot of money. Just when it seemed as if the league was poised to take off to another level, finally putting its past behind it, something always happened to sabotage it, as if it couldn't transcend its past, no matter how hard it tried.

That's what Cousy thought, anyway.

The Celtics would have a big crowd at the Garden, a chance to make a symbolic statement, and they would invariably lose. Especially to Mikan and the Lakers. Or in the playoffs. They would lose, the big crowd would leave disappointed, and it was almost like starting from scratch again. To Cousy, the Celtics had become a microcosm of the league.

Most teams traveled by bus or train. And still Walter Brown and the Celtics were not making money, were still having trouble generating real interest. One reason was the decided lack of coverage by the Boston media, most of which had no interest in basketball, seeing it as decidedly second-rate.

This was not surprising. Most veteran sportswriters had little use for basketball in general, and for pro basketball in particular. The sportswriting giants of the day, men like Red Smith and Jimmy Cannon in New York, avoided it almost completely, moving from baseball to college football to spring training, with only the big prizefights and the big horse races thrown in. These were the sports with mass appeal, the ones with the big crowds and the heroes that all but grabbed America by the throat. To the older sportswriters, the ones whose names resonated with the sporting public, basketball was little more than filler, the only occasional exception being a big college doubleheader in Madison Square Garden. To them, basketball was a graceless game played by genetic freaks, a game with no real history, no real tradition.

The attitude of the Boston press was similar.

In the beginning no one had known a lot about basketball. Some, of course, wanted no part of it. Some, like Sam Cohen, the editor of the *Record-American,* who became friendly with Auerbach, began championing the Celtics. Others liked Cousy, believed he could do no wrong, something of which they were forever reminding Auerbach. Especially Cliff Keane of the *Globe,* who seemed to have a propensity for getting under Auerbach's skin.

Jack Barry of the *Globe* was one of the few writers who actually liked basketball. He kept telling Walter Brown to hang in there, that the Celtics were going to make it in Boston. But it was Dave Egan, possibly the most widely read Boston columnist of the day, who was the first Boston sportswriter to publicly acknowledge how good Auerbach was, the same Dave Egan who made a large part of his reputation in those days by trashing Ted Williams.

The Celtics also had a new radio voice, Johnny Most having replaced Curt Gowdy in 1953.

No one could possibly have known the impact Most would have on the Celtics when Auerbach first hired him, that his raspy, distinctive voice would become the sound of the franchise, one of the constants for nearly 40 years. Nor that Most would evolve into one of the most colorful personalities in the league's history. But as Most once said, "I wasn't born. Damon Runyon created me."

No doubt.

The creation began in the Bronx, where Most grew up an only child, of Bavarian ancestry, another kid chasing the sports dream. He parlayed a limited football ability to a stint at the University of Alabama, where he was a reserve quarterback, what he called "a spectator with a number on my back." He then transferred to Brooklyn College, where he was a linebacker on a team quarterbacked by Allie Sherman, who would go on to coach the New York Giants.

Afterward, he scratched his way around several radio stations in New York City, paying his dues. It was the heyday of New York and every night Most was on Broadway, the New York of guys and dolls, a Great White Way of Nicely Nicely Johnson and Nathan Detroit, characters as New York as an egg cream. The big names in broadcasting then were Mel Allen and Red Barber, two men with distinctive styles. Most also spent a year working with Bill Stern, one of the legends of sports radio. Then he became second banana on the Knicks' games with Marty Glickman.

Auerbach had been looking for a broadcaster who was going to pump the product, and Most didn't need anyone to tell him that twice. From the first time he did a game everything was filtered through a green lens. The good guys wore green. The bad guys wore the other colors. The game was a morality play, Good versus Evil. There was no in-between in Most's world. You were either a hero or a villain. Once, in the late fifties, he said Wilt Chamberlain's eye had gotten in the way of Bill Russell's elbow.

He called Cousy "Rapid Robert," had nicknames for just about everyone, and in his view of the world no Celtic ever committed a foul, and the Celtics were always playing against seven men, two of them wearing striped shirts. He was the ultimate homer, and he wore that distinction as if it were a merit badge.

Suffice it to say Most was never burdened by the truth. Tom Heinsohn often told the story of the time Most was saying on the air how one of the Celtics was doing a great job guarding Hawks star Bob Pettit:

"He's in his jersey, he's in his socks, he's in everywhere he can be. Here we are in the third quarter and Pettit only has . . . 32 points."

Or consider his feud with Al Bianchi, a tough guard for Syracuse:

"Bianchi is a poor excuse for a human being," Most said on the radio one night. "He gets humiliated out there because he couldn't defend a one-arm midget. And he knows it. He thinks he's a hard-nosed player, but he's nothing more than a coward."

Bianchi was nearby, heard what Most had said, and stared at him. Most began to laugh at him.

"What's the matter, Al? The truth hurts."

"I'll never do an interview with you again, you jerk," Bianchi shot back.

"Who cares about you?" Most replied. "You're nothing but a scrub, anyhow. Al, do me one favor, will you? Retire before someone exposes you for what you are, a no-talent fraud."

Most also shared the NBA lifestyle. He spent his days on the road sitting around in the lounge, chain-smoking cigarettes, and telling war stories. He finished the day sitting in the coffee shop, chain-smoking more cigarettes and telling more war stories. By the end of his career his face was a bas-relief of lines and creases, as if every Celtics injustice down through the years was etched there. To him, it was all theater.

"It's all entertainment, baby," he used to say. "That's what it is. It's showmanship. I didn't get here on my looks."

To a young franchise searching for fans, Most seemed to have been delivered from Central Casting.

The other thing that was becoming clear was Walter Brown's growing frustration with the limitations of his team. Not that they were bad. Far from it. They were good. They scored a lot of points. They were the most entertaining team in the league. They were always in the playoffs, had even been to the Eastern Conference finals in '53 and '54. They just weren't good *enough*.

And for Brown, who had become the ultimate fan, often falling victim to his emotions, this ate away at him.

"I have three players getting more money than the entire Philadelphia team," Brown said one day at a weekly basketball luncheon at the Hotel Lenox in Boston's Copley Square, the day after the Celtics had lost to the Warriors, Cousy scoring only four points. "But what they're doing is reading their press clippings. I have the most expensive team in the league and I can lose just as easily with a cheap ballclub."

Auerbach also chipped in:

"Cousy is back to where he was three years ago," he said. "He is trying too much of that behind-the-back razzle-dazzle. He makes a spectacular play, but we lose the ball. Cooz can make this team, or he can kill it."

Cousy quickly found out about these comments, and was irate. He went on a Worcester radio talk show later that afternoon.

"I don't understand this trade talk," he said on the air. "I'm pretty upset about it. I don't understand why those statements about me were said at the luncheon in Boston today. If the Celtics aren't happy with me I want to be traded."

The next day the Boston papers announced Cousy wanted to be traded. The underlying tension that had been there between Cousy and Auerbach from the beginning seemed about to explode. But Brown and Auerbach quickly defused it.

"Look," Auerbach told Cousy the next day. "Nobody's trying to trade you. I hope you got that straight."

"Good," Cousy replied. "I don't want to go anywhere. If the Celtics traded me I'd quit."

Then Brown publicly defused things more.

"Maybe I ought to fire myself," he said. "I'm so eager to have a winner that I'm more of a fan than an executive. I get upset when I lose games. I'm going to keep my mouth shut, and I've asked Red to keep his mouth shut, too."

Still, the league was in trouble, in ways that went beyond economics.

Most teams played very deliberately, a style of play that turned off fans. The worst game had probably been played in November 1950 when the Fort Wayne Pistons won a game in Minneapolis against the Lakers by the score of 19–18. It was really very simple in those first few years: If a team was winning in the fourth quarter it would simply hold the ball, thus slowing the game's pace to a deadly crawl. To get the ball back, the losing team was forced to commit fouls, many of which were more like body blocks. It got to the point that Curt Gowdy, who was doing the Celtics' games on radio, believed that the league could never survive, that no one wanted to watch basketball being played this way.

The best team in the league was the Minneapolis Lakers, a team that revolved around George Mikan, the NBA's most dominant player. He was 6-foot-10, big and rawboned, almost unstoppable once he got the ball inside. He was complemented by two bruising forwards in Vern Mikkelsen and Jim Pollard. So the Lakers' game plan was simple: Walk the ball slowly up the court, wait for Big George to get in the low post, and then pound the ball inside to him. Effective? Absolutely. Entertaining? No.

The Celtics were the Lakers' antithesis. They ran. They had three great scorers in Macauley, Cousy, and Sharman. They had Cousy, already the best show in the game, so they were the most entertaining team. They drew well on the road. They just weren't big enough.

"Macauley was built more like a small forward, but he was forced to be our center," Cousy said. "But there was no way he could guard Mikan. And he knew it. We'd be walking down the street and Macauley would stop and lean against a lamppost, look up, and say, 'Hi, George.'"

The rules then also said the only time a player shot free throws was if he were fouled in the act of shooting, so it was not uncommon for players to foul whenever their opponents had a step on them. This was called "tactical fouling," to the extent that the last minutes of games too often turned into glorified wrestling matches. During the 1953 finals an average of 80 fouls were called in each game.

Enter the 24-second shot clock.

It was the brainstorm of Danny Biasone, the owner of the Syracuse Nationals, who had made his money owning bowling alleys and was known to sit on his team's bench and bait the referees. He arrived at the figure of 24 from monitoring the '53 finals, where he decided the average shot was taken every 18 seconds. So 24 seconds it became.

It changed the game. In one season combined scores jumped nearly 14 points to 93 a game, with considerably less fouling and stalling than there had been.

The NBA game was getting better, even if not enough of the American sporting public seemed to notice.

Basketball in Rockaway became a sort of rite of passage in New York City. Eventually, if you were a serious player, you found Rockaway Beach, 18 blocks along the water that in the thirties had been known as "Irish Town." The 13-mile stretch from Breezy Point to Far Rockaway was where people streamed to in the summer to escape the city's stifling heat, complete with party lights that were hung on the bungalows.

The court was across the street from the beach, right there with the motels, the too-small bungalows, the dance halls, and the bars playing the summer music.

Cousy had found it the summer after his freshman year at Holy Cross.

He and his friends from St. Albans would go to the beach, ogle the girls, play ball, go back to the beach, maybe go to McGuire's bar afterward for a few beers, maybe a block away. The games were three-on-three, half-court, and extremely competitive.

The centerpieces were the McGuire brothers. There was Dick, then a big star at St. John's. He was a few years older than Cousy, and Cousy looked up to him, admired the way he played, especially his ability to pass the ball and make his teammates better. He had played against Dick McGuire in church leagues when they had both been younger, but this was different. And there was Dick's younger brother Al, not the talent his older brother was, but more defense-oriented, someone who got by on toughness, on attitude.

"It was the first time I thought this was pretty good stuff," said Cousy. "The first time I had an identification as a basketball player."

The connection between Cousy and the Brothers McGuire continued to the NBA. Dick became a star with the Knicks, later being called "Dick the Knick," and might have been the closest thing to Cousy as a passer. His only flaw was his reluctance to shoot the ball. But he played low to the floor, and was very quick. He and Cousy were always a great matchup when they played in those early years.

Cousy and Al McGuire would be linked later, something McGuire claimed probably kept him in the NBA a couple of years longer than he should have been. Once, McGuire saw *Boston Globe* sportswriter Cliff Keane in the locker room after a game. Knowing Keane was a huge Cousy fan, McGuire pointed to his more famous brother Dick and said in a voice loud enough for Keane to hear:

"You can't cover Cousy," he said. "I own Cousy."

The next time the Knicks played the Celtics in the Boston Garden a sellout crowd showed up to see Cousy go against the brash New Yorker. So what if McGuire quickly fouled out? So what if it was all self-serving? So what if McGuire couldn't have stopped Cousy with a gun? So what if McGuire once brought a knife and fork to the middle of the court before a game with the Celtics? It was all great theater, something McGuire always intuitively understood.

Not many players could stop Cousy.

In retrospect, Cousy is remembered as the consummate point guard, and there's no question that was the main part of his game, his lasting legacy as a player. But he was a scorer, too, especially in the early years of his career. From 1951 through 1955 he led the Celtics in scoring, and in '54 had been second in the league behind Philadelphia center Neil Johnston.

"Bob wasn't a great shooter, never shot for a particularly high percentage," Sharman said. "But he was a great scorer, and a great clutch shooter."

Cousy got the idea for a players' union in 1953, not because he had some ideological belief in the rights of labor, but from the pragmatic view that in a league as fragile as the NBA the players needed to have a strong voice, that they had almost as much of a stake in the league as the owners did. It was Cousy's belief, one shared by many players, that for the league to be assured of survival it had to become more big league, less bush league.

"We need class," Cousy had told writer Al Hirshberg the year before. "We've got to stabilize so we can demand respect."

"Is that your job?" Hirshberg asked him.

"It's everybody's job," Cousy said, his brown eyes flashing. "We can't go around apologizing because we're professional basketball players. We've got to have pride—pride in ourselves and in our teams and in our league. What's good for the NBA is good for us all—and what's bad is bad for us all. We need a players' association, so we can fight for these things."

Although he'd never been in a union before, he believed a union could only help the players, improve the working conditions, specifically the ridiculous schedule, one that saw each team play more than 20 exhibition games before the season started, and sometimes had teams play exhibition games during the regular season. Once, the Philadelphia Warriors had taken two weeks off during the regular season to go touring in Canada because they needed the money. The regular season often seemed more about survival than basketball, always on the move, like some page out of professional basketball's barnstorming past.

Cousy became the unofficial sounding board for gripes, everything from the feeling that certain teams and certain players got preferential treatment from referees, to the fact that the refereeing often seemed to vary from city to city. He also believed he was one of the few players in the NBA whom the league office would be afraid to take any retaliatory action against.

In the summer of 1954 he wrote a letter to a player from each of the league's eight teams. Each player was a veteran, one he thought would suffer no recriminations if there was a backlash from the league. In order to find out what the leaguewide sentiment was, he asked the players to poll their respective teams.

Within three weeks he heard from everyone except Andy Phillip, who played for Fort Wayne, and that was because the Pistons were owned by Fred Zollner, who was publicly antiunion, and threatened to fire any of his players who joined.

Walter Brown was the opposite. He supported Cousy, one more example of his concern for his players, sometimes even to his financial detriment.

Cousy did not like NBA president Maurice Podoloff, considering him an arrogant little bastard, someone who was forever making Cousy wait outside his office when he went to New York to talk about union issues. He felt Podoloff cared little about the concerns of the players, that getting concessions from him was next to impossible. Eventually, five requests were given to Podoloff, the most important being the establishment of a 20-game limit on exhibition games, after which the players would share in the profits.

None of the requests were radical demands, and it would be 1957 before the Players' Association was fully recognized by the league, but even in its embryonic stage the union further demonstrated Cousy's growing stature within the game. And as his stature grew Cousy became more cognizant that he had squandered some of his educational opportunities at Holy Cross, that he'd been too preoccupied with basketball, something he now came to resent. So he set out to rectify the situation. One thing he did was take five words he didn't know from the dictionary every Monday and try to use them during the week.

He also started reading more.

At first, it was the crime novels of Mickey Spillane, a pulp writer in the early fifties. They were violent and sexual, written in a quick, spare style, depicting a world in which antihero Mike Hammer strode through a world of leggy blondes and gangsters. In an era in which television and movies were usually bland and tame, depicting a sanitized America that was making the transformation from the cities to the suburbs, Spillane's books spoke of a much edgier place, the tensions running beneath the placid surface.

Later, Cousy graduated to biographies, books on history, intent on broadening his interests. Most of all, he set out to transform himself the way he had once transformed his game, by focus and attention to detail. In a sense, this was the most American of ideals, this belief in the future, the idea that one could grow as the country was growing. Thinking of Cousy scouring through the dictionary every Monday looking for five new words to add to his vocabulary resurrected images of a young James Gatz compiling his lists in F. Scott Fitzgerald's *The Great Gatsby*, believing that if he only worked hard enough and dreamed big enough he could one day become Jay Gatsby, that he could change himself from his meager midwestern beginnings into someone who walked across the velvet lawns of seaside mansions in the summer twilight, that in an America full of promise anything was possible.

Cousy believed in the same thing, this sense that you could script your own future. Why not? Hadn't he already come so far from the Manhattan tenement where there hadn't been any running water, from the little house in St. Albans full of too much tension, from the childhood where there had never been enough money? Hadn't he come so far from those playground days in O'Connell Park, all the way to the biggest arenas in the country? Hadn't he always set out to get what he most wanted?

In retrospect, this is probably not surprising. All around him was an America in the midst of tremendous change, a country that was rushing toward the future. Eisenhower was in the White House, the police action in Korea had ended in 1953, and even if the threat of communism created the country's new fascination with fallout shelters, America was an optimistic place. The new ideal was the new house in the new suburb, with dad coming home from some undetermined job at the office to water the lawn before using the barbecue in the backyard, while mom stayed home to raise the kids, who went to new schools during the day, then played Little League in the early evening. Then at night everyone sat in the living room and watched television, which by now had become mainstream culture, very different from 1948 when there had only been 500,000 television sets in the entire country.

This was the new American Dream and it came into everyone's living room every week in television shows like *The Adventures of Ozzie and Harriet, Father Knows Best,* and *Leave It to Beaver.* They were all remarkably similar, the new, idealized American family living in clean, well-lighted homes in some generic suburb where trouble was some kid hot-rodding too fast through the neighborhood. In this new America there was no anger, no divorce, no abuse, no drugs, no problem that couldn't be solved in a half-hour, minus the time for the commercials, of course.

For there were no serious problems on these television shows of the mid-fifties. No racism. No frustrated women unhappy with doing the cooking and the cleaning and taking care of the kids. No rebellious kids chafing at the antiseptic conformity they saw around them. No unhappy families. There were no ethnics, save for Ricky Ricardo on *I Love Lucy.* Instead, the main characters were "American," with their Anglo-Saxon names, their understated manner, their unchallenged belief in the system. These shows depicted an America that had come far from the Depression and World War II, one that was prosperous and optimistic and believed that the future was limitless.

The mid-fifties also saw the proliferation of what was to become known as popular culture, along with the birth of several new things that eventually would become American icons: McDonald's, Disneyland, *The Tonight Show,* frozen dinners, *TV Guide,* Kentucky Fried Chicken, Holiday Inns, *Playboy,* Marilyn Monroe, Elvis Presley.

Not that Elvis invented rock 'n' roll. It had been around since the early fifties, a hybrid form of Negro rhythm and blues and white country and western music, but it was the swivel-hipped Presley, with his pompadoured hair and insouciance, who became its unofficial evangelist. It was rock 'n' roll, with its rebellious spirit, that later became the chief spawning grounds of the counterculture of the sixties.

It wasn't just music that was changing. Sports were changing, too. For one thing, they were becoming more popular, fueled by television that was no longer just in the big cities, but was now in everyone's living room, making professional sports accessible in ways they hadn't been before.

But the NBA was still, for all practical purposes, a regional league. It didn't go west of Minneapolis. It didn't go south of Philadelphia. There were only 8 teams. Salaries were still comparatively low, the players getting five dollars a day in meal money. There were too few games on television, and there was little national cachet, at least not when compared to baseball, the Triple Crown, and the big prizefights. The NBA had been around for almost a decade now, already much improved from its humble beginnings, yet in many ways it still seemed minor league, always swimming against the sports tide.

Chapter Six

On January 9, 1956, Bob Cousy was on the cover of *Sports Illustrated,* a magazine then in only its second year.

The article, written by Herbert Warren Wind, who would become a nationally renowned golf writer, was called "Magician at Work." It featured six pictures of Cousy in his road uniform, with "Boston" on the front and the number 14 underneath it, going behind his back, complete with the caption that said stop-action photography shed light on Cousy's behind-the-back artistry.

"Today, 27 years old, a discernibly improved player in his sixth season as a pro, Cousy is regarded by most experts as the greatest all-around player in the 64-year history of basketball," wrote Wind, who goes on to quote Joe Lapchick, the famous ex–New York Celtics player and then coach of the Knickerbockers.

"I've seen Johnny Beckman, Nat Holman, that wonderful player Hank Luisetti. Bob Davies, George Mikan—the best of the big men—to name just a few. Bob Cousy, though, is the best I've ever seen," Lapchick said. "Cousy does everything. He always shows you something new, something you've never seen before."

The article depicted Cousy as pro basketball's greatest attraction, who almost by himself had carried the league to a popularity it had never had before. It said he was now making about $20,000 a year, also starting to get some of the outside gravy that other stars in the more high-profile sports had been getting for years.

It was Wind's contention that Cousy did things with the ball that not only no one had done before, but no one was doing now. Like the pass off the dribble, the reverse dribble, or the behind-the-back transfer where he shifted the ball from his right hand to his left and then shot a left-handed layup, all the while in the air. The only person mentioned in the same paragraph was Marques Haynes, the old Globetrotters star who seemed to be able to do everything with a ball but make it talk, but Haynes was largely dismissed because of the level of competition, the sense the Globetrotters were almost a vaudeville act. It was another indication of how much the world of professional basketball had changed in the past decade.

Wind also wrote that, contrary to popular perception, the overwhelming majority of Cousy's game was textbook, conservative, that his greatness "lies in the fact that he is fundamentally a playmaker and that his legerdemain, far from being empty showboating, is functional, solid basketball."

But it concluded this way: "From now on the new stars will play like Cousy. You can see his influence in backyards throughout the country. Where all the kids used to be practicing special shots, you now find them trying to do something with the ball in the style of the master and submitting rather stoically, when the maneuver fails, to that inevitable comeuppance: 'Who do you think you are, anyway—Cousy?'"

The article was significant for several reasons: Foremost, it came in *Sports Illustrated,* a slick new magazine from Time, Inc., in New York City with ambitions as big as the city that had spawned it. This wasn't *The Sporting News,* a recapitulation of newspaper stories geared to ardent baseball fans. Nor was it the preseason basketball magazines, with their limited circulation and narrow scope. This was an ambitious, new magazine from one of the biggest media giants in the country, one that coveted a mass audience, one in which tennis and golf were considered as important as baseball and boxing, one targeted for a more affluent, suburban America, one in which both spectator and participatory sports had become part of the country's new post-war vision of itself.

It was also the first time the NBA had been on its cover, the magazine's message that professional basketball was no longer a dance-hall league, roller derby in short pants. No longer was the NBA simply something that existed on the periphery of American sport, something squeezed in between college football and Major League Baseball. And no longer was Cousy just a professional basketball player, his name known only to basketball fans. He was now stepping into the landscape of celebrity, now known to people who had no real interest in basketball, who probably couldn't name five players in the sport, right there in the same constellation of America's new sports stars, men like Ted Williams, Mickey Mantle, Willie Mays, Rocky Marciano.

Cousy was already doing endorsements, the first NBA player to do so since Mikan. He represented a chewing gum company, a seamless basketball, toothpaste, a Canadian sneaker, Roman Meal Bread. In the summer, he had Camp Graylag. In fact, one of the pictures in the article was of Cousy at his camp, in a white T-shirt and sweatpants, watching kids go through a drill.

The year before, he'd been the star of the All-Star game in Madison Square Garden when he'd scored 10 of the East's 14 points in overtime, causing the sportswriters, who already had voted to give the game's MVP award to Minneapolis's Jim Pollard, to rip up their ballots. The summer before, he had been one of the leading athletes from all sports who had met with President Eisenhower at the White House to talk about how sports could contribute to the nation's campaign against juvenile delinquency.

Now *Sports Illustrated* was saying Cousy "has opened the road to better basketball." The underlying premise was that professional basketball was more than just a game played by goons and genetic freaks, but it could be a game of artistry, too.

Baseball was still the sports king, certainly, in the middle of one of its golden eras, especially in New York, the media capital of the world, the place where myths were created. Mantle. Mays.

Duke Snider. They were the three centerpieces of the continuing discussion about who was the best center fielder in New York. The National Football League, which had been floating around since the twenties with only a modicum of success, was still two years away from the title game between the New York Giants and the Baltimore Colts that was decided in overtime, brought to a captivated audience by national television, the game universally recognized as the one that ushered in the NFL's modern era.

The early fears that the NBA wouldn't survive had evaporated. Later, Cousy would remember that the players always knew they had a great game, knew that all they needed was more exposure. They would sit around in those cramped, sweaty locker rooms and talk about how the best athletes were in the NBA, how basketball was the best game, how all they needed was more television to bring them into more living rooms. This was now starting to happen. Not in one defining moment, but slowly, gradually.

The *Sports Illustrated* article was one more example the NBA was changing. It wasn't the only one.

Mikan had retired before the start of the 1954–55 season. Big George had been the league's dominant player, and would later be called basketball's best player in the first half of the 20th century. His departure ended a certain era, paving the way for Syracuse to win the NBA title in the spring of '55. The Lakers had won the three previous titles, five in all, and Mikan had been the pro game's first larger-than-life star, "Geo Mikan vs. Knicks" appearing on the Garden's marquee one night. He was so big in those early years that he would often come in the day before a game on the road to promote it.

But now Mikan was gone, and with him went a certain style of play. The game was quicker now, the 24-second shot clock doing what it was intended to do. There wasn't enough time to walk the ball up the court and wait for the big center to trot into place, then force the ball inside to him.

Ben Kerner had moved his Milwaukee team to St. Louis, where they were now the St. Louis Hawks. Kerner also had the league's new young star in Bob Pettit, the league's scoring leader. The scoring average had climbed to nearly 99 points a game, more proof that the 24-second shot clock had changed the pro game. There was a slew of talented young players entering the league, led by Pettit, who had gone to Louisiana State University, and had been the rookie of the year in 1955. There were more games on television.

Cousy was now 27, in the prime of his basketball life.

The Celtics were one of the league's better teams, yet it was as if they were still caught in a holding pattern. They had the league's best backcourt in Cousy and Sharman, two players whose skills blended perfectly, who would later become the prototype of the modern backcourt, the point guard and the shooting guard, although no one used those terms yet. Still, Cousy handled the ball and ran the break. Sharman ran himself off screens and waited for Cousy to get him the ball.

The Celtics also had a great offensive player in Macauley, and a rising young star in Frank Ramsey, the ex-Kentucky great who had joined the Celtics in 1954, even though he had another year of eligibility left at Kentucky. Ramsey had been signed by Auerbach while sitting in the Red Sox dugout, the Celtics playing an exhibition game in Fenway Park. He was another of the kind of players Auerbach liked, players who were winners, who had known success, and had both the personality and temperament to fit into a team. His Madisonville, Kentucky, team lost in the 1948 state finals to an Owensboro team led by Cliff Hagan, later a teammate at the University of Kentucky. As a college sophomore Ramsey led the Wildcats to a 32-3 record and a national title. He was six-foot-three, blond, with multidimensional skills. He was pigeon-toed and heavy-legged, but that belied a kind of sneaky quickness.

The drafting of Ramsey was the first of many shrewd draft moves by Auerbach, a sort of preview of the ones that eventually got Russell and Larry Bird and solidified Auerbach's reputation as the craftiest executive in NBA history. He had first known Ramsey in the Catskills, and when it came time for the draft he remembered him. His acquisition of Ramsey added another talented player to the Celtics, someone who could take some of the pressure off Cousy, Sharman, and Macauley.

After Ramsey's first loss as a Celtic, teammate Ed Macauley saw him crying and asked what was wrong. Ramsey replied he wasn't used to losing.

"You're going to lose a lot of games in the pros," Macauley told him.

"Well, it ain't going to make me cry any less," Ramsey replied.

He missed his second season due to a military commitment, but had returned in the fall of '55. He was conservative, both by nature and in his dress. He was always thinking about money, talking about it. He loved looking for loopholes in the tax law. But from the beginning Ramsey helped make the Celtics better. Eventually, Auerbach came to use him as a sixth man, energy off the bench, someone whose presence instantly changed the game's equation, another skilled player into the mix, a Celtics tradition that later would also include John Havlicek and Kevin McHale. It was another Auerbach innovation, another example of how he was never restrained by convention. Ramsey would go on to play for nine years, establishing a reputation as a great clutch player. And when the playoffs started, Ramsey always got real serious. To him, the playoffs were money time, no small thing in a league where everyone worked in the off-season, where no one ever seemed to have enough money.

"You're playing for my money now," Ramsey would tell his teammates.

He had a slight stutter at times, a condition that once led to this classic encounter with Auerbach.

"Having trouble with your F's?" Auerbach asked one night.

"Fuck you, Red," Ramsey replied. "How are those F's?"

Later, in 1963, Ramsey would take some heat for writing a story for *Sports Illustrated* on how to draw fouls in the NBA, but even that was an example of how Ramsey was the perfect Auerbach player. Auerbach wasn't interested in basketball ethics, or sportsmanship, or any of the issues that got debated in college seminars. He was interested in winning, and players who would do the things necessary to win. Ramsey was that kind of player.

Another new player that year was Jim Loscutoff, who had gone to the University of Oregon. He quickly became Auerbach's whipping boy, to the extent that Loscutoff used to tell the other players that when he quit the game the first thing he was going to do was drag Auerbach into an alley and beat the hell out of him. He thought Auerbach treated people badly, especially in the beginning, and that he was obnoxious.

Loscutoff was six-foot-five, 225 pounds. He was sandy-haired and tough. He was another of Auerbach's enforcers, replacing Bob Brannum, who was gone after the '55 season. They were there to protect Cousy and Sharman, to protect the Celtics' skill players. They were the floor cops, and Auerbach's strategy was as simple and direct as a school-yard fight: Mess with my stars, and Loscutoff will take your head off. He eventually became known as "Jungle Jim," and was quoted in *Saga,* a national magazine, as saying, "I play in a jungle where the trees swing back, and the only thing I have to protect myself is my bare fists and a jockstrap." The article was titled, "Confessions of an NBA Hatchet Man."

He was never much of a scorer, nor was he particularly athletic, at least not in the ways that word would come to be interpreted. In truth, he was a holdover from the game's early days, rugged white guys who played because they were physical and tough, not because they had great basketball gifts. Brannum. Dick Hemric. Jack Nichols. In a sense they were the same basketball prototype.

The Celtics finished the '56 season as the highest-scoring team in the NBA, averaging 106 points a game, as Sharman, Cousy, and Macauley all averaged more than 17 points a game. Cousy led the league in assists for the fourth straight year. Sharman was the best free throw shooter in the league for the fourth straight year. They were both named to the NBA's All-First team, along with Neil

Johnston at center, Pettit, and Paul Arizin, the great scorer of the Philadelphia Warriors. For Cousy, it was the fifth straight year he'd been named to the NBA's first team.

But the Celtics didn't have enough rebounding, which translated into giving up too many points, and they lost in the first round of the playoffs to Syracuse, in what was then the Eastern Conference semifinals.

To Cousy, it had become the ultimate frustration. One year, after being eliminated again from the playoffs, he sat on the floor in the locker room and cried. Now, he felt that same overwhelming sense of failure. Once again, he had poured everything into a season, all his sweat and hard work, heart and will, and once again it hadn't been enough to lead his team to the NBA's biggest prize. Once again, there was the painful realization that for all his growing celebrity and all the cheers, all his accolades and accomplishments, he had certain physical limitations in a game that kept getting bigger, limitations that prevented him from being able to lead the Celtics to a title, no matter how well he played.

But he also knew the Celtics had gone as far as they were physically able to go. In fact, in his first six years in the league, he never felt the Celtics underachieved, or that Auerbach hadn't gotten the most out of them. He had always felt they'd gone as far as they could, that Auerbach had pushed all the right buttons; they simply were not big enough.

Auerbach believed his team was talented enough to win the whole thing, if only he could find someone to get his skill players the ball. What good was it to have the best running game in the NBA if they had no one to get the ball off the backboard and into Cousy's hands? What good was it to have the most entertaining team in the league, if they didn't have a realistic chance of winning the whole thing? He needed a big man.

And he had a plan.

Bill Russell was the most dominant college player in the country in the winter of 1956. The year before, he had led the University of San Francisco Dons to the NCAA title, and was in the process of doing it again. Eventually, Russell's Dons would win 56 consecutive games. Utah coach Jack Gardner called USF the greatest college basketball team ever assembled.

And just as Holy Cross had been an unlikely national champion in 1947, the Dons' amazing story was almost as improbable. Phil Woolpert, the lean, bespectacled coach, had been hired in 1950 to coach golf and tennis, and to supervise the intramural program, in addition to his basketball duties. Like Holy Cross, USF was also a small Jesuit school, with under 4,000 students. Also like Holy Cross, the Dons practiced in an old barn that had broken windows and a floor that was warped because of the damp weather. The only recruiting the school did was in the San Francisco area.

USF was just another small school with a struggling basketball program until a gangly six-foot-seven kid from McClymond's High School, across the bay in Oakland, had been seen by a volunteer scout. Russell was as green as grass when he first entered USF, seemingly having more potential as a high jumper than a basketball player. As the story goes, the first advice Woolpert gave him was to grow to seven feet. He almost did. Two years later he was over six-foot-nine and his world had begun to change. The next year it did. Teaming Russell with a local kid named K. C. Jones, who had been a football star in high school and dunked a ball against LaSalle in the '55 title game, even though he was only six-foot-one, USF became the best team in the country, a preview of the game's future.

Not only was Russell six-foot-nine, with long arms and a huge wingspan, he was athletic. He could run. He could jump. And when he blocked a shot he seemed to come out of nowhere to do it. In a game where big players were essentially immobile, even the great ones like Mikan, Russell was basketball's future. In a college game that was overwhelmingly white, USF was different in that respect, too, as both its stars, and some others, were Negro.

USF's incredible run didn't come without a certain backlash, however. There were even some alumni who criticized the presence of so many Negroes on the team, an incident written about in a *Sport* magazine story.

Said one alumnus about the racial composition of the USF players: "They are scarcely representative of the school. Perhaps a rule should be established that only three can be on the court at any one time."

Woolpert angrily responded: "Anyone who claims there should be a discrimination toward a Negro or a Protestant or a bricklayer's son on an athletic team or in a classroom is not representative of this school either."

Strangely enough, Russell was not named the MVP of the 1955 tournament, that honor going to Temple's Hal Lear. But there was no question who the most dominant player in the country had been for two years.

Yet there were doubts about Russell's potential as a pro.

He was essentially a nonshooter. Even though he was an excellent rebounder and dominated college players defensively, would he be able to do that in the appreciably rougher NBA? Could someone really be a dominant player if he was so raw offensively? That was at the root of the skepticism, and though it would soon be revealed as completely misguided, no one, Auerbach included, knew back then in the winter of '56 what kind of impact Russell was going to have on the NBA.

There was also the rumor that the Globetrotters were going to make a big push for Russell. The world had changed for Abe Saperstein and his 'Trotters. No longer did they have a stranglehold on every good Negro player. The Globetrotters were still very popular, still a big draw, but the perception of them had changed. More and more they were seen as a vaudeville act, a contemporary minstrel show. More and more they were on the periphery of professional basketball, their days as one of the best teams in the world as antiquated as the old dance halls. Saperstein needed another big name, and in the winter of 1956 it appeared it might be Russell. The word was Saperstein was going to offer Russell as high as $25,000 a year, maybe more, huge money for a basketball player.

But Saperstein made a strategic mistake when he went to San Francisco to woo Russell. He directed all of his comments to Woolpert, essentially treating Russell as if he weren't intelligent enough to make decisions for himself. Russell wanted no part of either Saperstein or the 'Trotters.

Auerbach had never seen Russell play. College basketball was not being nationally televised then, not even the NCAA Tournament. Besides, Russell played on the West Coast and the NBA didn't go west of the Mississippi River. To most basketball fans in the East the big center from San Francisco could have been playing in some parallel universe for all they knew. But Auerbach had heard of Russell from his old college coach Bill Reinhart, whose George Washington team had been routed in a tournament by San Francisco when Russell had been a sophomore. Reinhart told him Russell was going to be a great player. That was enough for Red. Well, almost. He asked Freddie Scolari, one of his old players from the Washington Caps, to check up on Russell, and Scolari sent back a glowing report. He also asked Don Barksdale, who had played for the Celtics from '53 to '55 and was from the West Coast, to find out about Russell. Was he tough enough? Was he a good teammate? Was he unselfish? What was he like off the court? Was he coachable? Would he fit into both the NBA in general and the Celtics in particular?

These were the things Auerbach always wanted to know about prospective players, qualities that, to him, anyway, were almost as important as talent. In this sense, he was ahead of his time. He knew a professional sports team was like a family, full of the inherent tensions and potential problems that run through every family. He knew the season was too long, and that teams spent too much time together, so if just one person did not fit in, the entire group could be disrupted. He knew he wanted players who had come from winning programs, who knew what it was like to win, who were able to subordinate individual ambitions to win.

He also knew that assembling a team is not just about getting the most talented players you can, but getting players whose games fit together. What good was it to have five great players if they all needed the ball to be effective? What good was it to have five great players if they all wanted to be stars? So he put his teams together like a chef making a great stew, a little of this, a little of that, his skill players, his enforcers, other guys who knew their roles. And he made it work not only by lip service, but by paying players for what they contributed to winning, not simply by stats. His players soon came to learn that simply putting up big numbers didn't necessarily translate into big dollars. They had to help the Celtics win.

But even after he was convinced that Russell was exactly what the Celtics needed, how was he going to get him?

The Celtics had the third pick in the '56 draft. The first pick belonged to the Rochester Royals and their owner Lester Harrison, whose relationship with Auerbach was tempestuous at best. The second pick belonged to Ben Kerner's St. Louis Hawks, the same Ben Kerner whom Auerbach once had worked for in Tri-Cities. How were the Celtics going to get Russell with the third pick?

Eventually, the acquisition of Russell would get Auerbach his coaching immortality, not to mention the universal respect he had always sought, but it essentially happened due to the realities of the time. In retrospect, maneuvering around the Royals proved to be the easier of the two challenges, a scene out of the NBA's past. Lester Harrison also owned the arena in Rochester, and like most arena owners, was constantly looking for attractions to fill up his building. Walter Brown owned the Ice Capades. One thing led to another, and the Royals agreed to take Duquesne guard Sihugo Green with the number-one pick, and Brown agreed to send the Ice Capades to Rochester for some extra dates.

Kerner was more difficult.

But Auerbach had an ace in the hole. It was no secret St. Louis wasn't ready for a Negro player, even one who had been as dominant a college player as Russell had been, so Auerbach suspected Kerner would trade the pick for the right player. That player became Macauley, who was from St. Louis and had been a huge star there in college. On the surface, the trade seemed to make sense: The Celtics would get the big man they coveted, someone whom the Hawks probably didn't want, anyway; the Hawks would get their prodigal son, with rookie Cliff Hagan thrown in.

Getting rid of Macauley, who would go on to be inducted into the Basketball Hall of Fame, was no easy thing. He'd been the Celtics' inside offense, one-third of the team's firepower. He had also been one of Walter Brown's favorites, and Brown would never have traded Macauley until Macauley came to him and said it was all right, that he was ready to go back home to St. Louis. In addition to Russell, Auerbach also knew he was getting Tommy Heinsohn, a six-foot-seven scoring forward from Holy Cross, someone who qualified as a "territorial pick" in the draft. That was a practice, which lasted until 1966, by which teams had the rights to college players who played within a 50-mile radius, a way of building up the fan base.

Heinsohn was someone who, in theory anyway, could make up for the loss of Macauley's offense. Plus, Auerbach felt he had no choice.

Then he saw Russell play.

It was at the University of Maryland, a benefit game the Olympic team was having. Auerbach and Walter Brown flew down to see it.

"It was the first time I had ever seen the kid play and he stunk out the joint," Auerbach said. "No offense, no defense, nothing. They had some high-school kids on the other team and they looked better than my guy. I looked at Walter, and he looked at me, and neither of us said a word.

"Then a great thing happened. I had invited Russell and a couple of his friends to have dinner with Walter and me at my house after the game. We got there first and waited. Pretty soon they arrived and the first thing Russell did was stick his hand toward me and say, 'I'm sorry.'

"For what?" I asked.

"For the way I played tonight, I don't usually play that way.

It's the worst I've ever played in my life and I'm sorry you had to see it."

"If you do," Auerbach replied, "you better stay in Melbourne [Australia, where the Olympic team was headed], because I won't be in Boston. I'll be back coaching junior high in Brooklyn."

Tom Heinsohn came to training camp in the fall of '56.

He had been raised in Jersey City, where his father worked for the National Biscuit Company, and his mother for Woolworth's. He came of age during World War II in an Irish and Italian neighborhood, and in his words, "I was the bad guy," the German kid who was afraid to go outside because kids would beat him up. Instead, he spent his time making model airplanes and learning to draw, something he would do for the rest of his life—until the day his father took him outside and made him fight the biggest kid.

"My father said, 'Don't start anything, but finish what you start,'" Heinsohn wrote.

He went to St. Michael's High School in Union City, New Jersey, and he quickly learned that if you were a basketball star people "looked at you in a special way." And star he was. His name was in the papers. He was picked by Haskell Cohen, then the NBA's publicity director, to be on *Parade* magazine's All-American team. He was invited to play in the North-South All-Star game in Murray, Kentucky. College coaches such as Dudey Moore at Duquesne and Ken Loeffler at LaSalle came to his house to recruit him. He visited North Carolina State, and had a tryout at Niagara. He could have gone to any college in the country. It was only six years after Cousy had come out of high school, but already college recruiting was changing, becoming more sophisticated, the world opening up to great high-school players with decent grades. Especially to those who were six-foot-seven as Heinsohn was.

He decided on Holy Cross, primarily because Togo Palazzi and Earl Markey, two Holy Cross players, were also from Union City.

His first day he walked around the campus in a powder-blue suit and pegged pants, out of place on a campus where most kids wore gray flannel suits. He soon adjusted, though, and by the time he was through at Holy Cross he was one of the best college players in the country, the Crusaders having won the NIT in '54. He passed up an invitation to the Olympic trials the following year to barnstorm across the country with the Globetrotters, playing for a college All-Star team that went up against the 'Trotters. They played 21 games in 19 days, and he was paid $3,000.

He had been a junior when he first heard the Celtics were interested in him, but in his customary fashion, Auerbach threw the first public shot.

"The kid is lackadaisical," Auerbach told one of the Boston papers. "He doesn't hustle. He doesn't have the right attitude. He doesn't have the proper temperament. He doesn't mix it up under the boards."

Heinsohn knew little about Auerbach, other than the fact that he'd seen the Celtics play a couple of exhibition games in Worcester and that Auerbach smoked cigars. Now here was Auerbach trashing him in the press, demeaning him as a player. He wasn't sure what to do. He even thought about going to play AAU ball for the Peoria Caterpillars, the only basketball alternative to the NBA. It was all reminiscent of what Auerbach had done to Cousy six years earlier, Auerbach's way of putting the rookies in their place, establishing who the boss was, but of course Heinsohn didn't know that. He just knew Auerbach essentially was saying the Celtics weren't all that interested.

Then Cousy called Heinsohn. They didn't know each other, Heinsohn briefly meeting him one night during his college days when the Celtics played an exhibition game in the Worcester Auditorium. But they shared the Holy Cross connection, and both had played for Buster Sheary.

"They're interested in you," Cousy said. Cousy knew all too well about Auerbach's way of handling local college stars, his way of using the press to establish that he was the boss.

"They have some way of showing it," Heinsohn said.

"Forget what you read in the papers," said Cousy. "They are interested in you, and want to see you."

Cousy said he would drive Heinsohn to Boston.

"What kind of contract should I ask for?" Heinsohn said.

"Make your own deal," Cousy said.

So Heinsohn walked into Auerbach's office in the Boston Garden. It was full of stuffed bears, and a gruff Auerbach who essentially told Heinsohn that he was now a Celtic, and oh yeah, take that T-shirt you wear under your uniform and shove it, you are a Celtic.

Rookies had to carry the ball bags. And from the beginning he was Auerbach's whipping boy, right there with Loscutoff. Auerbach was always yelling at one of them. Heinsohn was always too heavy, too lazy, too something. Eventually, he realized this was simply a ploy on Auerbach's part, for Auerbach knew both he and Loscutoff could take it. Heinsohn also came to know that Auerbach never motivated anybody the same way, that he intuitively understood which individual buttons to push. He knew never to criticize Cousy or Russell. He knew never to yell at Sharman, who didn't take it well, and might just retaliate by punching Red in the mouth. He rarely yelled at Ramsey, who might take the criticism to heart. Heinsohn was perfect. Auerbach could yell at him, and in doing so could get his message to the entire team. So it was Heinsohn who was too heavy, Heinsohn who wasn't playing defense intensely enough in practice, Heinsohn who wasn't running wind sprints hard enough, Heinsohn who was smoking too many cigarettes, Heinsohn who was always doing something wrong. Once, after a great first half where he had put up big numbers in both scoring and rebounding, he said to Auerbach, "How am I doing now?"

Heinsohn soon learned what Cousy had learned six years earlier, namely that Auerbach's greatest coaching skill was his ability to direct his players' passions, their emotions.

Heinsohn had no trouble adjusting to the league. He was very skilled for a six-foot-seven player, could pass, and also put the ball on the floor. He had grown up playing all positions as a kid, and that experience suited him well now that he was in the NBA. He liked to run and immediately fit into the Celtics' fast-paced style. He could score, and he wasn't bashful about getting shots up, either. In time he would be called a gunner, even nicknamed "Ack-Ack," for the sound a machine gun makes. But none of that ever bothered him. From the time he first arrived in training camp Heinsohn was very secure as a basketball player. He was even known to periodically take a hook shot from the corner, the kind of shot that was viewed as basketball sacrilege.

"Are you kidding?" Knicks star Dick McGuire said. "You can't get away with that stuff in this league."

"You ain't seen nothing yet," Heinsohn shot back.

Maybe most important of all, at least at the start of the season, was that he could also rebound. With Macauley gone, and with Bill Russell in Melbourne, Australia, with the Olympic basketball team, that was essential.

From the very beginning Heinsohn realized Cousy was as good as advertised, maybe even better. "He was a one-man team offense," said Heinsohn. "The only time we ever called a play was maybe coming out of a timeout. We never called one coming up the floor. Cooz just ran things. He would make things happen. If you got a half-step on your man he would get you the ball. And if you weren't running as hard as he wanted you to early in the game he'd throw the ball just off your fingertips to make you run harder."

Because they both lived in Worcester they would ride into Boston together every day, alternating the driving. So Heinsohn quickly got to know Cousy in ways another rookie never would have. He quickly learned how intense Cousy was, how much he wanted to win. But he saw, too, Cousy's dry sense of humor.

"I was the little brother," Heinsohn said. "Cousy was the captain, the star of the team, the boss man. But he accepted me. I think he realized that I could help the team, and that I was committed to winning. We became close. It wasn't like we were with each other all the time, because he had roomed with Sharman on the road and continued to do so. But we palled around together."

From the beginning Heinsohn was the class clown, a combination of his personality and the fact that he seemed oblivious to criticism. Cousy was always needling him, saying he took too many shots, but Heinsohn never stopped shooting. Beneath the surface, though, he was very perceptive. He quickly saw that even though Sharman didn't run or jump very well and had a well-deserved reputation as a shooter, he was excellent defensively, tough, tenacious, a real bulldog. He also had a temper, and Heinsohn also quickly saw that Auerbach had more trouble getting along with Sharman than with anyone else.

Heinsohn was also the only Celtics player who knew what the Celtics were getting in Russell. He had played against him as a college player, in a game in Madison Square Garden in 1955, in the Holiday Festival, and had been outscored by him. He knew how good he was. In truth, he had never seen anyone play defense like that.

Russell would lead the U.S. Olympic basketball team to the gold medal, nine months after he had led San Francisco to the national title. He didn't arrive until late December.

When he finally arrived nothing was ever the same again.

Not for Bob Cousy.

Not for the Celtics.

Not for the NBA.

Not for basketball.

Chapter Seven

You could buy a new Dodge for $2,200, a three-bedroom house in a new suburb for a little over $20,000, and spend two nights at the Hyannis Inn on Cape Cod, complete with breakfast and dinner, for $12.50 a person. In movie theaters you could see Cecil B. DeMille's *The Ten Commandments,* starring Charlton Heston and Yul Brynner, and *Fear Strikes Out,* the story of Red Sox outfielder Jimmy Piersall's emotional breakdown, featuring Anthony Perkins and Karl Malden.

It was April 13, 1957, and the Celtics were playing the St. Louis Hawks in the Boston Garden. It was Game Seven of the NBA Finals, the Garden was full, and the game was on national television, no less. It all seemed a long way from the "Milkman's Special" back there just five years ago, the game that had started at midnight.

The Celtics had swept the Syracuse Nationals to win the Eastern Conference, the first time they ever had done that. They also had the best record in the league, another first. They seemed destined to win their first world title, which figured to be sweet validation for Walter Brown, who had always believed in the Celtics, even in those years when no one else seemed to. Dave Egan, the acerbic *Record* columnist, whose vendetta against Red Sox star Ted Williams already had become part of Boston sportswriting lore, was calling the Celtics an almost legendary team. Still, they had to beat the Hawks in the seventh and deciding game, and even though they had won seven out of the nine games against the

Hawks—a below .500 team for the year—during the regular season, the Hawks were not pushovers.

They had upset the Celtics in the opening game of the NBA Finals, and had evened the series at three games apiece, winning the sixth game in St. Louis by just two points to force a seventh game. They were led by Bob Pettit, then in his third year in the NBA, and ex-Celtic Macauley, two of the top scorers in the league, and had picked up the veteran guard Slater Martin during midseason. They also had the sure-shooting Cliff Hagan, who had gone to St. Louis in the trade that had brought Russell's draft rights to Boston, and huge Charlie Share in the middle, the man Auerbach had selected over Cousy in the 1950 draft. The Hawks had not had a great year, with Red Holtzman being deposed as coach in midseason and replaced by veteran backup forward Alex Hannum. Somehow, though, they had survived, now only a game away from the NBA title.

The series had also featured Auerbach punching Hawks' owner Ben Kerner in the mouth before the third game, after the two had argued over the height of one of the baskets in Keil Auditorium in St. Louis. The argument had started when Sharman, the best foul shooter in the league, kept missing his free throws in the pregame warmups, his shots always coming up short, and complained to Auerbach that the basket was too high. Auerbach had come out to the middle of the court, screaming that the basket should be measured. Kerner also came out on the court to see what was going on, yelling at Auerbach as he did so, calling him "bush," and as Kerner approached him Auerbach turned around and landed a wild right to Kerner's chin.

Kerner, who was known throughout the league as "Benny the Boob" for his decision to bring the Hawks to St. Louis in the first place, retaliated with a slap, which grazed Auerbach, then said, "Not only are you bush, but you can't throw a punch, either."

"Ben, why don't you go put some ice on that fat lip I just gave you?" Auerbach shot back.

Was it the legacy of the bad blood that existed between Auer-

bach and Kerner from those early days in Tri-Cities when Auerbach had quit in midseason in a dispute with Kerner over the
owner trading a player? Or was it just Auerbach in the heat of the
moment, combative and aggressive? Either way, it seemed to set
the tone for the rest of the series. Hannum called the Celtics
"hatchet men," and Celtics owner Walter Brown countered by
saying Hannum had always been a butcher, and was lucky to be
in the league.

"He cussed me out," Red told the press afterward, trying to
defend his punching Kerner. "What he called me was unprint-
able. I wasn't going to take that."

"Aw, all I called him was a busher," Kerner said. "He's a big
sorehead. That stuff he was pulling was bush. With all the talent,
he still has to pull tricks like that."

Auerbach was fined $300 by NBA commissioner Podoloff for
"unbecoming conduct," but all it really did was add to Auerbach's growing reputation as one of the bad boys of basketball,
even if Auerbach felt badly about it afterward, saying Kerner had
always been one of the classiest men in the game. In retrospect,
the game was one of the defining moments in the evolution of
the NBA, called the game that solidified the NBA as a major
sport, but some of that is probably hyperbole. This wasn't Fort
Wayne in the NBA Finals, as it had been the year before. This was
two major-league cities, teams from two different parts of the
country, two of the best baseball towns in the country, two
places that had a resonance with sports fans across the country.
As did the top players.

The NBA first team was Cousy, Sharman, Pettit, Paul Arizin of
the Philadelphia Warriors, and Syracuse's Dolph Schayes. Arizin,
Pettit, and Schayes were the three top scorers in the league, with
Sharman and Cousy being seventh and eighth. Russell was fourth
in rebounding, although his average of 19.6 was the highest in
the league. These were names that were known to sports fans, not
just those who followed professional basketball.

The Hawks were an all-white team, and in many ways mirrored what the NBA had been in its first decade. The Celtics, with Russell, were what the NBA was to become.

Game Seven was one of the most dramatic playoff games ever played. There were 38 lead changes. Every time it seemed the Celtics were finally going to take command, the Hawks would somehow resurrect themselves and come charging back. With just 13 seconds left to play Cousy was at the free throw line. The Celtics were one point ahead. All he had to do was make the two free throws and the game would be over. It seemed like a sure thing, as Cousy always had been an excellent free throw shooter. He made the first.

Then the Hawks called a timeout.

Suddenly, Cousy was nervous, as if he no longer could block out the enormity of the situation. He hadn't really been nervous in a basketball game since he had played on the junior varsity back at Andrew Jackson High School. His ability to control his nerves, to focus and block everything else out, always had been one of his great strengths. The Celtics were in a huddle during a timeout, Auerbach giving instructions on what to do once Cooz made the foul shot, because everyone knew that there was no way in this big bad world that Bob Cousy was going to miss this free throw, and all Cousy could think of was what would happen if he missed.

He did miss.

Missed so badly that his shot didn't even hit the rim.

For the first time in his basketball life Cousy had come to know what "choking" was. Pettit then made two free throws in the closing seconds that sent the game into overtime. And at the end of the first overtime Hawks reserve Jack Coleman made a basket to force a second overtime.

The Celtics' attempt to win their first-ever NBA title was turning out to be a lot more difficult than anyone had expected.

Much has been made of "Celtic Pride." It's one of those concepts that's grown through the years, equal parts romance and myth, to the point that now, the common perception is that all the Celtics players were like brothers, one big happy fraternity where everyone hung out together like some basketball version of *Happy Days*. It was always more complicated than that.

In retrospect, much of the team's success occurred because the players knew they needed each other if they were going to be successful and came to understand that the whole was better than the individual parts, even though some of the individual parts were outstanding. They all had certain skills, certain specialties, and what made them a great team was that these individual specialties were blended together.

"None of us had to strain to understand that we had to complement each other's specialties," Russell once said. "It was simply a fact, and we all tried to figure out ways to make our combination more effective."

In Russell's view that kind of togetherness was simply pragmatic, and had little to do with the popular image of Celtic Pride, a team where the players were together both on and off the court. In essence, the core of the Celtics' success was that several talented players realized the Celtics played together because it was the best way to win.

Maybe it was simply that both Cousy and Sharman realized that, for all their individual acclaim, they never really won anything until Russell and Heinsohn arrived to help them. Or that Russell knew he simply didn't have the offensive skills to carry a team all by himself. Or that Heinsohn knew that, for all his wondrous scoring ability, he needed Cousy to get him the ball. And there's no question the role players not only understood who the stars were, but also understood that their own survival on the team depended on their doing what they did best, whether that was Loscutoff doing all the dirty work, or Ramsey bringing a lift off the bench.

Maybe it was the fact that all of them had come of age in an era in which playing the game the right way was considered important, and helping your teammates was as important as scoring yourself. Certainly, that was the way Cousy had learned the game in the St. Albans of his youth, as it was the way Russell had learned to play at the University of San Francisco. They were two unique superstars in the sense that the things they did best on a basketball court had nothing to do with scoring.

Would the Celtics have been different if both Cousy and Russell wanted or needed to take a lot of shots to be great?

No question.

If nothing else, it would have changed the delicate equation of the team concept. Certainly there would have been the potential for disharmony, simply because lesser players tend to resent the fact that the stars not only make more money and get more attention, but also get the ball more. If nothing else, the Celtics would have been fundamentally different.

Instead, their two glamor players had individual games that were unselfish by nature. Cousy liked nothing better than to make the pass that led to the score. Russell liked nothing better than to prevent the other team from scoring. At their core, they were the ultimate team players, not only in attitude, but more important, in the way they wanted to play.

Red Holtzman, who had coached the Hawks for half of the year and would go on to achieve his slice of NBA coaching immortality with the Knicks in the early seventies, believed the Celtics were the first team to create "the big inning" in professional basketball, his way of saying the Celtics played for the home run, the quick scores, the fast breaks that ran opposing teams right out of the building, ultimately robbing them of their resolve.

Why not?

Hadn't that always been the way Auerbach had wanted to play, the kind of basketball he'd learned at the feet of Bill Rienhart at George Washington, back when hardly anyone played that way? Hadn't that been the way his early Celtic teams had tried to play, even when they had never rebounded enough to be able to get out on the break as often as they wanted? Hadn't he always believed you had to take a lot of shots, that the team that took the most shots usually won?

It had also been Cousy's dream, the way he had always wanted to play. Now with Russell, he could. In essence, it was simple: Russell would get the rebound and find Cousy for the outlet pass. There was a small irony in this, in that Russell was not a particularly good passer. Give him the ball in the low post and the offense often seemed to slow to a crawl, for Russell simply didn't see the open man very well, and lacked the necessary passing skills to deliver the ball if he did. But he could throw an excellent outlet pass, sometimes even before he came down from a rebound. To see him rebound the ball, then turn in the air and throw the ball to Cousy before his feet hit the floor, was to see another aspect of the game's future, the wondrous athleticism of big men who had previously been labeled clumsy and unathletic.

With the ball in his hands it was Cousy's turn. Even if his behind-the-back dribbles and his ball-handing wizardry captured the public's imagination, Cousy's true basketball genius showed when he had the ball in a transition situation. He had an intuitive sense of where everyone was on the court, thanks to his exceptional peripheral vision, the fact that he could look straight ahead and still see almost 180 degrees. He also knew things, instinctive things, a library full of basketball intelligence that he could summon instantly. He knew he could give the ball to Heinsohn on the wing, because Heinsohn could both catch a hard pass and put the ball on the floor. He knew not to throw Loscutoff the same pass, since his hands were not as good as Heinsohn's and he wasn't skilled enough to put the ball on the floor and take it to the basket, even if he caught it. He knew not to throw difficult passes to Satch Sanders, whose hands were suspect. He knew not to give Russell a low pass, that the big guy liked the ball up where he could go get it. He knew Sharman liked to come behind him, so that if Cousy started to penetrate to the basket and the defense collapsed around him, there would be Sharman behind him for the bail-out pass and the open shot.

He knew he had to reward the big guys who got the defensive rebounds and also ran down the floor on the fast break, even if that meant giving them the ball at the expense of someone who might have a better shot; he knew that if you didn't reward the big guys for running the floor it wouldn't be too long before they wouldn't run anymore. Often Russell would never come over half-court after getting the rebound. He would throw the outlet pass and essentially trot to half-court as the play took off without him, both as a way to conserve energy and because he figured he was out of the play anyway. But on those times that Russell ran hard up the court after getting the rebound, Cousy rewarded him.

No one had to tell him these things. They were simply things he had come to know, as if all his basketball, all the long hours he had spent practicing his craft, the long road that had begun in O'Connell Park, had led him to this team, this moment in time. He was the quarterback of the best team in the world, playing a style that was uniquely suited both to his talents and to the way he saw the game.

Even if he had just missed the biggest free throw of his life. Against the Hawks. In the seventh game of the NBA Finals.

The first game of the NBA Finals, in the Boston Garden, had gone to two overtimes. Cousy and Sharman, the two who had been the best backcourt in the game for several years now, both had great games, accounting for nearly half the team's points between them. But it hadn't been enough, as Pettit had 37 to lead the Hawks to the upset.

The series would be an affirmation of Pettit's greatness.

He was in his third year in the NBA, and was another Cinderella story in professional basketball, someone who had been cut from his high-school team in Baton Rouge, Louisiana, his first two years. But he had spent two years working on his game, dedicating himself, and when his coordination began catching up with his body, he began getting better and better. By the time he got to LSU he was six-foot-nine, a rare blend of size and outside shooting ability, someone who could score both inside and out. He had been the rookie of the year in 1955. Later, Pettit would say that the key to his success was that he was never satisfied, that every time he reached a goal he quickly set another one for himself. He was one of the first basketball players to do extensive weight training, something that, decades later, would be routine for all players.

And he would get a chance to send Game Seven into a third overtime.

Shortly into the second overtime Heinsohn fouled out. He had scored 37 points and grabbed 23 rebounds, an incredible game. When he left the court he was in tears, completely spent emotionally. At first, he headed for the locker room, then he turned and sat down on the bench. He wrapped a towel around his face and buried his head between his knees. He stayed there for the rest of the game. Later, during a crucial timeout, the entire team on the floor around Auerbach, Heinsohn remained on the bench, a solitary figure, his face in a towel.

With one second left two Loscutoff free throws put the Celtics up, 125–123. But the Hawks weren't dead yet. Alex Hannum, the Hawks' player-coach, came up with a last-second play, something he had learned in his early days with the Rochester Royals. The play was simple: He told Pettit to go down the court and stand near the Celtics' foul line. The plan was for Hannum to inbound the ball and throw it the length of the court off the backboard, at which point the ball was supposed to bounce back to Pettit. It was a play the Hawks used to fool around with, and Hannum could throw it off the backboard 50 percent of the time. He hit it this time, dead on. The ball caromed off the backboard, and went back to Pettit, just like Hannum had diagramed it. Pettit took a last-second desperation shot.

"I caught the ball and shot in one motion and it rolled around the rim and out," Pettit said.

The Celtics were the NBA champions.

When the game ended, Cousy was ecstatic, jumping high into the air. It no longer mattered that he had only made two baskets in the entire game, or that he had missed the crucial foul shot that might have won the game without having to go to two overtimes. It no longer mattered that he and Sharman, the great backcourt that had carried the Celtics through so many games and so many years, had been a combined 5 for 40 from the field, maybe as bad as they'd ever been together. Suddenly forgotten was the tension, and the frustration, and the unrelenting pressure he had felt the entire afternoon, the feeling that he'd spent so long climbing up the mountain only to get so close to the top and not be able to get there, each time falling back and having to start over, like some basketball Sisyphus. Instantly forgotten was the fact it had taken seven years to get to this point. So there he was in joyous celebration in the middle of the floor, as the crowd swarmed down from the stands, crowding the court. It was the first championship for a Boston professional sports team since the Bruins had won the Stanley Cup 16 years earlier.

Afterward, he didn't remember how he got back to the locker room. The small room was packed with a mob of reporters and photographers.

"My nervous system is shot," Auerbach said.

He had been thrown into the showers by some of the players. Now he stood there in his wet clothes. He was 39, and he had come very far from that time he had decided to leave the security of high-school teaching to cast his fate with an upstart professional basketball league.

"This is a great team," he said. "The fellows refused to quit, and finally came through. This is a great day."

Years later, he would say the first championship is always the sweetest, that there was never another one that meant as much as that first one against the Hawks.

Auerbach changed into a sweatsuit and started moving through the room, congratulating the players.

"I never saw such a game played by a man under pressure," Sharman said, motioning toward Heinsohn. Then he moved the 15 feet or so over to where Heinsohn was.

"Tommy," he said. "That was a wonderful basketball game. You're really a great basketball player."

"Don't you ever feel any pressure on a basketball court?" Heinsohn was asked by a sportswriter.

"Pressure?" he yelled. "'Course I feel pressure, like everyone else. But if the shot's there, take 'em. So I took 'em. What the deuce is a guy supposed to do with that ball? Eat it? Let them eat it if they want to."

But Heinsohn was also effusive in his praise for the Hawks, especially Hagan and Pettit.

At one point Auerbach shaved off Russell's goatee, while Russell laughed. The goatee had been controversial all year, for the simple reason that no one else in the NBA had any facial hair. From the beginning it had been the outward sign that Russell was different, and was going to do things his way.

It had only taken until Russell's first game for Cousy to know that the Celtics had gotten more than they had expected with the rookie center. Until then, Cousy figured they were simply getting someone who was going to rebound for them. That was the word, anyway. Russell wasn't going to score, and no one ever said anything about him blocking shots, or playing the kind of defense that was going to change basketball. No one expected Russell to be a savior.

But from the moment Cousy first saw Russell he knew he was

looking at something different. The NBA centers then were Larry Faust of the Pistons, Harry Gallatin of the Knicks, Charlie Share of the Hawks, Neil Johnston of the Philadelphia Warriors, Johnny Kerr of the Syracuse Nationals, and Clyde Lovellette of the Minneapolis Lakers. All were white. All were products of the early years of the NBA, and had come of age in the Mikan era. All shared certain similarities as players. To Cousy, they were all clumsy, Frankenstein types, immobile, even someone as awesomely effective as Mikan.

Not Russell.

All you had to do was look at him to know he was an athlete, someone who could run and jump and do all the athletic things smaller players could do. Even without training camp, even missing the first several weeks of the season, Russell grabbed 16 rebounds in his first game against the St. Louis Hawks, even though he didn't start and only played 21 minutes. It was in the Boston Garden in front of 11,052 people. It was also on national television, and you didn't have to be a visionary to know Russell, as raw as he was that first game, was something the NBA had never seen before, a big man who was as athletic as anyone in the league.

A couple of weeks later, over New Year's weekend, the Celtics played two games in Philadelphia. The Warriors' star was six-foot-eight center Neil Johnston, who not only had led the league in scoring three times, but also had led the Warriors to the NBA title the previous spring. So this was to be Russell against Johnston, perhaps the first definitive test for Russell. But by the time the weekend was over two things were apparent: The league had never seen anything quite like Russell, and Johnston had been embarrassed.

The staple of Johnston's game was a hook shot he took from almost a standing position. That, and a line-drive jumper. But he jumped so poorly that Russell quickly realized he could block virtually any shot that Johnston took. As soon as he did, Johnston was almost helpless, as if the future of the game was suddenly in his face. On the second night Russell held Johnston scoreless for 42 minutes, so dominating that Warriors owner Eddie Gottlieb kept screaming that Russell was both goaltending and playing an illegal one-man zone.

Russell, and his new wife, Rose, had arrived at Boston's Logan Airport on a cold, slushy December day. They were met by Walter Brown, who soon endeared himself to Russell by saying Russell should not be penalized for playing in the Olympics and that Brown would pay half the money Russell was supposed to forfeit from missing the first part of the season.

Russell already had a strong sense of racial pride, already had decided he was never going to be the stereotype of the Negro, the laughing boy seeking favors. He decided he essentially would volunteer little, would speak only when spoken to, would do what his new team paid him to do, but on his terms, true to himself. He already had discovered some hard truths, not only about the ephemeral nature of sports fame, but also about his place in America. He had been invited to the White House in the summer of 1955. It was only a few months after the University of San Francisco had won its first national title, and even though Russell had another year of college eligibility left he was invited to be on Eisenhower's commission on physical fitness, along with Cousy, baseball stars Willie Mays and Hank Greenberg, baseball commissioner Ford Frick, and prizefighters Gene Tunney and Archie Moore, among others. Afterward, he had traveled to Louisiana to visit relatives, only to quickly discover that it didn't matter that he'd led his college team to the national championship, or been invited to the White House. In the Deep South he was "just another black boy, just so much dirt, with no rights, no element of human courtesy or decency shown to me and mine."

Later, he would say he wasn't particularly close to anyone on the Celtics his first year, that not only had he arrived late, he had also arrived with a bit of a chip on his shoulder. But from the beginning there was the persona Russell gave to the public, and the one his teammates saw.

"He was laughing all the time," Cousy said. "Russell always has been very outgoing when he feels comfortable. We didn't know how militant he was then."

There were indications he was different, though. Once, in Madison Square Garden, for a game against the Knicks, Heinsohn's family was there, and he was going up to the other players and getting autographs for them. Until he got to Russell. Russell wouldn't sign. Not even for a teammate.

That was just one of his idiosyncrasies.

He also did none of the traditional things Celtics rookies were always asked to do. He didn't carry the ball bags. He didn't go fetch sodas for the veterans. He didn't have to pay for all the taxis, then have to hunt Auerbach down to get reimbursed. That was Heinsohn's role. Russell was exempt.

But his most important idiosyncrasy was that he was one of the first superstars who did not care about scoring points, no insignificant thing. And that did not happen simply by accident. It was the result of his belief that winning was the ultimate form of athletic expression, and in order to give his team the best chance of winning he was going to have to subordinate some of his individual goals.

It was a lesson he first learned during his sophomore year in college. That was the year he decided he was going to be a great basketball player. The epiphany happened at halftime of a game in Provo, Utah. He had been challenged by Phil Woolpert, the USF coach, and went out and played in the second half with a fury he hadn't played with before, as though he had finally found a way to channel all his anger into the game. But the team underachieved during the year, and afterward Russell came to understand his attitude had been one of the factors in the team's lack of success, and that never again was he going to concentrate on individual goals at the expense of the team. That had become an article of his faith through those last two years at San Francisco, the one he brought with him to the Celtics.

He entered the NBA with doubts about his offensive ability. He knew he didn't shoot well. He knew he wasn't a great scorer. He knew that in all the traditional ways, he wasn't supposed to be a great player, not in the way basketball had evolved, anyway. But he knew he could help a team win. There was no doubt in his mind about that. Years later, he talked about how he certainly had a huge ego as a basketball player, but it was a team ego. That was how he came to judge himself. Not by how many points he scored, or how many awards he won. Not by any of the traditional standards of measure. But by how his team did.

So when Auerbach told Russell that the only thing he really had to do was rebound, that he would never be judged by how many points he scored, any pressure Russell felt joining the NBA evaporated. He also instantly realized that Auerbach knew what he was talking about. From the beginning Russell and Auerbach had a good relationship. Not that they were ever particularly close, but not only did Russell respect Auerbach as a coach, he sensed Auerbach respected him as a person, no insignificant thing for a young black man who had spent his early years in segregated Louisiana.

Russell had learned lessons growing up that he always carried with him. He had heard the stories of the way both his grandfather and father had grown up, his grandfather not having the chance for an education, his father going to a colored school in Monroe, Louisiana, then working in a paper bag factory, in something called a "Negro job." As a young child he had heard the story of when his mother had gone to town wearing a new dress only to have a cop say, "Who do you think you are, nigger, a white woman? Get out of town before sundown or I'll throw you in jail."

He had ridden in the colored section of the train from Louisiana to St. Louis, on his way with his mother and brother to meet his father in Oakland, where he had gone for work. When his mother had died when he was 12 his father had taken him and his older brother back to Oakland from Louisiana, telling them the entire way that it was time for them to learn how to cook, how to clean, time for them to grow up. More important, Russell came to realize that both his grandfather and his father were role models in the very best sense of the word, proud, hard-working men, men who were true to themselves.

"I went to bed just a boy," he once said. "I woke up the next morning proud—so very proud—to be a Negro."

This was how Russell grew up, even if he wasn't always aware of it at the time. These were the lessons he brought with him to Boston. Not only was Russell the first black superstar in the NBA, he was a young black man positioning himself for a changing America. He knew what he thought, knew what he believed, and nothing was going to get in the way of that.

Russell spent the first few minutes of his first professional game on the bench. Midway through the first quarter he entered the game to a tremendous ovation. In addition to his 16 rebounds, he also blocked three of Pettit's jump shots, something that almost never happened. He even blocked an 18-foot shot by Macauley, seemingly coming out of nowhere to do so.

He also blocked shots in a unique way, not by swatting the ball as hard as he could and knocking the ball out of bounds, but almost gently, keeping it in play, trying to block it so a teammate could get it and start the fast break. Auerbach had never seen anything like it, and came to view it as almost a pass.

Knicks coach Joe Lapchick liked to say that in the NBA "they ask you the question right away." He was referring to toughness, the legacy of the NBA's bruising past when, if you didn't fight back, you were virtually run out of the league, a take-no-prisoners Darwinian world. From the beginning, Russell proved his toughness, taking no nonsense from opposing players, using his elbows as weapons, clearly making a statement that he would do anything to protect his turf.

"Well, there it is, boys," Russell yelled in the jubilant locker room, after Auerbach shaved off his goatee. "Or I mean there it isn't. No more goatee. It's down the drain. I promised to do it and now no one can ask me about the thing anymore."

"What was that goatee all about, anyway?" asked *Boston Globe* sportswriter Cliff Keane.

"Well, I came here with it and somebody on the team asked, 'What's that thing, anyway?' and I told him I was going to keep right on wearing it until we won the division title. Then I decided to wear it through the playoffs. And I said that if we won I'd take it off. So it's down."

He paused a beat.

"Let's see," he continued. "That's three championships in a year for me. NCAA. The Olympics. And with these fellows."

He sat down. But he didn't stop talking.

"I was never so scared in my life. Did I say I was scared? Man, I was shaking all over my body. See me leap out there when it was over? Felt like jumpin' all night long."

Russell had pulled down 32 rebounds and blocked five shots, one of those blocks coming near the end of regulation when he had sprinted down the court to block a Jack Coleman layup, a play Heinsohn said was the greatest play he ever saw in basketball.

"What did the Rook get anyway? Thirty-seven points?" Russell now asked.

"Hey, Rook," he called over to Heinsohn. "Quite a day. You're great."

Heinsohn did radio interviews, posed for more pictures.

"Want to be my agent?" he asked around the room. "Sign me up quick. I'm going for a big price."

Later, he would say he hadn't realized how important winning the title had been to Cousy and Sharman. Then again, he hadn't been there in the early years of the decade.

Cousy sat in front of his locker, too tired to do anything else. Yes, he'd had a poor shooting game, but he'd played all but a few minutes. He also had passed out 11 assists. Now, he sat there, emotionally drained, in the middle of a joyous celebration, and all he could think of was the long journey it had taken to get there, all those nights in those crummy little locker rooms in the early years of the NBA, back when it seemed as if the Celtics were light-years away from winning an NBA title, and it was always going to be his fate to never win, to end every season in frustration. All those nights of small locker rooms where there never seemed to be enough hot water, all those nights of too few fans rattling around in too big arenas, all those nights on the far side of glamor.

"We finally did it," he said, almost to himself.

Later that night, at a celebratory dinner, he would say that he felt very happy for Walter Brown.

"We wanted to win for Mr. Brown," he said. "If it wasn't for his perseverance there wouldn't be any Boston Celtics, and we'd all be playing somewhere else."

The next day, the game story of the Celtics' winning the NBA title was on the front page of the *Boston Sunday Globe*, right there with a new column by Kay Furcolo, the wife of Governor Foster Furcolo, on how she spent her days, and a story about how Hollywood tough guy Edward G. Robinson was selling his three-million-dollar art collection to Greek shipping magnate Spyros Niarchos.

There were two pictures above the game story. One had Heinsohn kneeling on the floor, his face in his hands, too nervous to watch the final seconds. The other showed Auerbach on the sideline, arms extended, obviously yelling something.

The game story, written by Jack Barry, who had been one of the few sportswriters who had actually liked the Celtics from the beginning, jumped to the sports page. There it competed for attention with one that said all the *Globe* baseball writers were picking the Yankees to win the pennant, and Bruins' coach Milt Schmidt saying his club must start playing better hockey, the B's being down 0–3 in the Stanley Cup Finals against the Canadiens.

There was a banner headline saying, "Celtics Win Title, 125 to

123." Underneath were two large pictures, one of Arnie Risen throwing a driving left-hand shot over the Hawks' Jack McMahon, the other of Cousy throwing up a one-hander.

On another page, a drive by Heinsohn eluding Hagan and Pettit is stripped across the top, and the obligatory locker-room shot of Auerbach, Cousy, Ramsey, and Loscutoff in celebration. In another picture, Auerbach is shaving off Russell's goatee, while a jubilant Heinsohn stands behind him.

"It's my greatest day in basketball," Walter Brown said. "I've waited for this for a long time. There have been rough times, but now every minute has been worth it."

Cousy was the MVP of the National Basketball Association, the first time a so-called "small man" had been so honored in the 10-year history of the league. He'd been surprised. To him, the MVP had always been the "big man's award," out of reach.

But now his team had won a world title, and he was the MVP of the league. He had come far from that first practice with the Celtics, back when he was just the skinny kid from Holy Cross whom Auerbach had made go back to the locker room and take off the T-shirt underneath his uniform top. As had Auerbach, Walter Brown, and the Celtics as an organization. It had only been a handful of years since Brown had been forced to mortgage his house to keep the team afloat, only a few years since Auerbach believed he had to educate the public to what professional basketball was all about, just a few years since all those nights in the Boston Garden when there had been too few fans, too little interest, when the Celtics seemed to play to the sound of one hand clapping. It was as if some Maginot Line had been crossed, and if that first world title didn't eradicate all the Celtics' problems, it certainly gave them a legitimacy they never had before. They still might not have been able to outdraw the Boston Bruins in the Boston Garden, they still were nowhere near as popular in Boston as the Red Sox, but they were the best basketball team in the world, and no one could take that away from them.

And Cousy was being called the best player, complete with the MVP award to prove it, too. In just 13 years he had gone from someone who had been cut from his high-school basketball team to the best basketball player on the planet. In just 13 years he had gone from an unsure adolescence to the very top of the world he had created for himself.

Chapter Eight

In the fall of 1957 Cousy published an autobiography. It was called *Basketball Is My Life,* and it was written with Al Hirshberg, a sportswriter for the *Boston Record-American,* someone he had known from the time he had first joined the Celtics.

It's a typical sports autobiography for its era, written to cash in on Cousy's popularity. It was written in the first person and skims effortlessly along the major points in Cousy's life, with heavy emphasis on his young years in St. Albans, his troubles with Doggie Julian, his courtship of Missie, the machinations that eventually brought him to the Celtics, and, finally, the Celtics' first NBA title. The tone is self-depreciating, understated.

It was still a time when people knew very little about sports stars, other than what they did on the field. There were no drugs. The sports page didn't look like a police blotter. The problems in society hadn't come into the locker room, and on those rare occasions when they did, fans were not told about them. No one knew how much money athletes were making. Off the court they almost seemed not to exist, as if they were packed in ice between games and kept inside the arena somewhere. No one knew where they lived, or how they lived, or what they thought about, other than the obligatory postgame locker-room quotations, or thoughts on the upcoming game.

So *Basketball Is My Life* was relatively groundbreaking for the times, even if it was as sanitized as the fifties themselves. There was no mention of his family's dysfunction, no mention of the fact that after his first summer in the Catskills when he'd just graduated from high school Cousy knew he was never really going home again. There were few mentions of his demons, the relentless drive for perfection. If his nightmares were discussed, the reasons for them were glossed over.

There are clues to the inner drive that would dominate his life, some foreshadowing. One was his sleepwalking, which spoke of inner tensions trying to get out. Perhaps the worst sleepwalking incident occurred one year when he was at his camp in New Hampshire, when he went running out of his cabin in the middle of the night, punching open the door and diving clean through the screen door, all the while feeling people were chasing him. He then collided with a black Buick that was parked outside, pushing a distressed Missie away all the while, and kept on running until he hit a tree. A couple of weeks later he essentially did the whole thing again, running 200 feet downhill over rocks in his bare feet. When he awoke he was crouching behind a tree. He was also naked.

When he finally went to see a psychiatrist he was told he had an "anxiety complex," and it was not just coincidence that many of these episodes happened during the summer, when he had fewer outlets for the pressures building inside him.

"You're on a strict schedule in camp, with no place to go, and your mind has trouble accommodating to the change in routine," the psychiatrist told him. "Your mental attitude corresponds exactly to the dream. People are holding you back and you are trying to break loose."

Another driving force was his social conscience, something that had been evident in the way he had befriended Chuck Cooper in his first year in the NBA. Decades later, he wasn't exactly sure where the seeds of his view of the world had been planted, but they were always there. Maybe it was because he had grown up feeling a little different, always a bit of an outsider, thus his inherent sensitivity to other outsiders. Maybe it was the residue of his Holy Cross education, the awareness that it's the

Jesuit tradition to give back. Whatever, he always felt a certain embarrassment about the attention he received, that all athletes and entertainers received, even at a time when he was the MVP of the league.

The NBA was still a "slam bang league," though, the heavy remnants of the past still as much a part of the game as fouls and sweat. The Celtics still played a half-dozen or so "home games" in Providence, Rhode Island, because Lou Pieri, who owned the Rhode Island Auditorium and had once helped out Walter Brown financially, owned a piece of the team. The building was old and drafty, a reminder of the early days of the professional game, to the extent that once in the mid-fifties the Celtics had played with the floor so slippery, the players were sliding on every play. Still, the game had been played, because the show had to go on, right?

Players still got hit with just about everything in Syracuse. Bottle caps. Cups of soda. Pennies. Virtually anything fans could throw at them. The word was Rochester owner Lester Harrison would shut off the hot water in the visitors' locker room if his team lost, and that often he and his brother would scalp tickets outside the building. Officiating was still inconsistent at best, referees often taking a barrage of abuse from fans and coaches alike. There were still too many fights. There were still instances of guys being signed for a weekend, then shipped out the next week, as though, for all the improvements, the early days of professional basketball were like some demon that couldn't be completely exorcised.

Only three of the original franchises—Boston, New York, and Philadelphia—remained from that meeting at the Hotel Commodore in New York City back in June 1946. The Philadelphia franchise had passed to Eddie Gottlieb, who had gotten some of his financial backing from Abe Saperstein of the Globetrotters, so the Warriors sometimes traveled with them, playing the understudy to the 'Trotters. The NBA schedule was also a leftover from the barnstorming days, too many nights with players crammed into cars driving through winter nights to make the next game.

There was still the sense that the players were third-rate traveling salesmen. The big men often slept in beds that were too small, their feet dangling off the end of the bed. Everyone had a roommate, and the meal money was less than $10 a day, so the players on the road were always looking for cheap places to eat. When teams played back-to-back on the road the players had to wash their own uniforms, hanging them on the hotel radiators.

All too often there were games being played in small cities around the country for no discernible reason, other than that the owners thought they could make a quick score in some new venue. The Fort Wayne Pistons even played some home games in Miami, of all places, because owner Fred Zollner had a winter home there.

There were often doubleheaders in Madison Square Garden, which meant that on a given evening one-half of the entire NBA was in one building. Afterward, many of the players would go to a nearby bar on Eighth Avenue called Friendly's. Some nights there could be as many as 25 players in there, their gym bags in the front of the bar.

Earl Strom, a young referee, was making only $40 a game, plus expenses, even in his fifth year in the league.

But the league was changing, too.

The Fort Wayne Pistons had moved to Detroit, to Olympic Stadium. The Rochester Royals had moved to Cincinnati and a 14,000-seat arena. There were now eight teams in the league, and if the NBA still did not go west of Minneapolis, or south of St. Louis, with the exception of Syracuse, it wasn't in minor league cities anymore, either.

Several months earlier Ed Linn had written an article in *Sport* magazine asking the question, "Is the NBA Big-League?" The premise was that the league was getting better, was in the process of transcending its past of dull games, screaming coaches, myopic management, and dirty play; that the 24-second clock and the nationally televised Saturday games were giving the league a respect it never had before. Linn also reported that all the vital statistics in the game were up, everything from shooting percentage, to free throw percentage, to team scoring average.

More important, Linn's article pointed out that franchises were actually starting to make some money, the Knicks having their first profitable year in 1954, the Celtics a year later. But it was Linn's contention that the NBA could not legitimately be called big league until more of the biggest cities in the country were represented, specifically Los Angeles, Chicago, and San Francisco.

In December of '57 *Sports Illustrated* published a special issue on college basketball. There were scouting reports on all the major conferences in the country, and a big story on Frank McGuire, the former St. John's coach who had found another life at the University of North Carolina, called "Dixie's Yankee Hero." But the gist of the issue, what made it meaningful, was that it was one more emphatic example of not only how basketball was growing, but how the perceptions about it were changing, too.

There were full-page color photographs of new field houses at Kansas, Maryland, and Ohio State, spacious arenas that could seat more than 14,000 people. There were six pages called "Art on the Court," all designed to show readers that basketball really was an art form, not just "the apparently aimless swirl of 10 young men racing down a polished hardwood floor." And the centerpiece was an article called "The American Game," in which Roy Terrell wrote that this most American of games "has circled the globe and captured the fancy of both players and fans of virtually every country on earth."

Interspersed, though, you could still see the bias against basketball, the old perceptions that the big man was too dominant, and there was too much whistleblowing from the referees. Terrell wrote that basketball "at times, can look a little foolish."

Still, the college game was rebounding from the scandals of

the early fifties. It would never recapture the dominance it had in New York City. College basketball was becoming more of a national game, fueled by new gymnasiums and new stars. The NBA had never been more popular. Its stars were now nationally known, profiled in magazines, quoted in wire service stories, part of the growth of spectator sports, vastly different from just a decade before.

And if professional basketball was changing, so was the country. For the first time white American teenagers were being exposed to Negro culture, primarily through music and sports. As Negroes were in the beginning stages of the Civil Rights struggle, sports and music made them accessible in ways they hadn't been before, thus beginning the slow chipping away at many of the stereotypes, like water against sedimented rock. If the decade was still, in many ways, conformist and defined by a growing materialism, the tremors that would shake the country in less than a decade were already present. The publication the year before of Jack Kerouac's *On the Road,* the book that became the anthem of the Beat Generation; the rise of rock 'n' roll, the music that would become the soundtrack for a new generation; the emergence of Negro sports stars; all were harbingers of the decade to follow.

The Celtics had the best record in the league in the 1957–58 season and appeared headed for their second straight title. Then Russell turned his ankle in the third game of the NBA Finals against the Hawks, crumbling to the floor in Keil Auditorium in St. Louis, and the power shifted, the Hawks going on to win in six games, redemption for the year before. Pettit had 50 points in the deciding game, securing his eventual legacy as one of the greatest players in NBA history, the prototype of the big forward who could shoot and score. Still, there was no one in basketball who didn't believe that the Celtics were the best team in the NBA, that if Russell hadn't gotten hurt a second banner would have been hanging from the rafters of the Boston Garden.

They had won 14 straight to start the year, had finished the season with 5 more wins than they had the year before, even though Loscutoff missed most of the year with a knee injury. Sharman averaged 22 points a game, Cousy was the assist leader for the sixth straight year, and Russell averaged 22 rebounds a game, the most ever in NBA history. It seemed as if the Celtics were poised to win their second straight title, until Russell lay on the floor in the third game, didn't play in the next two, and gamely came back in the sixth game in St. Louis, one the Celtics had to win just to stay alive and get the seventh game back to the Boston Garden. But he wasn't effective, and Pettit scored 50 to finally give Ben Kerner his world title.

The Hawks would be the last all-white team to win the NBA title, even if no one realized a certain era had ended. They also went on a 21-game exhibition tour shortly after they won the championship, because Kerner still had to make money.

The Celtics came back to win in 1959, beating the Minneapolis Lakers in four straight, the first time that had ever been done in the NBA Finals, after surviving a tough seven-game series with their old nemesis Syracuse. After the final game the players carried Auerbach off the court, then got into an elevator that was supposed to take them down two levels where their locker room was. But the elevator wouldn't work, so they found a small shower room and threw both Auerbach and trainer Buddy Le-Roux into the shower. To them, it was the title they would have won the year before if Russell hadn't gotten injured, their second banner in three years, the reaffirmation that they were the best team in basketball.

No one ever came into the NBA with the kind of anticipation that surrounded Wilt Chamberlain. He had been a celebrity since he was a freshman at Overbrook High School in Philadelphia. In many ways he was basketball's first prodigy, discovered early, growing up in the middle of fame's crosshairs. Years later we would see the same scenario played out over and over again, a conga line of basketball wunderkind that included Lew Alcindor, Moses Malone, Darryl Dawkins, Bill Cartwright, Ralph Sampson, Patrick Ewing, and others. They came from different decades, and different parts of the country, but they all shared three things: They were roughly seven feet tall as high-school players, they were black, and they were supposed to possess otherworldly potential, the kind that promised national titles to any college fortunate enough to land them.

Wilt was the first.

He was already nearly 6-foot-11 at only 12 years old, called "Dipper" by his friends, supposedly for the time as a child when he had to dip his head to get into a room. Even as a kid, he was never gawky or awkward, like some immobile circus freak. He could run. He could move. He was graceful. He was so dominating a high-school player that he led the "Brook" to three straight public school titles and a 53-3 record. He had 90 points in one game, 74 in another. His senior year he averaged 44 points a game.

He was fawned over, courted, and he learned early that his size and his growing celebrity could get him things, allowed for him to be able to play by different rules. In the summer before his senior year he was guided to Kutscher's Country Club in the Catskills by Haskell Cohen, the NBA's director of publicity. He was a bellhop for the summer, earning $26 every two weeks, plus tips. And he got a lot of tips. He was forever being asked to come back to the guests' rooms and bring extra coat hangers, anything, because he was such a curiosity.

Ironically, his coach at Kutscher's was Auerbach, who spent summers there augmenting his income with the Celtics. As the story goes, Wilt scored 26 points in the first half against B. H. Born, an All-American at Kansas, after which Auerbach asked Wilt, "Why don't you go to Harvard when you get out of high school?"

But this time Eddie Gottlieb was too quick for Red.

Gottlieb, who had been born in Russia, had founded a team called the South Philadelphia Hebrew Association in 1918. They were known as the SPHAs, and they played all the touring professional teams in the thirties and forties before morphing into the Philadelphia Warriors when the Basketball Association began in 1946. Gottlieb was the owner, president, and coach of the Warriors, a short man who knew how to hustle. He had coached Philadelphia to a title in 1947, the first year of the BAA, talked the NBA into something called the "territorial draft rule," which bound high-school and college players to the teams within a 50-mile radius. Thus, the Warriors owned Chamberlain's NBA rights once his college class graduated.

Chamberlain went to Kansas, supposedly turning down more than 200 other schools. Kansas was one of the glamor college basketball programs in the country, coached by the legendary Phog Allen, and when Chamberlain finally committed to the Jayhawks, Allen supposedly gushed, "With him, we'll never lose a game. We could win the national championship with Wilt, two sorority girls, and two Phi Beta Kappas."

Freshmen were not eligible for the varsity then, but Wilt was no secret. In a preseason public scrimmage against the varsity he had scored 40, with 30 rebounds. He was clearly the best player in the school, already being said to be ready for NBA greatness. From the beginning Chamberlain's career at Kansas was under a microscope, the rumors constantly swirling that Kansas had bought him. He drove around the KU campus in fancy cars, although the only time the school was penalized was for supposedly buying him tires. He stayed at Kansas for three years, but never won an NCAA title. The closest he got was his sophomore year, Kansas losing in three overtimes to a North Carolina team that had five players from metropolitan New York, coach Frank McGuire's so-called "underground railroad." Even now, it's regarded as one of the most famous championship games in NCAA history.

At the end of his junior year he quit Kansas to sign with the Globetrotters. Saperstein paid him $65,000 a year, a princely sum in an age when the average NBA salary was $15,000. Chamberlain loved the 'Trotters. He was allowed to shoot jumpers and handle the ball, even play guard at times, things he wasn't able to do in college, and he liked the clowning aspect, too. He was still a curiosity piece, but for the first time in his basketball life there was little pressure on him.

When he finally arrived in the NBA in the fall of 1959 he treated professional basketball like he had treated every other basketball game in his life. He was too big. Too coordinated. Too athletic. Too strong. If he got the ball close to the basket he invariably overpowered the man who was guarding him, simply turning and dunking. Gottlieb said Chamberlain was "Babe Ruth all over again." He was so dominant that a young writer in New York named Jimmy Breslin wrote a magazine article titled, "Can Basketball Survive Wilt Chamberlain?"

It was a legitimate question. Chamberlain was an inch over seven feet and weighed roughly 270 pounds. He was the biggest player in the league, and even in the NBA it was as if he were a man playing against boys.

Except when he was matched against Bill Russell.

The first meeting between the two giants drew a standing-room-only crowd in the Boston Garden on November 7, 1959. Barry Gottehrer, a New York City freelance writer, covered the game for *Sport* magazine.

The article was part of a special issue of *Sport,* called "The Negro in American Sport," which had grown out of a discussion at the Biltmore Hotel in New York City between several editors of the magazine and tennis great Althea Gibson, football player Buddy Young, Larry Doby—the first black player in the American League—and Jackie Robinson.

Two of the most significant things that came out of this discussion were the consensus that Negro players could not expect to get the kind of endorsements that white players could get, and the realization that Negro players tended to segregate themselves on teams, due to comfort level, even if Robinson thought that was a bad precedent, "that it isn't good for Negroes to band together in cliques on ballclubs."

Gottehrer's story opened with how he was offered a $3 ticket for $10 on the afternoon of the game.

"Just tryin' to do you a favor, Mac," the ticket scalper whispered.

Russell had spent a quiet afternoon playing with his young son Buddha and helping his wife, Rose, repair a shelf in the bathroom.

"My husband hasn't said much about tonight's game," Rose Russell said. "But I know he's been thinking about it. Some of the things sportswriters have said about Bill have hurt him. He's a proud man. I'm not worried. I'm sure he'll do okay."

What they had been saying for a few years now was that though Russell was obviously a great player, he was just the caretaker to the role of the best center in the game, a distinction that already belonged to Chamberlain, who was still only in the nascent stages of his NBA career. In fact, some people thought that Chamberlain would have been the most dominant player in the NBA if he had entered the league out of Overbrook High School, that he was simply too big and too coordinated to be contained.

Wilt had spent most of the afternoon lying diagonally across two beds in a room in the Hotel Lenox in Copley Square. If both he and Russell were low-key on the afternoon of the game, they also knew the significance of the upcoming showdown.

And showdown it was.

It had all the atmosphere of a championship prizefight, complete with fans who crowded around the court as the two teams warmed up. Chamberlain spent much of the warmups dunking, to the delight of the crowd. He was four inches taller than Russell, and 40 pounds heavier. He was averaging 40 points a game, an unheard-of figure.

There is a picture from that night, taken before the game. The two are standing together, Wilt in his dark uniform top with

"Phila" on it, over the number 13. He is wearing satiny shorts and
high white socks that are topped by white knee guards worn on
his shins. Russell is in his white uniform with low black sneakers.
They are standing together, but not looking at each other, as if
linked, but separate, too.

Chamberlain finished with 30 points, but he took 38 shots to
get them, twice as many as Russell, who finished with 22 points.
Unbelievably, they had 63 rebounds between them. And in the
end the Celtics won by nine.

In many ways that game was a microcosm of a rivalry that
would become one of the greatest in the history of American
sport. To this day, who was greater is one of basketball's great
unanswered questions. Chamberlain always scored more points,
ultimately had the better stats, while Russell and the Celtics
invariably won. The two of them would go on to play 142 games
against each other over the course of a decade, Chamberlain averaging nearly 29 points and 28 rebounds a game, as compared to
Russell's 14.5 points and 23.7 rebounds. Wilt scored at least 50
points seven times against Russell, once even 62. But in 10 years
Russell's teams won nine championships; Chamberlain's teams
won one.

"I didn't play as well as I should have," Chamberlain said afterward in the runway that led to the visitors' locker room, "but I'm
not taking anything away from Russell. He's just great. He gets the
ball off the boards and gets it to Cousy and Sharman. I thought
he would play me closer but he stayed back and then moved in
on my jumper. Nobody ever did that to me before. He sure can
box out under those boards."

Cousy had played a great game, 24 points and 11 assists. The
next week's *Sports Illustrated* said this: "The occasion was turned
into a double feature by Boston's Bob Cousy, who evidently had
not been told what the big attraction was supposed to be. In any
event, he dominated the game as he has so often done in recent

years—though without added recognition, simply because we have come to take this incredible athlete for granted.

"Last Saturday, after nine years as a professional, Cousy displayed a dozen sleight-of-hand tricks with the basketball that no one had ever seen before. He set up his teammates for scores all night and made 24 points."

But, he too, was like a backup singer on this particular evening, even if he took a great delight in upstaging the Wilt-Russell showdown.

"Wilt's got all the guns," Cousy said. "But he's got to learn to play with four other men. He can't do it alone in this league, like he did in college. Bill has learned this and we work well together. Bill's a great ballplayer. I think he proved that tonight."

Russell was in the Celtics' locker room.

"He's the best rookie I've ever seen," he said of Chamberlain. "I wish I was that good when I started. You've got to keep your hands on him and bother him all the time. This guy's no freak. By the end of the season, he could be the best basketball player of all time. When you're that big and good—and man, his potential's unlimited—there's no stopping him.

"I think I'm a little quicker defensively but he's so strong you can't lean on him. I weigh 210 pounds and you saw how he picked me off the ground. I'm glad he's in the league finally. He'll bring more people and I'll make more money."

He smiled after he said that.

"He's a great ballplayer," he continued, "but that doesn't mean Bill Russell is finished. I'm proud of the way I played tonight."

He should have been. He had outplayed and outfought the most celebrated rookie in the history of professional basketball.

It was the start of a strange dance between these two giants of American sport. They soon became friends. Chamberlain would eat at Russell's house in suburban Reading when the Warriors played in Boston, a favor reciprocated when Russell played in Philadelphia. They began calling each other by their middle names, so that Russell became "Felton," and Chamberlain "Norman." It was as if they had always known it was their respective fates to be linked, intuitively realizing they never could escape each other, even if they wanted to, as though they lived in some universe that was different from the one everyone else lived in. In a sense they did. They were both a generation ahead of themselves, the advance guard of big, athletic men who would change basketball forever.

It was a complicated friendship, too. How could it not be? They were always being compared to each other, measured against each other, all in a very public forum. Eventually, Chamberlain began to chafe at the role he was always being placed in, Goliath to Russell's David. He didn't like that it was Russell who came to be portrayed as the smarter player, more cerebral, more multifaceted, while Chamberlain was perceived as simply being a giant. There was one theory, later promoted by Wilt himself, that he took so many fallaway jump shots from the left side because he wanted to be admired for his skills, even though he later said he could have scored even more if he had remained inside in the paint, using both his height and his strength to overpower the man guarding him.

But that was Chamberlain. In retrospect, many of the things he did in his life were an attempt to disprove the perception that he was just some dumb giant, important only because he was bigger than everyone else. He hated being called "Wilt the Stilt," because that only drew attention that he was a freak. He wanted to be seen as smart and urbane, a skilled player, not just a goon. He had run track at Kansas, partly to show he was a great athlete, not just a basketball player. He had also been a disk jockey for a while at the Kansas student radio station, doing a show called *Flipping with the Dipper*.

In that sense, both Chamberlain and Russell wanted to be seen as Renaissance men. Music. Clothes. An appreciation of the finer things in life. A yearning to do well in business, too, not just in basketball. Those were the things they sought. This, too, was consistent with the times, that most American of ideals, that you could transform yourself, continue to evolve. There was no doubt both Russell and Chamberlain were not content to be dismissed as genetic freaks, no matter how much money they made.

If they were alike in many ways, though, their games were remarkably different. Russell was the ultimate team player, not only in terms of attitude, but in terms of skills, too. His rebounding, his shot blocking, the fact he didn't need the ball to be a great player, all made him unique. Chamberlain was the antithesis. He needed the ball. He always had had the ball, knew no other way to play. He was a scorer, pure and simple, and things worked best when his teammates passed him the ball and got out of his way. That was the way Eddie Gottlieb wanted him to play, for Gottlieb believed in that oldest of show biz adages: Stars put people in seats. On the Warriors, everything was geared to getting Wilt the ball. He determined how the Warriors played, the offense waiting for Wilt to get situated in the low post, similar to how the Minneapolis Lakers had played with Mikan. The Celtics were a fast-breaking, free-flowing team. The Warriors were Wilt and everyone else.

To Cousy, it was basketball sacrilege.

He knew he couldn't have played with Chamberlain, at least not the way he played with Russell. The Warrior guards were all instructed to wait until Wilt got down the floor. No freelancing for them. No pushing the ball up the court. They were strictly subjects in Wilt's kingdom, planets revolving around the sun. Cousy knew that everything he did on the floor, all the things that made him the player he had become, the pushing the ball, the fast break, the instinct that was at the very heart of his game, would be nullified by playing with Chamberlain.

"There was no way I was going to wait for Wilt to come up the floor," he said later in his life. "That would have muted the way we played. I just don't think his game would have complemented the rest of us."

Would it have been different if the Celtics didn't have a big man themselves, and Chamberlain had kept beating them? No doubt. But Cousy and the Celtics had Russell, and they always won. What did they need Wilt for?

Cousy had heard of Chamberlain when he had still been in high school. Not that that was unusual. You couldn't be around basketball and not hear about this Philadelphia high-school kid who was going to change the game. But when he first saw him, Cousy considered Wilt almost a Frankenstein-type player, certainly the biggest player he had ever seen. But Cousy looked at Wilt more as a specialist than a basketball player, didn't think Chamberlain understood his role as a basketball player. He saw he didn't make a full commitment to defense, didn't make his teammates better. In fact, it was just the opposite.

Cousy certainly never held Wilt in awe, as others did. Years later, Cousy thought he probably didn't give Wilt enough credit when he was playing, didn't give him his due as the great offensive force he was, that he was so into himself and the Celtics that Wilt's large shadow didn't intrude on his world. Nor did he have any real relationship with Chamberlain. Their teams played against each other, then they moved on in their own worlds.

"But it wasn't as if I disliked him," Cousy said, in retrospect. "I always had the sense he was happy to be Wilt. There was no chip on his shoulder. He didn't seem to have Russ's issues. If he did, he didn't show it. Nor did he lose his temper very often. He was always complaining that he was getting picked on because he was bigger than everyone else, and he was probably right about that. But I never looked at Wilt as a power player, even if he was the biggest and strongest man I had ever seen at the time."

In fact, the only time Cousy saw any evidence of Chamberlain's temper was an incident with Sam Jones, during a playoff game in the Boston Garden.

"Wilt was in a rage, and he was coming after Sam, so Sam picked up a chair," remembered Cousy. "Sam said something like, 'If I have to fight you, I'm not going to fight you fair.' Everyone was trying to intervene, but I thought the incident was more comedic than anything else."

But Cousy came to believe that Wilt's presence in a game made his and his teammates' jobs easier, for the players they were guarding rarely did anything on offense, everything was so geared to waiting for Wilt to get into the low post and then giving him the ball and watching him do his thing.

Except for Russell, of course.

Russell was never cocky when it came to playing Chamberlain. Wilt was so big, so strong, so potentially dominant, that Russell soon learned he couldn't stop him as he could other players. So the goal became to take things away, try to minimize him. Instead of Wilt getting 40, maybe he could hold him to 32. Instead of Wilt being able to do what he wanted, the goal became to make him work, make him take more difficult shots.

Much of it was little things. Chamberlain liked to settle in the low post to the left of the lane, much as Mikan had before him. That way, with his back to the basket, he could spin to his left and dunk with his right hand. That was his signature move, and against most opposing centers he could do it, simply using his superior size and strength to overpower his defender.

So Russell's strategy was to try to beat him to the spot, make Chamberlain set up farther away from the basket, make Wilt put the ball on the floor to get to the basket, then use his superior quickness to get in his way. Whenever Chamberlain had to put the ball on the floor, Russell thought he had the advantage.

Wilt also had deficiencies, as dominating as he was. He didn't have a hook shot. He didn't have a jump shot. He had the dunk. He had a finger roll that he shot in the lane, usually when he was blocked from getting in for the dunk, and he had a fallaway shot from the left side, which he tried to bank off the backboard. So Russell tried to block Wilt's move into the lane and make him take the fallaway instead, a much lower-percentage shot, one that took Wilt out of any rebound situation. Then, when the game was close, Russell would try to get up closer and bother that shot, making Wilt shoot even more of a fallaway, making it an even more low-percentage shot.

Later in their careers, as their roles became more and more cemented in the public's perception, Wilt tried to prove his game was as well-rounded as Russell's, that he could do all the things Russell could do. Wilt would also become more idiosyncratic as the years went by.

From his first year in the NBA, Wilt had been flamboyant. One of the first things he did was buy a Bentley, which went for $22,000, supposedly one-third of his first-year salary. For a while, early in his career, he lived in New York City, in a posh apartment near the corner of Central Park West and 97th Street, where he owned Big Wilt's Small's Paradise, a Harlem nightclub. He lived with two Great Danes and commuted to Philadelphia in the Bentley.

At the end of his first year he announced his retirement. He had averaged 37.6 points and 27 rebounds a game, had scored at least 50 points seven times, and said he had nothing to prove anymore. It was a theme he would cling to intermittently through his career, that the NBA was a bush league, and he had done everything he had set out to do in it. But it would not be until 1967, eight years after he came into the league, that he first won a title.

Already, the Celtics were establishing themselves as a great team. And as with all the great teams, the whole was better than the sum of the parts, even if many of the individual parts were great. Whether it was by accident, design, or a combination of both, the players had become specialists: Russell for the rebounds that fueled the fast break. Cousy orchestrating the break, running the offense. Sharman coming off screens, hitting the medium-range shot, over and over again. Heinsohn the scoring forward, both inside and out. Sanders, strong defensively, but a complementary player offensively, didn't need the ball, was content to set screens and see others get the shots.

Then Ramsey coming off the bench, doing a little of this, a little of that, the best sixth man in the game. Or Loscutoff would come off the bench and crush someone, give the Celtics an unmistakable physical presence.

There were others in bit parts through those years, mostly a sprinkling of veterans who had been around the league for years and were content to finish with the Celtics, where their salaries were augmented by playoff money. Arnie Risen, who had won a title with Rochester in '51 and joined the Celtics in 1956, backing up first Macauley, and then Russell. Jack Nichols, who had played for Auerbach both in Washington and in Tri-Cities and was a dental student at Tufts in addition to coming off the bench for the Celtics. Andy Phillip, the veteran who came over from Fort Wayne to back up Cousy and Sharman on the '57 title team. Gene Conley, one of the few who played both professional baseball and basketball, pitching in the major leagues for 11 years while backing up Russell for three years. Conley, who never ran from a fight, achieved his slice of infamy a couple of years later when, after too many beers, he left a Red Sox bus in Manhattan traffic with the idea of going to Israel.

They were all handpicked by Auerbach, selected as much for their attitudes as for their ability. Auerbach had always understood chemistry, one of those words so many other coaches gushed about, all the while stocking their rosters with players who didn't seem to exhibit any. Part of that, no doubt, was that Auerbach always wanted to be in control, knew a coach *had* to be in control. He always had known that, which was one of the reasons he had jumped all over Cousy in the beginning, letting the hometown hero know right away that he was in charge. In his own way, he did it with all his players. He quickly established the parameters, let it be known from the outset what the terrain was going to be.

He also had known from the beginning of his coaching career that the players' games had to complement one another. It wasn't good to have too many shooters. He believed in having players whose individual games blended with others. Cousy now knew that Auerbach recognized talent, knew how to acquire it, how to motivate it.

And from the beginning Auerbach paid people based on what they contributed to winning. Not by their glowing stats, the traditional standard of measure. Not by reputation. But by what he saw with his own eyes, what he thought each player brought to the whole. In retrospect, this might have been Auerbach's true coaching genius. He created an environment where winning was the Holy Grail, and everything he did reinforced that vision. All coaches paid lip service to winning. Everything Auerbach did was in pursuit of it.

He also had the benefit of longevity. Coaches came and went; Auerbach was always there, or so it seemed. By the 1959–60 season he and Syracuse coach Paul Seymour had the most seniority of any coaches in the league.

More important, the Celtics had a definite stability.

The core of the team was now in its fourth year. Everyone knew their roles. Everyone got along. Everyone knew what it took to win. So every year the Celtics would go to training camp and all they really had to do was get in shape, something Auerbach passionately believed in.

The scenario never changed.

They would run and run, then run some more, as everything they did, everything they were as a team, fed off the fast break; the Celtics played at a quicker pace than any other team in the NBA. This always had been Auerbach's vision, the reason the team had been put together the way it had been, and as the seasons went by and the titles accumulated that got reaffirmed. New players joined the team because they could fit in, not necessarily because they were the most talented players available. Auerbach had his stars. What he needed was players who could complement those stars.

They won again in the spring of 1960, too. They beat Wilt and the Warriors in the Eastern Conference finals. And again, they beat the Hawks in the Finals, just in case there was any lingering doubt who the better team was.

Another banner hung in the rafters of the Boston Garden, the third one in four years.

Chapter Nine

By 1960 Boston was as segregated as any major city in the country. The Italians were in East Boston and the North End. The Irish were in South Boston and Dorchester, a legacy of the potato famine that sent scores of immigrants to America, to Boston. The blacks were in Roxbury, removed from downtown geographically, as well as spiritually, tucked away in the city's west side, out of sight and usually out of mind. Blacks comprised roughly 10 percent of the city's population and none of its power structure.

Ironically, the early blacks had gotten along well with the Brahmins, Boston's unofficial ruling class. Slavery had been outlawed as far back as the 18th century, and by the middle of the 19th century blacks in Boston had achieved a degree of freedom unprecedented in the United States. Schools had been desegregated as far back as 1855. Boston had been at the center of the abolition movement, founded at the African Meeting House, the city's first black church. The movement's two main goals had been the eradication of slavery in the South and the end of discrimination in the North. Many blacks were educated, cultured, closely aligned with whites. That had begun to change, as the city's ethnic makeup changed. More blacks, uneducated, unskilled, arrived from the South, establishing divisions in the black community. The poorer blacks competed with the Irish for marginal jobs, increasing tensions that would last for generations. From 1940 to 1960 the black population in Boston tripled, as the influx of more uneducated southern blacks flooded the city and settled into ghettos.

And even though there had always been a distinct black community in Boston, blacks in Boston were almost invisible, geographically isolated in Roxbury, and economically isolated by the
realities of the era.

This was the city Russell found himself in, and it soon became
apparent he had little use for it. Maybe that was inevitable. It was
soon apparent he was not someone who could be put in a tidy little package and called "a credit to his race," like the prizefighter
Joe Louis, not someone who was going to acquiesce to the status
quo. It was also soon apparent he was a sports star the likes of
which Boston had never seen before.

In 1958 he had written a story in *Sports Illustrated* saying he
didn't like white people because they were white, and that, con-
versely, he liked most Negroes because they were black, and that
he thought of even the most downtrodden of Negroes as brothers. He had also suggested that race was the reason he never really
had gotten his due as a player, from being beaten out of player of
the year in his college conference by Kenny Sears, to losing out as
college player of the year to Tom Gola in 1956, to coming in second to Heinsohn as the NBA rookie of the year in 1957. Three
years later, in his autobiography *Go Up for Glory,* he qualified his
statements, not exactly taking them back but saying they were
made out of emotion.

Regardless, he was Boston's first black sports star, in a sports
landscape where the Red Sox didn't have their first black player
until 1959, the last team in the major leagues to integrate. The
Red Sox were owned by Tom Yawkey, who owned a plantation in
South Carolina and was described, in the manner of the times, as
a gentleman sportsman. He had bought the Red Sox in 1933,
doted on the stars, and spent money lavishly on the team. The
team was his plaything, to the extent that when the team was on
the road he used to take batting practice at Fenway Park, or have
picnics on the outfield grass with his wife. Yawkey was many
things, but socially progressive was not one of them. It's part of
Red Sox lore how they could have signed Jackie Robinson in

1945, and Willie Mays four years later, and in the mid-fifties Yawkey surrounded himself with some of his drinking buddies. One was manager Mike "Pinky" Higgins, who, according to Cousy biographer Al Hirshberg, once said, "There'll be no niggers on this team as long as I have anything to say about it."

This was the sports landscape in Boston. If the Celtics had had Negro players before, in Chuck Cooper and Don Barksdale, they had been role players, with minimum impact.

Russell was different.

From his height of six-foot-nine, with a goatee to boot, to the fact that he was so dominant a player, such a presence, he made people deal with him. Traditionally, all the Celtics' rookies had to pay their dues. They had to carry the bags of basketballs, fetch the Cokes for the other players, pay for the cabs, all the subservient things. Russell never did any of them. Later, he said he was never asked, that "with my size and temperament, I could avoid a lot of harassment by scowling or looking glum at the right time."

Auerbach called the black players "Schvartzes," the Yiddish word for blacks, although in American colloquial usage it had, in a certain sense, come to mean "nigger." It was an insult, but to Auerbach it wasn't any big deal, because he insulted everyone anyway.

In fall 1960 the Celtics now had four black players. They were still called "Negroes" then; it would be roughly seven more years before the term "black" began being commonly used.

One was Sam Jones, and he was another one of the players who contributed to the perception of Auerbach being two steps ahead of the other coaches, seemingly arriving from nowhere. Actually, he had gone to college at North Carolina Central, a small black school that played college basketball in virtual anonymity. He had come to Auerbach's attention through Bones McKinney, the Wake Forest coach who had been on the Celtics for a while in the early fifties, and as he had with Russell a year earlier, Auerbach put a lot of credence in what his ex-players told him. In a sense, he had to. The Celtics didn't have any scouts looking at college players. Nor were college games on television, at least not many, not even the NCAA Tournament. Instead, NBA teams relied on college reputations, often drafting players they had never seen. So it was with Sam Jones. From the time he came to training camp in fall '57, though, he was a steal, better than anyone ever could have dreamed he could be. He was six-foot-four, big for a guard in those days, and rangy and athletic, too. He was also a great shooter, often using the backboard in ways no one had ever done before. The only reason he didn't start right away was that he played the same position as Sharman, still one of the best guards in the league.

K. C. Jones, who arrived a year after Sam, after two years in the Army, had been a college teammate of Russell's at San Francisco.

It had been K.C. who had shut down the celebrated Tom Gola in the 1955 Final Four, using his speed and toughness to compensate for the fact that the six-foot-seven Gola was five inches bigger than he was. But K. C. Jones had been a high-school football star in San Francisco, and he dogged the bigger Gola the entire game, holding him to just six field goals. At one point he stole the ball, rushed down the court, and dunked, the first time he had ever done so in his life. By the end of the game the Dons had won by 14, Jones had scored 24 points, and LaSalle's veteran coach Ken Loeffler said he'd never seen a better college team than San Francisco.

Jones said it was at San Francisco that he learned about togetherness on a basketball team, that it was a team that figured out that if you played together and stuck to your roles anything was possible. Afterward, he had spent two years in the Army, and always believed that, as a third-round draft pick, the two-year wait had been the reason he had made the Celtics in the first place, with some of the veteran backup guards no longer there.

But K.C. came to the Celtics with the reputation of being a nonshooter, and in the beginning the word was he was on the team primarily because he was Russell's friend. There was little question about his defensive tenacity, or that he knew what it was like to be on winning teams, a quality Auerbach always coveted. He, too, had played on the Olympic team in Melbourne.

The "Jones Boys," as they came to be known, also knew they had to wait their turn. That was the Celtics' way, Auerbach's way. You paid your dues. They were the understudies to Cousy and Sharman, joining the best team in the game. Their role was not only to spell the two backcourt superstars, but also to apply defensive pressure. Often, they would come into the game together, pick up opposing guards in the backcourt, shadowing them up the court in ways Cousy and Sharman did not, making the Celtics a different team, at least defensively.

The rookie was Tom Sanders, whose nickname was "Satch," supposedly in honor of Satchel Paige, the legendary pitcher of the old Negro Leagues. Sanders had been an All-American at New York University and arrived at the Celtics' training camp wearing glasses and large white knee guards. His role was simple: Guard the opponent's best forward, and essentially stay out of the way on offense. He later became known for calling President Kennedy "baby" at a White House reception honoring the Celtics, but that had been more out of shyness than cool. The Celtics did not run any plays for Sanders. He essentially was a nonshooter, and if he were going to get the ball it probably was going to come by getting rebounds off the offensive glass.

"The black guys hung together," said Cousy. "They would go to the movies together. They would spend time in the locker room together. They would sit and laugh at everything. They would create humor out of the most ordinary of everyday situations. And the rest of us were not part of their sense of humor."

No one laughed any louder or more often than Russell. Ed Linn, a Boston writer, once said, "If thunder were played on an English horn instead of a kettledrum, you would have some idea of the pitch and tone of Russell's laughter."

It was just one more aspect of a complex man. Certainly, it was something the average fan never heard. Russell already had said that "I owe the public nothing, and I'll pay them nothing," and by 1960 it was also apparent he had little use for the hypocrisy he saw around him. In the parlance of the times, he was militant and made no secret of the fact. His public face was of a scowling, almost menacing presence, full of anger and old hurts, either real or imagined. He had little use for the sports establishment, something that remained throughout his life. When he was approached in hotel lobbies he often blew people off, maybe the classic scene coming when someone came up to Russell and said, "I'm sorry to bother you, but . . ."

"Then don't," Russell snapped.

Auerbach was always trying to educate people about how good Russell was, how incredibly dominating a basketball player he was. It was a basketball version of spreading the Gospel, but it never seemed to really take, for whatever reason. Maybe it was because Russell wasn't a big scorer, or that you had to know basketball, understand its nuances, to fully appreciate the impact Russell had on a basketball game. Maybe it was his persona, the fact that he wasn't particularly likable, not easy to root for, however great he was. Or maybe it was simply race, that in America then, and in Boston no less, Bill Russell was never going to get his due.

One of the great unanswered questions is why the Celtics didn't draw better when they were clearly the best basketball team on the planet. Was it merely because Boston was a bad basketball town, never really able to transcend its past, or was much of it racial, the unfortunate fact that the city was not going to embrace a team that kept getting blacker?

From the beginning Russell was unappreciated when it came to the public at large, even in Boston. Take the game story in the *Boston Globe* in April 1957, the day after the Celtics had won their first championship, the game in which fellow rookie Heinsohn had had his monster game, 37 points and 23 rebounds.

Jack Barry, who had covered the Celtics for years, wrote that it was obvious Heinsohn was the rookie of the year.

Then there was the relationship between Cousy and Russell.

There's no question each respected the other as both a player and a teammate. That had been the case from the beginning. But it was more complicated than that, too.

"I used to joke with Bob Cousy, and I admired what he stood for and the way he conducted himself," Russell said later. "I thought he was the smartest man I ever played with, and I had too much respect for him to get sucked into the jealousy others tried to promote between us. Still, I can't say I was ever close to Cousy; we never sat down and had a real conversation the way real friends would."

Russell went on to say this was true of many of his Celtics teammates, that there was simply too much pressure and too much competition to share your hopes and fears with people in the same business, that the kidding they all shared helped them win, and enabled them to have fun doing so, but it didn't necessarily make them the best of friends.

Cousy essentially had similar thoughts.

"We were never unfriendly," he said of Russell. "I think my shyness prevented us from being closer. It made me gun-shy. Given my situation, the fact that I was the veteran, the captain, I should have been the one to initiate things more. But because he was so sensitive I really didn't know how to handle Russell. And when you don't know how to handle things you tend not to. So it was like we were mutually guarded around each other."

The slice of irony was that Cousy's wife, Missie, was probably closer to Russell than her husband was, because Missie had befriended Rose Russell.

The other small bit of irony was that Cousy and Russell had certain similarities, not the least of which was that neither one had been a basketball prodigy as a kid, Russell having been the last kid picked on the jayvee team as a junior at McClymond's High School in Oakland, so little thought of that he had to share a uniform with another player. They also shared a certain competitive drive, one that was so internalized it surfaced in idiosyncratic ways. In Cousy's case it was his sleepwalking. In Russell's, it was his practice of throwing up before big games.

He did it so often that eventually it became a sort of weird good-luck charm. The players and Auerbach would be in the locker room waiting to go out on the floor, the tension starting to rise, nothing left to be said, then all of a sudden there would be the sound of Russell throwing up in the nearby bathroom and everyone sort of relaxed; they knew the big guy was ready. And if the big guy was ready they were going to be all right.

Cousy quickly came to realize, as many of the other Celtics did, that there were almost two Russells. There was the difficult, sometimes even hostile, public Russell, the one who wouldn't sign autographs and seemed to have no use for people, the one whose racial anger was always there, as visible as one of his sharp elbows when he came down with a rebound.

And there was Russell the teammate, who within the confines of the team unit would laugh and joke and be one of the guys. As if there were two sides to his personality and they were always competing with each other.

Another similarity was that they both believed they were men playing a child's game, as if for all their success, all the banners that kept going up in the rafters of the Garden, they did little that contributed to society in any profound way. Cousy was forever saying that "one good teacher is worth the whole lot of us," and was almost embarrassed when people made a fuss about him, or any other athlete.

"I don't consider anything I've done as contributing to society," Russell said. "I consider playing professional basketball as marking time, the most shallow thing in the world."

They also both had the ability to stand in front of their peers and admit mistakes. It was not uncommon for them to come into a huddle and say that they were the ones not playing well, that they had to do better. It was a quality that gave them immense respect from their teammates.

They shared something else, too, both a bottomless pride and a need to win. Not a will to win, thought Heinsohn, whose locker was between them in the locker room. A lot of players had that. No, thought Heinsohn, the trait Cousy and Russell shared was a need to win, a sense that winning helped heal some dysfunction in their makeup; other players wanted to win, Cousy and Russell *had* to win.

After the first couple of years, Russell's dislike for practice became apparent. He often loafed, went through the motions, expending as little energy as possible. He viewed practice as essentially meaningless, at least for him. Later in his career, he would have days when he simply wouldn't practice at all, would simply sit on the sidelines as the practice session went by in front of him. Yet within the team this became accepted, for the simple reason that once the game started, and the lights went on, Russell played with a certain fury.

Cousy believed Russell's aggressive behavior on the court was what made him a great player, and he theorized that in a league that was overwhelmingly white, this was what fueled Russell, the one arena when he could get "whitey." It was this ability to channel his anger that made him great, Cousy thought, and if that were indeed the case, then so be it. Let Russell hate the other team's white guys, let him take his rage out on them.

Cousy also came to believe Russell didn't really like basketball, it was just something he happened to be great at.

If by 1960 Russell had emerged as a genuine superstar, there was no question Cousy was infinitely more popular, not only in Boston, but nationally as well. He was the one with the endorsements, the one who got the biggest cheers, the most attention. Heinsohn later said it best: In those days Boston was Red Sox country, it was hockey country, and it was Cousy country. He could do nothing wrong, and the sportswriters were always making sure no one ever forgot that.

It's perhaps understandable that Russell would come to resent this. Later, he talked about the countless times he would be in the locker room and someone would come up to him and say, "Let me shake your hand. I've just shaken the hand of the greatest basketball player in the world, Bob Cousy. Now I want to shake the hand of the second greatest."

It was not what Russell wanted to hear, and it lent credence to his theory that no matter what he did he was never going to be a genuine sports hero in Boston.

But if the white players and the black players could sometimes seem to exist in parallel universes, they got along, too. There were never any significant problems. None that lasted for very long, anyway. They were not simply a collection of individuals who shared the same locker room. They were a team in the very best sense of the word. Heinsohn believed it became a basketball version of the Cosa Nostra, "this little thing of ours."

K. C. Jones would later say he never thought in terms of race. In his early years maybe that was because he was too concerned with trying to make the team, hang in the league. After that, there were occasional parties at someone's house, and it was simply understood that everyone was invited.

"From the day I first met my teammates and coach," Russell said, "I experienced something very different from what I had before: a real family whom we called team."

Russell went on to say how in his first game he was called for goaltending and in an instant Auerbach was off the bench and screaming at the refs, a visible sign that Auerbach was always going to fight for his players. Russell came to believe that both Auerbach and his teammates were always there for him.

Another incident that happened after his first practice with the Celtics had a considerable influence on Russell. The team's center had been Arnie Risen, a six-foot-nine skinny veteran who had been a very good player in the league with the Rochester Royals before coming to the Celtics in the twilight of his career. Russell obviously had been drafted to replace him, but after the first practice Risen approached Russell and said that he had some things to tell him.

Risen began telling Russell about some of the different centers in the league, tips on how to play them. Russell never forgot that. Not only was it a testimony to Risen's character, but it was one more sign to Russell that the Celtics were all about winning.

One year, there was a party for Russell at a country club in Reading, the suburban town north of Boston where he lived, and the whole team went. Heinsohn recalled how Russell was touched by the gesture, yet when Russell later sought to buy a bigger home in Reading, neighbors circulated a petition. Later still, his home was broken into and someone defecated in his bed.

So race, and the ramifications of race, were always there. How could they not be?

Cousy soon realized Auerbach dealt with race by not dealing with it, that he treated the Negro players the same as he treated everyone. He made fun of them. He occasionally berated them. He never let any of the players forget he was the boss, the one who controlled their fates. Russell later said that if you crossed Auerbach you were finished as a Celtic. But that was no different from the way he treated the white players. In part, that was the way he related to all people, always putting them on the defensive, making them deal with him. That was his way of being in control.

He was not particularly close to any of the players. Occasionally, he might go to the movies with a couple of them on the road in the afternoon, in those hours when everyone was just killing time until the game that night, but he never went out with players after the game. Auerbach and Russell became closer as the years went by, but even as late as 1966, when Russell had been with the Celtics for nearly a decade, he said he and Auerbach weren't particularly close.

Cousy certainly understood the black players' hunger, their drive, their desire to use basketball and the NBA to make money, have a better life. Hadn't he been the same way? To him, they were similar. Hadn't he come out of a ghetto experience, too, at least in those early years off East End Avenue in Manhattan? He also always had had an affinity for the underdog, whether it was the result of being picked on as a young child because he talked funny, or always feeling he was the outsider, the kid from the home life that didn't work. From his Jesuit education at Holy Cross, to his senior thesis on the persecution of the Jews, to his sensitivity to Chuck Cooper that night in North Carolina, his natural instinct was to side with the underdog.

There was a pragmatic aspect, too.

The black players made the Celtics better, and in a bottom-line business that was all about winning there was no getting around that. Just as Walter Brown had told the other NBA owners in 1950 that he didn't care if Chuck Cooper was polka dot or plaid, and just as Auerbach was oblivious to race, so were the players. They wanted to win, and the black players helped them do it.

That was Ramsey's view, anyway, and all the stereotypes of the time suggested that he should have had the most difficult adjustment dealing with black teammates, someone who, by his own admission, sounded like a white, southern hick. But he didn't. They were his teammates, they helped him win, and winning put money in his pocket. Years later, Ramsey said it probably helped that several of the Celtics had spent time in the service, had been exposed to different people, had to learn to deal with them.

Would it have been different if the Celtics didn't win?

Probably.

There were rumors that racial divisions existed on some teams, but that was never the case with the Celtics. Ramsey tells the story of the time he was on the court with Russell, Sanders, and the Jones Boys, and Russell leaned over to him and said with a laugh, "Just remember, Frank, there are more of us than you."

Since the league began, only 22 black players had played in the NBA through the '57 season. Now, 20 percent of the league was black.

Still, the overwhelming majority of the league was white, and in Cousy's view, little had changed. He came to believe that the slow integration of blacks into the league helped the racial situation, made it less of an issue than it might have been otherwise.

To his mind, the white players certainly didn't feel threatened, and on the Celtics, anyway, it was never an issue. Plus, Cousy never saw the black players as a group, for he knew their individual differences. Yes, Russell had a complicated personality, but K. C. Jones was a sweet man, shy and almost withdrawn in those early years. Sam Jones was more militant. He could be moody, had times when he seemed to be off in some private funk somewhere, something that could last for a couple of weeks, to the point that when his mood finally brightened his teammates would say, "Sam's back from vacation." Satch Sanders was delightful, and had many different interests.

To Cousy, though, they were all basketball players, all his teammates. He believed that, by its very nature, basketball created a bond between players, because unlike baseball, for example, everyone's success depended on everyone doing well. At those times when he saw the black players in terms of race, it only made him feel more sympathetic toward them, for he had learned as a child that prejudice was wrong, back when his mother railed against the "dirty Germans," and those rants made him uncomfortable.

Still, it would be a mistake to think that this was about civil rights. To Cousy, Auerbach was not so much racially progressive as simply a man who wanted to win. That was his lifeblood, and if black players could help him do it, so be it.

Later, Cousy believed that, as well as the players got along, to the extent that they periodically did things as a group, the white players could have been more sensitive to the situation, could have done more things to challenge the status quo, such as inviting their black teammates to their country clubs, a gesture that would have had symbolic meaning.

But he never did, even though he joined the NAACP and became very active in Big Brothers, requesting a black kid as his first "little brother," and often taking him to Blessed Sacrament, his church in Worcester, even though he knew it upset many of the parishioners.

"In many ways I was in my own world," he said. "I should have been more sensitive."

There was a belief that there was an unwritten quota system in the NBA, a tacit agreement that there were to be no more than three blacks on any team. There was the belief in "white dollars," the perception being that it was white fans who went to the games, and white fans didn't like seeing too many black players.

What was too many?

That was the issue, a line in the sand that seemed to always be shifting.

Or as the old line went, two blacks at home, three on the road, and four if you're behind.

The clues of how basketball was going to change were there, in ways both subtle and as emphatic as a Chamberlain blindside screen. The two best big men in the league were black. And the best young player in the league was black.

His name was Elgin Baylor, and he had arrived in fall 1958. That first year he averaged 25 points a game, fourth in the league behind Pettit, Jack Twyman of the Cincinnati Royals, and Paul Arizin of the Warriors. He was six-foot-five, strong, explosive, and had the ability to stay suspended in the air, what would later be known as "hang time." He was another preview of what the NBA would one day become, an improvisational player who had the ability to go up in the lane and create a shot for himself, something the league had never seen before. He had come out of Washington, D.C., the youngest child of a father who worked as a public-school custodian and a mother who worked for the Department of the Interior. He was named after a gold pocket watch his father had, and occasionally had a nervous twitch that caused his head and shoulders to move forward, in what became a built-in head fake.

The District of Columbia was still segregated in the early fifties, and Baylor wasn't allowed to play in the parks close to his neighborhood. Instead, he played in the street, inventing himself as he went along. He didn't watch basketball on television because his family couldn't afford a set. He didn't model his game on anyone else, just did what came naturally. But the neighborhood was clean, lower middle class, and Baylor didn't grow up wanting. He went to a vocational high school where he made All-City in basketball, but didn't particularly like either the attention he was receiving or school, and dropped out after his junior year, going to work in a warehouse. He was talked into going back the next year to Springarn High School, in hopes of getting an athletic scholarship to college somewhere, but no one tried to recruit him, because he didn't have enough credits.

In one of those tiny twists of fate, Baylor had a childhood friend who was playing football at the College of Idaho and told his coach he had a friend back in D.C. who was a great football player. So what if Baylor's only football experience was once playing on a boys club team? Baylor went to the College of Idaho, a small school in Cardwell, Idaho, that had fewer than 500 students. He never actually played football there, his basketball ability being quickly discovered. But one night during his first year he walked into a dorm room and heard a radio broadcast of San Francisco playing LaSalle, a game in which Russell and Tom Gola were going against each other. He became so excited listening to the game he figured it would be great to actually play for an NCAA school, a thought that began a process that ultimately had Baylor transferring to the University of Seattle.

He really didn't know much about the NBA, but ironically enough it was Russell who first gave him his introduction, albeit indirectly.

"I'd met Bill in college at Corvallis, Oregon, in the Far West Regional," Baylor later said. "He was playing with a team of touring NBA players and got me tickets for the game. R. C. Owens, who went on to be a great football player, was a friend of mine, and he was in Seattle playing for an AAU team at the time. They needed an extra player and asked R.C. to play. He did OK, didn't embarrass himself. That was the first time I started thinking about the NBA. I got a little inspired watching R.C., because I knew I might be a little better than R.C. and he held his own with those great players."

Baylor averaged around 30 points a game in his two years at Seattle, and in 1958 he took his team to the NCAA championship game, becoming the tournament's MVP in the process. Then he left to join the Minneapolis Lakers for $20,000, the first pick in the draft.

Would he have ended up in the NBA if he'd stayed at the College of Idaho?

Probably. He was very talented, and the NBA was in search of talent, even if it came from obscure places. Auerbach's finding Sam Jones was testimony to that. And the racial barriers were starting to crumble, however slowly. But not always without a certain pain.

In his first season Baylor had refused to play a game in Charleston, West Virginia. It was the first time a player had refused to play, and it happened after Baylor and two of his black teammates had not been allowed to check into a hotel in Charleston.

He and veteran Vern Mikkelson, a white player who had teamed with Mikan for years, back when the Lakers were the best team in the NBA, and who had befriended the young Baylor, were at the front desk.

"You can stay, but the colored fellow can't," the desk clerk told Mikkelson.

"We have reservations for the whole team," Mikkelson said.

"Then take the whole team somewhere else," the desk clerk said.

So they did, the entire Lakers team going to a Negro hotel.

Baylor was livid. Normally, he was easygoing, not quick to anger, but he had already been barred earlier in the year from a hotel in Charlotte, North Carolina, and the Lakers had told him then it wouldn't happen again. Now it had. Late that afternoon he went looking for a place for a pregame meal.

"I couldn't find any place to eat, any place a Negro could eat," he said. "It ended up that we had some meat, I think, and made some sandwiches. That was the last straw."

In the arena, approaching game time, Baylor sat in the locker room and told his teammates he wasn't going to play.

"If we have a nine-man team I guess we split the playoff money nine ways, huh?" a white teammate grumbled.

Baylor fired back that they didn't care about his feelings, that they just wanted him to play for their own selfish reasons.

Rod Hundley, a white Lakers teammate who was from Charleston and was a sort of a folk hero in West Virginia, where he was known as "Hot Rod," made one last pitch to convince Baylor to change his mind.

"Elj looked me in the eye and I'll never forget his words," Hundley said. "He said, 'I'm not an animal. I'm a human being, and I want to be treated like one.' I said to him, 'Elj, don't play.'" He didn't.

Baylor was an instant star. He scored 55 points in one game. He was the rookie of the year, and made the NBA's first team along with Cousy, Russell, and Sharman. For the first time in the history of the league two players on the first team All-NBA team were black.

By 1960 there was a certain sentiment that Baylor was the best all-around player in basketball, bigger than Cousy, more skilled than Chamberlain or Russell, more athletic than Pettit.

Cousy thought he was the best small forward he had ever seen. After one game, in which Baylor had scored 63 points against the Celtics, Cousy had told Satch Sanders he had done a great job guarding Baylor, even if Elgin had scored 63 points.

"He could flat-out hang in the air," Cousy said, "and we had never seen that before. He would get up in the air in the lane and just seem to stay there, and then because he was so strong he could get bumped and still finish. I was much more impressed with Elgin than I was with Wilt."

Then came Oscar Robertson.

He came into the league in fall 1960, fresh off the Olympic team where he had teamed up with fellow NBA rookie Jerry West to win the gold medal in Rome, and had had an unbelievable career at the University of Cincinnati. It was there that he began being called "The Big O," leading the country in scoring three straight years. Robertson might have been the first small player to enter the league with the same acclaim Chamberlain did a year earlier, even if at six-foot-five he wasn't exactly small. What he was, though, was the prototype of a big man who could handle the ball with all the skills of a smaller man, the first great big guard. He had led his Crispus Attucks High School team in Indianapolis to two consecutive state titles and 45 straight wins and had been the most-recruited high-school player since Chamberlain.

In his first year at the University of Cincinnati people would pack the 7,800-capacity gym for the freshman games, then half would leave before the varsity games started. As a sophomore he had 56 points against Seton Hall in Madison Square Garden, in what was called at the time the greatest individual performance since the Garden had opened in 1934. He had outscored the entire Seton Hall team, in a variety of ways. He was 19 years old then, and after the game he was carried off the court by his teammates.

He entered the league with the Cincinnati Royals, who used a territorial pick to select him. In his second year in the NBA he would average a triple double for the year, but from the moment he arrived in the NBA it was clear he was a great talent, perhaps as talented as anyone who had come into the league.

He was also another look into the NBA's future. He had grown up in segregated Indianapolis and had battled racial prejudice throughout his youth. His high-school team had been the first all-black team to win an open state tournament in the United States. When Crispus Attucks had won its first title in 1955 the team had celebrated by riding on fire trucks through Indianapolis with the sirens sounding. Years later, Robertson would say it had been an unbelievable moment, basketball when basketball was innocent and fun.

He soon realized it was more complicated than that, though. He had seen his older brother fail to be recruited by Indiana because of his color. He came to see that, although he was given special treatment because of his status as a great player, the racial prejudice never really went away. He had played college games in the South where he'd been discriminated against. In a sense, he brought a sense of racial pride with him to the NBA that mirrored Russell's, one shaped by a childhood of poverty, perhaps best defined by the fact that he learned to shoot a basketball by tossing tennis balls and rags with rubber bands around them into a rickety peach basket.

He became more and more outspoken the longer he was in the league, and spoke out in 1964 about the unfortunate fact that Negro players do not get endorsements, saying that even the great Willie Mays was lucky if he had a couple, and that for all that Russell had accomplished, what endorsements did he have?

Cousy was certainly impressed with Robertson's skills. How could he not be? He was also well aware that Robertson was considered the heir apparent to Cousy himself as the best point guard in the game, yet he saw their games as being very different. In Cousy's view, Oscar was a scorer first, a playmaker second. Although Robertson certainly possessed wonderful passing skills, his first instinct was to score himself, unlike Cousy, whose first instinct was to pass. Cousy also saw himself as someone who loved transition basketball, orchestrating the fast break, finding the open man, while Robertson was more of a halfcourt player, maybe at his best when backing an opponent down with the dribble, before rising up for a jump shot.

To Cousy, they were two completely different players. In fact, there was such a size difference that Cousy never even guarded Robertson, even though they essentially played the same position, Cousy instead being matched up with the other guard in the Royals' backcourt.

Yet there was a certain competition between Oscar and him, for Cousy always responded to a challenge, and what was more of a challenge than seeing some kid come into the league who was being called the best guard to ever enter the NBA? After a game in 1961, in which Cousy had had a great game against Oscar and the Royals, he had admitted in a newspaper story that he had gone into the game with extra incentive. Just as he had liked upstaging the first Russell-Chamberlain encounter, he liked nothing better than to shoot down all the young upstarts, serve notice that he wasn't going away, that he was going to defend his turf.

To Cousy, Auerbach was a master at Psych 101, and that transcended the fact that he integrated the Celtics with apparent ease.

Auerbach knew Heinsohn needed to be pushed. So he pushed him. He knew Loscutoff needed a little goose once in a while. So he goosed him. He kidded Ramsey once in a while, but knew that he couldn't do that with Sharman. Auerbach also knew never to get on Cousy or Russell, that they were both intense and self-motivated, each bringing his own particular form of need and fury to the court every night, so it was best to let them alone.

He also knew he could get on everyone, as long as he did it collectively. So he would come into the huddle and scream and holler, saying that everyone had gotten lazy and spoiled, ranting and raving, the Auerbach of legend, but he would never personalize it, never pick on any one individual. Cousy also came to know that Auerbach would have a big blowup every couple of weeks or so, just enough to keep everyone focused, then things would cool down for a while.

The titles became Auerbach's validation. He had always been respected, but he had been dismissed, too, perceived in other cities as obnoxious, always yelling at the referees, stamping his feet, throwing his little tantrums, almost a caricature of a coach in a nowhere league, still being thought of, in Boston, anyway, as the guy who hadn't wanted Cousy. Winning began changing all that. Now he was perceived as shrewd and cunning, two steps ahead of the other coaches, someone crafty enough to end up with Russell.

To Cousy, winning that first title only made Auerbach cockier, more assertive, more sure of himself. Then again, Cousy had known from the beginning that Auerbach simply was not a lovable figure. He was too confrontational. Too aggressive. Too one-dimensional. Too driven. Always someone with a chip on his shoulder, just daring the world to knock it off. One of his tricks was to walk by and drop cigar ashes on people. But only if he liked them. To him, dropping his cigar ashes was a sign of affection.

In the off-season Cousy and Auerbach would sometimes take trips around the world together, basketball evangelists for the State Department, and if these trips were a form of bonding, they also pointed out to Cousy how difficult it was to get close to Auerbach, how just when you got through one layer, you were faced with another, always another.

"I would hear the same stories over and over again," Cousy said. "I did this. I did that. I made this much money. I. I. I. It was always the same."

They would go to the movies and Auerbach would fall asleep, snoring loudly. He would burp in restaurants, holler loudly for the waiter, the Ugly American. Cousy would cringe. He would sometimes get so upset at Auerbach that he would stop talking to him, a tactic that would immediately cause Auerbach to start behaving better. Cousy eventually began to believe that Auerbach was all but impossible to get really close to, because he was simply too self-absorbed, the world always filtered through a personal prism. He saw how Auerbach would never congratulate him, not really, even the night he scored 50 points in the playoff game against Syracuse, as if Auerbach were simply not comfortable doing that.

Auerbach rarely fraternized with the players, even on the road. He would take his ham on rye sandwich and his large Coke and go up to his room. Outside of playing cards on plane rides, he kept his distance, as if knowing that if a coach got too close to his players it only created problems.

"I'm not married to you," he would tell the players.

The message was implicit: I'm not married to you, so I can easily get rid of you. He would often walk by one of the lesser players and say, "I almost traded you today," something to send the message that the player was existing on a day-to-day basis, always having to prove himself.

Everyone was on a one-year contract. No one had an agent. The players were all individual planets floating around in Auerbach's solar system. He was the coach, the general manager, the traveling secretary, the everything, running the Celtics as if they were a mom-and-pop store. When they paid for a cab on the road it was Auerbach whom they went to for reimbursement, Auerbach who always nickeled and dimed them about it, always trying to get an edge, because that was Red and that's the way he did everything. It was Auerbach who established the rules, however arbitrary they might have been, whether banning mixed drinks or forbidding his players to eat pancakes.

It was Auerbach who was the drill sergeant during training camp, running his own little torture chamber, getting them to run more laps, do more wind sprints. You were loafing? Run some more. You thought it was easy? Run some more, then. Auerbach was the boss and he never let anyone forget it. Heinsohn says he learned early that you didn't challenge Red. He wasn't your buddy. He wasn't your friend, and to players who had grown up in an era when authority was not questioned, his style worked. Players would occasionally complain amongst themselves, or mutter something under their breath, or occasionally give Auerbach a look, but no one ever made an issue out of it, no one ever rebelled. Coaches were expected to be taskmasters. Coaches were expected to set the rules.

In the early years of the titles it was the players who got all the credit, the perception being that the Celtics were so talented that anyone could coach them, a theory that no doubt rankled Auerbach. Or at least Cousy thought so.

The NBA had become different for Cousy, not like some of

those early years when everything had seemed like such a grind, and every season had ended in disappointment. Winning had made it so. Winning was the great elixir. It softened the problems, neutralized any of the potential difficulties. It gave everyone a sense of purpose, made everyone get along.

Had the Celtics become the paradigm for race relations, one big extended family where everyone always got along, black and white together, everyone striving toward the same goal, some place where color didn't matter?

That has become the mythology, one that's grown more entrenched as the decades have gone by. It's a romantic notion, certainly, especially in a country where race has always been the apple in the American Eden, especially in the late fifties when race in America was being put under a microscope. Heinsohn says he saw only one racial incident in all his time with the Celtics, a time when backup Gene Guarilia called Sam Jones "Sambo" and Jones wanted to fight. It was quickly broken up, and Guarilia said that he hadn't intended any racial slur.

Race was always more complicated than that, as every team has its cliques, its resentments, its own internal rhythms, its secrets. The Celtics were probably no different.

Except for one thing:

They won.

The Celtics were the best team in the world and they acted like it. They never sat during timeouts, because other teams got tired, other teams needed a rest; not the Celtics. They wore jackets on the road. Most important, there were no players who didn't fit in, no one whose individual agenda got in the way of the whole. Inside the team there were unwritten rules, so unquestioned they might as well have been chiseled in stone: No one cared about points. No one complained that he didn't get the ball enough. No one complained about playing time. It was all about winning.

Part of this, certainly, was that the more the team won, the more money the players made. Ramsey wasn't kidding when he used to put the figures the players could make in playoff money on the locker-room blackboard. Auerbach even used this in his negotiations with players, telling them that, yes, he was probably offering below market value, but they were going to make up for it with their playoff money.

Carl Braun, another of the veterans whom Auerbach had picked up near the end of his career to be a backup guard, once heard Ramsey say, "I'd rather live year-round in Kentucky. I come to Boston to make money."

"That's when I knew what it meant to be a Celtic," Braun said.

But it was more than that, too.

Winning became like an addiction, a feeling the Celtics never seemed to get enough of. Those rare times when they lost two games in a row, the players didn't need Auerbach in their ears. Nor they did they need any fiery "win one for the Gipper" pep talk. They knew it was time to buckle down, get things righted. In those games when they weren't playing particularly well there invariably would come a moment during a timeout when they would all look at each other and just know: It was now time to play. Usually, that was enough, those few minutes when they turned up the pressure and turned a potential loss into another win. Cousy got so he could see it in the faces of the opposition, first the look of doubt, then the realization they were going to lose.

The Celtics were the best team, and if there were always a couple of teams who could challenge them, capable of beating them, especially on the road, they came to believe they controlled their own destiny. If they did what they were supposed to do, kept working hard on defense and playing their roles, they knew they could win.

And win they did.

In February 1959, on an afternoon in the Boston Garden during school vacation, the Celtics scored an astounding 173 points in beating Minneapolis before roughly 7,000 people. In the morning Auerbach had done a clinic for 4,000 kids and youth coaches in the Garden, as part of the club's continuing attempt to be basketball evangelists in Boston, and in the opening game Marques Haynes and the Globetrotters had played their longtime patsy the Washington Generals. The 'Trotters were still a popular attraction, but it was all about entertainment now. It was evident that Saperstein had lost his battle to control the great black players. They were all going to the NBA. Chamberlain had been his last great player, and that was only because his college class hadn't graduated yet, making him ineligible for the NBA then. The days of the Globetrotters' having a serious impact on basketball were over.

When the Celtics-Lakers game began, though, it seemed as if it were still a 'Trotters exhibition. Eventually, seven Celtics scored 20 points or more, and Cousy set an NBA record with 28 assists. He was already out of the game when word came down that he was one assist short of Richie Guerin's NBA record of 21. So Auerbach put him back into the game, where he quickly found Sam Jones on a two-on-one break to tie the record, then quickly flipped the ball to Loscutoff for another score to break it.

"That man Cousy is too much," the Lakers' "Hot Rod" Hundley said. "He's the greatest ever."

There was little question Cousy was the man.

Russell might have been the most dominant defensive player who ever played the game, Sharman seemed to make every open shot he took, and Heinsohn was an incredibly talented scorer, but Cousy was a certified star. He got the biggest cheers in the Boston Garden. He was one of the elite players people wanted to see on the road. He was the one with his face on the cover of magazines. He had a basketball named after him, his own sneaker. He did commercials for Hood Milk. He was a presence in ways other players were not, even the other great ones.

A few years ago referee Earl Strom wrote about his five decades as an NBA referee. At one point, he talked about the first time he did a game in the Boston Garden. It was the late fifties. Strom was from Pottstown, Pennsylvania, and at the center jump to start the game Cousy remarked on that.

Later in the game Cousy made a great move. Strom called him for traveling, as the large crowd booed.

"You know, Earl," Cousy said, walking over to Strom, "at the Pottstown YMCA you can think that maybe it's walking, but in the Boston Garden, when I'm doing this, it isn't walking."

"You're right, Bob," Strom replied. "In the Pottstown Y it's walking, and when I'm working in the Boston Garden it's walking, too."

"You're full of shit," said Cousy.

"Get out of here or I'll hit you with a T," Strom said.

"You don't have the guts," Cousy said.

Strom gave him the technical, the Garden erupted with deafening boos, and even though the Celtics won by 30 points, Strom and fellow ref Mendy Rudolph needed a police escort out of the Garden.

Years later, Cousy did not remember the incident, even doubted its veracity, saying there's no way he would have known that Strom was from Pottstown. Still, he was never one to let rookie officials make their reputations at his expense. There had come to be an air of basketball royalty about him, as if he were somewhat above all the petty bickering and rough play that still plagued the league. He had achieved a sort of legendary status, as if he were finally getting his due for all those early years when it sometimes seemed as if he were keeping the NBA afloat all by himself. Strom recalled a fight that broke out in a game in Philadelphia and how he went over and stood next to Cousy, for he knew no one would throw anything at Cousy, even on the road.

Lenny Wilkens, who has been in the NBA both as a player and as a coach for 40 years, tells a story of when he was a rookie and once stole the ball from Cousy, only to have a referee blow his whistle.

"How can you call a foul on a play like that?" Wilkens demanded.

"Because it was a foul," the referee said.

"Come on, you know better than that," Wilkens said.

The referee stared at him and said with a straight face, "You can't take the ball away from Bob."

Cousy was the man.

He was the most popular player, the one the fans related to the most. Certainly, the fact that he was white was a huge factor, as was the fact that he'd been around for more than a decade. In Boston, he had been around since that '47 season at Holy Cross. There was also no discounting that his flashy style was the root of his appeal. Little kids went to the playground trying to be Cousy, not Chamberlain. They tried to do things with the ball like Cousy did, not block shots like Russell did. There probably wasn't a high-school gym in the country that didn't have a couple of kids trying to throw passes behind their back, or over their shoulder, all to the consternation of a coach who, almost accusingly, would say, "Who do you think you are, Cousy?"

For Cousy still did things with the ball that other players didn't. Sam Jones remarked how Cousy would come down the court on a break and bring the ball behind his back with his right hand, as if he were going to pass it to the player on his left, only to bring it back and make a layup, a move Jones had never seen before. Ramsey talked about how Cousy could throw a length-of-the-court pass right off a dribble, how no one else did that.

More important, Cousy's game was accessible in ways the other great players' games were not. He was still the underdog, the result of his size, the little man in a big man's game, no insignificant thing in a sport that still suffered from the perception that it was a goon's game, that many of the best players were good simply because they were tall. No matter that the Russells and Chamberlains of the world were great athletes as well as being incredibly tall, could run and jump and move in ways that were redefining the game, or that Baylor was the consummate athlete. No matter that the NBA game was so much better than it had been in the early years of the fifties, full of better players, the increased proficiency of the jump shot, and the advent of blacks. Old perceptions died hard.

By the spring of 1961 Cousy was breathing the rarefied air of a true American sports hero, right there with Mickey Mantle, Arnold Palmer, and Rocky Marciano. To people whose knowledge of the NBA came through television or magazines, the casual fan whose interest in the game was peripheral, dependent largely on name recognition, Cousy was the biggest star. Jimmy Cannon, the influential columnist for the *New York Post,* the man who used to hang out with Joe DiMaggio at Toots Shor's in Manhattan, always said he didn't like basketball, but he loved Cousy. A lot of sports fans who had little use for the NBA loved Cousy, as though, on some level, he had come to stand apart from the league he played in. For Cousy had come to transcend basketball, a name everyone knew.

And this brought with it increased pressure, even if much of it was self-imposed. The MVP award in 1957 had changed everything. He was supposed to be the best, even though a new generation of players was coming that was more dominant, bigger, could score more, could put up bigger numbers. But it was more than that. He had to be the best. And if he knew that in many ways he was protected, surrounded by great players, part of a great team, so that he didn't have to be the only star every night, that didn't lessen the pressure. He had to be the best because he was supposed to be the best, and if he weren't, what did that mean?

Then there was the other question he could never escape. How do you stay on top? How do you sustain it?

It was a question that haunted him more and more, struck at his basic insecurity. Years later, he would believe that all players had a basic insecurity that came from being seminude in front of 13,000 people, the feeling that there was no place to hide. But he didn't know that in 1961. He just knew that he was a little man in a big man's game, always having to run uphill, waking up in the middle of the night knowing that the next night he had to go up against Slater Martin, or Larry Costello, or Oscar, players who were going to battle him, push him, extend him.

How do you sustain it?

Especially when he knew his physical skills were starting to decline. Not in any dramatic way, or in one defining moment. Not in anything anyone else would really notice. But he knew. Where once he could do almost anything he wanted to on a basketball court, now he knew that came with an asterisk: He could do almost anything he wanted to do on a basketball court. Sometimes.

This showed more in the playoffs, the games more important, the tension ratcheted up, the defensive pressure more intense. He knew he no longer could always be the man, the "go-to" guy. That though his ball-handling and playmaking skills were still as good as ever, he couldn't get to the hoop as easily as he once had, was bothered more by quick guards than he once had been.

So he learned to pick his spots. If some young guy was playing him tight, all psyched to shut off the great Cousy, he wouldn't press things in the beginning, content to just be in the flow of the game. Later in the game, his defender tired, not quite as hungry as he had been earlier, maybe going underneath the screen instead of fighting over it as he'd done earlier, Cousy would try to strike at the key moment.

He learned to take a running one-hand shot off his right foot, instead of his left, a supposed basketball sacrilege. But it was something he felt gave him a slight edge, the ability to get a shot off when maybe he wouldn't have in the traditional way. To him, it was simply one more improvisation.

He became known for the dramatic basket, the one that broke the other team's will. Like how sometimes he would simply take the ball up the court by himself in transition, get into the lane and throw a running hook over the outstretched hand of the opposing team's center. Or come down and throw in a running one-hander before the defense was established. Even if he was no longer the scorer he'd been earlier in his career, no longer could carry the Celtics the way he had once been able to, he never lost the ability to make the big shot.

It was another spring, another title.

It was getting to be a familiar scene. The Celtics had been 57–22 during the regular season, then had dismissed Syracuse in five games in the Eastern Division finals, even surviving a brawl in the Onondaga War Memorial Auditorium in the fourth game.

"Police Quell Fans As Celts Top Nats," the *Boston Globe* head-line said the next day, complete with pictures of Loscutoff being neutralized by a helmeted cop, and another one showing Loscut-off and Auerbach confronting taunting fans in the front row as rows of other fans stood and jeered them.

The *Globe* called it a "near full-scale riot, only the rugged strong-arm unit of Syracuse police cooled off the uprising."

In the finals once again the Celtics were matched up with the St. Louis Hawks. But this time the series only went five games. It was all too apparent who the best team in basketball was. There was another victory celebration in the locker room, complete with Auerbach, his clothes soaking wet from being dunked in the shower.

"This is the greatest team ever assembled," Auerbach said. "And there are two reasons for that. One is that all these guys get along together and play as a unit. On some teams the players get into each other's hair over a long schedule. That doesn't happen here.

"And the other reason we're so damn good is the quality of our people. We always got someone ready to explode. Any one of them can tear you apart. One night it's Heinsohn. The next night it's Cousy. Then Sharman. One night it's Ramsey and Sam. And, of course, there's Russell. Somebody's always picking up the slack for us.

"With most teams you can win if you stop one guy. Stop Chamberlain and you win. Stop a Pettit, a Baylor, a Schayes, and you win. But you can't stop the Celtics that way. That's why we're the best."

It was not just hyperbole.

An incredible eight players from that team would eventually be inducted into the Hall of Fame.

It was also a team in its prime.

Russell was 27, and was the MVP for the second straight year. Heinsohn was 26, and had been the team's leading scorer for the second straight year. Loscutoff was 31. Sharman had just finished his last season with the Celtics, although no one knew it at the time. He was 35, and though he had averaged 16 points a game and again had led the league in free throw shooting, he also had Sam Jones nipping at his heels. Everyone knew Jones was a great talent who only needed more playing time to fully blossom. Jones was 27, and had been coming off the bench for four years now.

Six players had averaged in double figures. Cousy had averaged 18 points and seven assists a game, second in points behind Heinsohn. He was 32 years old. Once again, he was at the top of the world he had created for himself, the quarterback of the best basketball team in the world, maybe more famous now than he'd ever been, even with the arrival of Chamberlain, Baylor, and Robertson.

But his life had never really changed.

Yes, he made more money. Yes, there were more endorsements. Yes, he was more famous. But his day-to-day life changed hardly at all. There was still the barnstorming around New England during training camp, every night another small gym in the middle of nowhere, or so it seemed. There were still the practices at the Cambridge YMCA, a building with all the glamor of an old sweat sock. There were still the games, his personal little pilgrimages into some private hell, that left him drained and depleted afterward, emotionally spent. There was still the travel, which he was beginning to dislike more and more. He still roomed with Sharman on the road, as if they were still in college, instead of adults with families of their own. He still spent summers at Camp Graylag, a summer retreat away from the world and its growing pressures, where he ate with the kids, gave out the mail over a microphone, and played ball with the campers at night. He still lived in Worcester with Missie and the two girls, still tried to have as normal a life as possible.

That was one of the reasons he still lived in Worcester, even though it would have been both pragmatic and certainly geographically easier to have lived closer to Boston. But being geographically removed was perfect for Cousy's temperament, provided him with a convenient excuse not to do things he didn't want to do, whether it was to make public appearances or socialize, whatever. In Worcester he could somewhat hide from celebrity's increasing demands. In Worcester, he could focus on the life he'd lived since he first joined the Celtics in fall 1950. In Worcester his daughters could have a normal childhood, or at least as normal as possible with a father who was one of the leading professional athletes in the country.

"I was very proud of him and all that, but I really never saw him change," said Missie Cousy. "I would have bopped him if he did. I didn't marry a big head."

Missie's family was the most important thing in the world to her, and she was determined that her daughters would grow up as normally as possible.

It was almost as if there were two parts to his public persona. There was the Bob Cousy on the court, sure of his skills, sure of his teammates, secure in the belief that if they all played to the best of their abilities there was no other team on the planet that could beat them. And there was the Bob Cousy who was almost scared of having the spotlight on him, as if in a perfect world he would simply disappear in a puff of smoke after the game, go off into some private place where no one could touch him.

But of course it was not as simple as that, for he was also extremely pragmatic, always tried to take advantage of a situation. He knew his increased fame made him more marketable, put more money in his pocket, but he also knew it was a Faustian pact, a tightrope he was constantly walking. As if the discomfort he felt in public situations was the price he had to pay for everything else.

Mostly, Cousy lived inside the cocoon he had created for himself. He didn't like speaking in public, so he rarely did it. He knew he talked funny, didn't always articulate as well as he wanted to, and he simply wasn't comfortable doing it. He didn't like people in large groups, so he tended to avoid them. He rarely hung out with other athletes. He knew Ted Williams a little, had been at some appearances with him, respected him for his independence, but it wasn't as if they hung around together. He really didn't know Rocky Marciano at all, even though Marciano was from Brockton, the gritty mill city about a half-hour south of Boston. If Cousy certainly enjoyed the money he could make from his celebrity, he didn't like its demands, and usually did whatever he could to ignore them. He had come to understand that, at some level, anyway, his childhood had stunted him, shaped him in ways he was just beginning to deal with. He saw how Missie was better with people, more open and accessible, infinitely more comfortable, free of the demons of doubt and insecurity that plagued him. He came to understand he had paid a psychic price for all those childhood years where love was never articulated and rarely demonstrated.

He had come to know that though his talent had made him a star, he didn't have the personality to enjoy being a star. He didn't like making small talk with strangers, didn't like being on display. He liked to be home, was starting to realize that the time he missed with his two daughters could never be made up. He had never really liked the travel in the first place, often trying to get home earlier than scheduled in those early years, taking all-night train rides, anything to get out of staying another night in some lonely hotel room. Now the travel only seemed more onerous, more demanding. He had never really been one to go out with the boys very much; now it was less so. As another banner went up into the rafters following the 1961 season, he wondered how much longer he wanted to keep on doing this.

Chapter Ten

He was going to quit at the end of the '62 season.

The Celtics had won another title, their fourth in a row, this time against the Lakers in the Finals, and he just figured it was time. The coaching job at nearby Boston College had been offered to him, and he saw that as a smooth transition into the rest of his life, still basketball, still in Boston, a job that would allow him to have more of a regular family life, without having to move.

But Walter Brown asked him to play one more year, and there was no way he could say no to Walter Brown. So Boston College promised to hold the job for him for a year and in the fall of '62, a time when the world was going through the Cuban Missile Crisis and two months after Marilyn Monroe had been found dead in her home in Los Angeles, Cousy once again went to training camp.

The 1961–62 season had seen another banner go up in the rafters of the Boston Garden, but it hadn't been easy, the Celtics having to survive two game sevens in the Boston Garden, both games coming down to the last two seconds.

The first had been against Wilt and the Philadelphia Warriors in the Eastern Conference finals. Wilt had averaged an incredible 50 points a game for the season, still the most productive season in NBA history, and had only sat out eight minutes the entire season. It was his third year in the league, and, in retrospect, he would never again have a season where he was so dominant. He had games of 78 points, 73, and even had 62 against Russell and the Celtics. And in early March, in a game against the Knicks in Hershey, Pennsylvania, a game watched by a little over 4,000 people, he had scored an unbelievable 100 points.

"When I got into the 80s I heard the people yelling for 100," Wilt said later. "I thought, 'Man, these people are tough. Eighty isn't good enough. I'm tired. I've got 60 points and no one has ever scored 80.' At one point I said to Al Attles, 'I got 80. What's the difference between 80 and 100?' But the guys kept feeding me the ball."

When he hit his 100th point with 46 seconds still remaining, fans stormed out on the floor, stopping the game. Wilt went to the locker room where the Warriors' PR man wrote "100" on a piece of paper and had Chamberlain hold it up to photographers, a picture that seemed to be in every newspaper in America the following morning, adding to Chamberlain's legend as basketball's Superman, a giant whose talent knew no bounds. He had been an amazing 28–32 from the foul line. Throughout the game the loudspeaker played "By the River," a record Wilt had recorded.

Afterward, never known for his modesty, he said that if the Knicks hadn't triple-teamed him he might have scored 140.

It was one of those games that only grew in stature through the years, becoming part of basketball legend. The game was not televised, so it became almost mythic. Had Wilt really scored 100? How had he done it? Even in a league that was undergoing an offensive explosion, one man scoring 100 points in a game was unbelievable, even if it was Wilt Chamberlain.

The Celtics had won a record 60 games during the regular season, and had done it without Sharman, who had left to coach the Los Angeles Jets in the new American Basketball Association, the league started by Abe Saperstein. But in the Eastern Conference finals they had been hard-pressed by the Warriors, complete with a fight in the fifth game in the Boston Garden, which saw Loscutoff square off against Warriors' guard Guy Rodgers and Sam Jones going up against Chamberlain. That was the skirmish in which Jones picked up one of the photographer's chairs and waved it at Wilt.

"If I'm going to fight him, I'm not going to fight him fair," Jones said.

In the seventh and deciding game, Jones got his retribution.

With just two seconds remaining on the clock, he hit a fall-away jump shot to break a tie. The Warriors quickly called time-out, then tried to throw a long pass to Wilt underneath, but Russell batted the ball away as the buzzer sounded.

Interestingly, the Lakers had watched that game from the front row of the Garden, having already gotten by St. Louis in seven games to qualify for the Finals, and no doubt believing their opponent was going to be the Celtics. Afterward, Lakers star Jerry West called it the best game he ever saw.

Then the Finals with the Lakers had come down to the seventh game in the Boston Garden also. They were the Los Angeles Lakers then, having moved from Minneapolis before the 1960–61 season, the move that truly made the NBA a national league.

The move was inevitable, given the fact that the Lakers had never been as popular in Minneapolis after Mikan had left, even with the brilliance of Baylor. In 1958 both the Dodgers and the Giants, the two teams that had combined with the Yankees to make New York the greatest baseball city in the world, had moved west. The move had been a boon to Major League Baseball, opening up the West, and now basketball was following suit. The advent of jet planes had improved transportation, and Los Angeles had a new city-built Sports Arena that sat 14,500 people near the University of Southern California campus. They would be followed in the fall of '62 by Wilt and the Warriors, who left Philadelphia for San Francisco.

So the '62 Finals had been the NBA's first coast-to-coast series. The Lakers were led by their great twosome of Baylor and West, "Mr. Inside" and "Mr. Outside," who had averaged 68 points between them.

Specifically, the game came down to the last two seconds, the score tied, the Lakers having the ball out of bounds. No NBA team had ever won four titles in a row, and for a while it seemed as if the Celtics weren't going to do it either. Frank Selvy, the Lakers guard who had once scored 100 points in a college game while playing for Furman, took the ball out of bounds. He was being guarded by Cousy, and the first time he tried to throw it in Cousy swatted it back. The second time he threw it in to "Hot Rod" Hundley, the Lakers' flashy guard from West Virginia, who was known as much for his colorful personality as he was for his game. Hundley was at the top of the key, and when he got the ball he was open. But he hadn't played a lot during the game, didn't feel confident he could make the shot. For years afterward, he used to lie awake at night wondering if he would have made the shot. He liked to think he would have, that he'd been born to make a shot like that. But he didn't take it. Instead, he quickly looked for West. But West was closely guarded by K. C. Jones. So he threw it to Selvy, who had come back inbounds as soon as Cousy had jumped in the air while trying to stop Selvy from in-bounding the ball, and was open along the left baseline. Selvy, about 18 feet away, got set to take the biggest shot of his life.

Selvy was 29, called "Pops" by his teammates, and if in college he'd been a great scorer, now, on a team where Baylor and West were the two superstars, he was just another part of the constellation. Still, he averaged 14 points a game, and everyone in basketball knew you didn't let Frank Selvy take open shots. Now he had one, both the Celtics' season and their streak of three consecutive titles hanging in the balance. But he missed, and the rebound was grabbed by Russell, who hugged it to his chest as the buzzer sounded.

The Celtics had escaped to overtime.

"It was a fairly tough shot," Selvy would say later. "I was along the baseline so I couldn't bank the ball. I thought the shot was good. It hit the front rim, then back. But all the time I thought it was good. I would trade all my points for that one basket."

During the timeout before the overtime West looked over and saw Russell sitting on a stool near the Celtics' bench. He looked drained, depleted. West thought the Lakers were going to win, that the Celtics were spent.

West was in his second year, already emerging as one of the game's new young superstars after a rookie year that had often found him tentative, unsure. Even then, he'd averaged 17 points a game, a foreshadowing of things to come. He was from a small hamlet near Cabin Creek, West Virginia, hence the nickname "Zeke from Cabin Creek," a skinny kid who began playing basketball because it was something he could do by himself.

He took his high-school team to the West Virginia state title in 1956, becoming a virtual folk hero in the process. Four years later he led the University of West Virginia to the NCAA championship game in 1959, before teaming with Robertson in the Olympics in Rome. He would go on to become one of the greatest players in NBA history, a ten-time All-NBA selection, then become known as one of the shrewdest general managers in the game while orchestrating the Lakers during the Magic Johnson era.

Now, in only his second year in the league, he had averaged 30 points a game, which left him fifth in the league in scoring, behind Chamberlain, rookie Walt Bellamy, the 6-foot-11 former Indiana All-American who had been a teammate on the Olympic team, Robertson, and Pettit.

Shortly into overtime Ramsey fouled out, the fourth Celtic to do so while trying to guard Baylor. Ramsey, his thigh heavily taped, having hurt his knee at the start of the season, had scored 23 points, once again coming up big in a huge game, but now he was gone. With no one else, Auerbach put in Gene Guarilia, a little-used rookie from George Washington, telling him to grab and hold Baylor whenever he could. Soon after, though, Baylor fouled out, too. He had scored 41 points and as he walked to the bench the Garden crowd gave him a thunderous ovation.

With him went the Lakers' chance.

Sam Jones scored 27 points, reaffirming his reputation as one of the rising young stars in the NBA, and Russell scored 30 points and grabbed 40 rebounds. And when the buzzer sounded, Cousy, who had dribbled out the clock in the game's dying seconds as the huge Garden crowd stood and cheered, ducked under the scorer's table as the fans once again stormed the court, in a scene that had become a rite of spring in Boston. As had the pictures of the celebratory Celtics locker room that ran the next day in the *Boston Globe*, like the one that showed Cousy pouring a bottle of champagne over Auerbach's head, as Red sat there in his white shirt and tie, his left hand holding an ever-present cigar.

Now he was in another training camp, his 13th as a professional player.

The rookie in the fall of '62 was John Havlicek, who had been part of the great Ohio State teams, though always playing second fiddle to Jerry Lucas. Havlicek, from a small town in Ohio, had been one of those three-sport stars in high school who had seemed to step out of the pages of a Chip Hilton novel. He was such a great athlete he'd been drafted by the Cleveland Browns, even though he hadn't played college football, and had been to training camp with the Browns, eventually being one of the last players cut.

Havlicek had arrived at the Celtics' training camp expecting it to be somewhat similar to what he'd gone through at Ohio State. It wasn't.

He had first come to Boston in the spring of '62, He had shown up with Jack Foley, the jump-shooting Holy Cross star who was the Celtics' third-round draft pick. He had come from the East-West All-Star game and the Celtics were playing Philadelphia in a playoff game. It was raining, and to Havlicek, the entire scene around the Boston Garden on Causeway Street resembled something out of an Edgar Allen Poe story, with solitary figures huddled in doorways and the Hayes Bickford cafeteria across the street. He signed a two-year contract, $15,000 the first year,

$18,000 for the second year, but he didn't know what to expect from professional basketball.

For one thing, he couldn't believe how bad the locker room was, how small and cramped. He couldn't believe that there were only four people in the office, and one of them was Auerbach. This was the Boston Celtics, the best team in the world? This was the NBA?

During training camp that fall the players stayed in the Hotel Lenox in Copley Square, the hotel where Auerbach lived during the season. They practiced at Babson College in suburban Welles-ley. Two of the other rookies were local, Chuck Chevalier, a little guard from Boston College, and Skip Chappelle, a guard from Maine. There was no playbook, and every day Auerbach would put in another play. If Auerbach found out you had eaten pan-cakes he fined you $25. It all seemed a long way from Ohio State.

Auerbach was always on Heinsohn about his weight. Either that or his smoking. The problem was every time Heinsohn stopped smoking he would gain weight.

The team practiced at Babson for about 10 days, and then they started playing exhibitions around New England, playing intrasquad games, driving in cars. Auerbach and Satch Sanders were the worst drivers, but Russell drove so fast the other players were afraid to drive with him. Auerbach was known for falling asleep at the wheel, so nobody wanted to drive with him, either.

Havlicek's early impressions were that K. C. Jones was quiet and rarely said much, something always seemed to be bothering Sam Jones, and Heinsohn was the social director. Cousy? He was something of a loner. Ever since Sharman had retired after the '61 season Cousy lived by himself on the road, a concession Auer-bach allowed him. After games, he would go into the trainer's room with a beer and a cigar, surrounded by media.

To Havlicek, life in the NBA was far from glamorous. He didn't like Boston, thought it was too crowded, too congested, an alien world very different from the small town Ohio of his childhood. He didn't even have a car, eventually taking a bus to practice that first year from the Sherry Biltmore Hotel where he lived with fellow rookie Dan Swartz and backup center Clyde Lovellette, who liked to wear cowboy hats and quick-draw people. The room had three beds, a TV, couch, bathroom, kitchenette.

Havlicek was the seventh man, and Ramsey became his role model. Ramsey taught him how to draw fouls, and how to leave his warmup jacket unbuttoned so that when Auerbach summoned him he was at the scorer's table in an instant. Essentially, Ramsey taught him how to be a sixth man, grooming him, as all the Celtics' veterans were supposed to do with the young players. That was part of being a Celtic, too.

Havlicek would go on to become one of the all-time great Celtics, but he was raw as a rookie. In fact, Cousy didn't view Havlicek as all that talented a player, not then. He didn't shoot particularly well, and had been a college forward who was now trying to make the adjustment to NBA guard, his ball-handling skills so suspect he often had to back the ball down the court. To Cousy, Havlicek was someone who could be brought along slowly because he was joining a veteran team that didn't really need him, one more example that the Celtics were different from most NBA teams, having the luxury to wait on young players.

Cousy loved Havlicek's attitude, though. He especially loved his competitive spirit, the sense that losing bothered him, playing poorly bothered him. He loved the fact that Havlicek handled being a rookie so well, going along with the hazing, getting along with everyone, immediately fitting in.

Virtually everywhere the Celtics went that year Cousy had been honored, with gifts and loud ovations, public thank-yous for what he'd done for the pro game. Wilt was the most dominant player in the league, and Baylor and Robertson were already superstars, but in many ways Cousy still had the magic. There was also the strong feeling, particularly among the media and people who remembered the early days, of just what Cousy had meant to the league's survival in those years.

It was easy to forget that. Or take it for granted. There were new stars, new cities. Players made more money. The NBA was very different than it had been just a decade before. Still, to those who remembered, it had been Cousy who, maybe more than anyone, had installed professional basketball in the American imagination.

One of the places he'd been honored was Madison Square Garden, the game's most famous arena, the place he'd played in the city championships in high school, the place that had once seemed like Shangri-La to a poor kid from Queens.

"This was always like a second home to me," he said to the crowd. "The biggest thrill, I guess, was in the '53 All-Star game we won in overtime."

There were no tears, though.

Those would come later, on "Bob Cousy Day" in the Boston Garden.

After the game in Madison Square Garden, Russell talked about Cousy.

"It's hard for me to put into words what he meant to me from the start," he said. "I liked him right away, and that's important. But then, he always had a pride, a dignity, and a winning attitude. We try, all the time, to make the Celtics synonymous with 'class,' and Cousy was always there to lead us. It may sound corny, but I consider the years I played with him the golden years."

Cousy's minutes in games were down; he was now usually playing between 20–25 minutes a game, as K. C. Jones got more time. During those stretches Cousy could still be as effective as ever, still an integral part of a team trying to win another title. As he was in the seventh game of the Eastern Conference finals, another big game in the Boston Garden, this time against Oscar and the Cincinnati Royals. It was April 10. Shortly afterward, the Supreme Court would hear about Mississippi governor Ross Barnett's efforts to block the admission of James Meredith to the state university.

It was a seventh game that would be remembered for the shootout between Sam Jones and Robertson, Jones ending up with 47, Oscar 43. It was one more reaffirmation that Jones was another of the great scoring guards now in the league, but Cousy also had another great performance, as if the clock had been turned back to 1957 and some old highlight reel had been taken down from the dusty shelves in the basketball archives and played one more time. Better yet, he had waited until the fourth quarter for his brilliance. Again, it had been treats from the same grab bag: a length-of-the-court bounce pass to Sam Jones, followed by a behind-the-back flip on the run to Russell, combined with big baskets of his own. He had finished with 21 points and 16 assists, but when the series was over and the Celtics were headed off to another Finals, it was a sign of the times: All anyone wanted to talk about was Robertson.

"That Oscar," said Russell. "I've just seen too much of him."

"Poor Sam was so happy to be out of that series he almost cried," Cousy said.

Two days later Martin Luther King was arrested in Alabama for defying a court injunction and leading a march of Negroes into downtown Birmingham.

Cousy rarely went out on the road anymore.

In fact, he rarely left his room. He would sequester himself, order room service, try to read, anything to pass the interminable time before the games would begin. Most of all, he went off into some private place where he could work himself into an appropriate state of mind. He had come to hate the players he had to go up against. Not as people, certainly. Some of them were his friends, people he'd competed against for years, and he had a deep respect for them. But not when he was getting ready to play them. Then they were the enemy, and he would lie in his hotel room and obsess about them, all but see them in his troubled sleep. He came to see them as wolves come to steal food off his children's table. Now, it was Frank Selvy, the man he had to guard when the Celtics played the Lakers.

Before the sixth game of the NBA Finals, the Celtics having a
3–2 lead, the team was staying at a motel outside Los Angeles. On
the marquee it said, "Welcome the Boston Celtics and Red Auerbach." When Cousy saw the sign he first figured Auerbach had
brokered another of his many deals, then chastised himself for
becoming so cynical.

Truth be told, though, he wanted it all to end.

He knew in his heart he could probably play for three or four
more years, that he still possessed the skills to function at a high
level with a great team, even in a reduced role, but he knew he was
mentally shot. It wasn't just the travel, which he had grown to
hate. Or the hotel rooms, which seemed to get smaller and smaller.
It wasn't just all the time away from his family, which made him
feel guilty, or the demands of his celebrity, which had become a
kind of jailer. It wasn't just the unrelenting pressure that always
seemed to be sitting on his shoulders, weighing him down, the
kind of pressure he never seemed to be able to shake anymore.

It was all of it.

The day before he had picked up Heinsohn in Worcester and
driven into Boston, as they had done for seven years now. They
had grown close over the years, certainly, but in many ways they
still had the same relationship they had always had, Cousy the
big brother, Heinsohn the little brother. Cousy always thinking
that, as good as Heinsohn was, he could be even better if he only
worked at it more. If he didn't smoke as much. If he lost some
weight. If he got in better shape. If he lusted after it more.

Heinsohn, in turn, felt Cousy was always needling him about
being a "gunner," always pointing out how many shots he took.
He saw Cousy as a demanding personality, with no patience for
mistakes or imperfections, whether his teammates' or his own.

He also knew Cousy wanted to go out the right way. He understood how Cousy had always been driven by his fear of failure,
much as Russell was. To Heinsohn, that was what made them so
competitive, so relentless in their quest to win. He remembered
his second year, 1958, the season they had lost to the Hawks in

the Finals when Russell had gotten injured. He had gone into the locker room, grabbed a beer, and sat on the floor. Sure, he was upset, but there'd be more chances. Life went on, right?

Then he saw Cousy crying, and knew Cousy didn't think like that. Cousy played every game as if it were his last.

They were such different people, such opposites. Heinsohn was always open and friendly with people, the life of the party. To him, being a great player on the best team in basketball was more than enough. Unlike Cousy, he didn't have to be the best.

Cousy knew all this about Heinsohn, of course, long ago had made his separate peace with it, even if he couldn't help himself from periodically mentioning it. But on this last ride into Boston together, it bothered him again. Then again, everything was bothering him. Heinsohn called the playoffs "the rubber-room time," and Cousy could relate to that. He didn't want to have to come back to Boston for a seventh game, even if so many people were telling him that would be a fitting way to end his career, dribbling out the clock in his last game as the Celtics won yet another title, replicating a scene that had happened the year before. But he didn't want to hear it. He wanted to win the sixth game in L.A. He didn't want to come back for another game in the Boston Garden. He didn't want to play another high-pressure game seven. He wanted it to be over.

Now, in the hotel room, waiting for the game that night, he was edgier than usual.

He was trying to read Allen Drury's *Shade of Difference*, the sequel to the best-seller *Advise and Consent*, but he couldn't concentrate. Instead, he tried to write a speech for an affair to be held in the future for cystic fibrosis, for which he was the Massachusetts honorary state chairman, and had been for seven years. That hadn't worked, either.

He went down to the lobby, went into a small room where Loscutoff was sitting with the Boston sportswriters: Jack Barry and Cliff Keane of the *Globe*; Bill McSweeney and Murray Kramer of the *Record-American*; Joe Looney of the *Herald*; Phil Elderken of the *Christian Science Monitor;* Howie Iverson of the *Lowell Sun;* and Lin Raymond of the *Quincy Patriot-Ledger.*

He felt a certain affection for all of them. In many ways they were his guys; many had covered him since his freshman year at Holy Cross. He had even given them watches at his retirement ceremony on St. Patrick's Day in the Boston Garden. They had never written a harsh word about him, nothing he ever had found fault with. That would come four years later, when Cousy would feel betrayed by the media.

At three in the afternoon he went into the hotel restaurant. Some other players were there, but he sat by himself. He ordered beef stew, but his stomach was too tight, and he ate very little. So he went back upstairs to lie down, hoping he could take a nap. He could not. All he could think of was Frank Selvy. What he did. What he wanted to do. What he was going to try and do defensively. He continued to lie there, obsessing about the upcoming game, this game that had the potential to be the last one he was ever going to play. As if all the years and all the games, all the plans and all the dreams that had begun at O'Connell Park in St. Albans and had taken him all over the world, had now come down to this one game.

He lay there, and after a while all the innumerable games he'd played in his life no longer mattered. In fact, nothing mattered. Not his success. Not his fame. Not his accomplishments. Not the fact that he was one of the most celebrated athletes in the country. Nothing. Except the fear he could feel sitting in his stomach. As if this were the night everything was going to fall apart, and he would be revealed for the fraud he'd always been, exposed as a pretender, a basketball version of the emperor with no clothes, not worthy of any of the acclaim he'd received. The raw, unadulterated, fear.

For the first time since he arrived in Los Angeles he felt ready.

There were, in effect, two locker rooms in the Los Angeles Sports Arena. They were separated by the trainer's room, and although all the other players were changing in one room, he went into the other room by himself. The other locker room was full of people. Show business people. People Auerbach knew. Auerbach liked people around him before a game. They helped to lessen the tension for him, kept his mind off the upcoming game. Cousy wanted none of it. He didn't want to see anybody. He didn't want to hear any funny stories. He didn't want to talk to anybody. He just wanted to sit by himself and brood about Frank Selvy.

By chance, Ramsey came into the room. He, too, wanted to get away from everyone. It had been a difficult year for Ramsey, and when things were not going well Ramsey became very moody; so moody, Cousy thought, that Ramsey made him seem like the life of the party. Still, Cousy had the utmost respect for Ramsey. He considered Ramsey the most mature of all of them, as if in this world of professional basketball, this world of arrested development, Ramsey was a true adult.

He and Ramsey made small talk about the game, the gist of which was that neither of them wanted to go back to Boston for a seventh game. The talk was intended to calm them down, but it didn't work. Both knew the Lakers had the psychological advantage simply because the game was at the Sports Arena, that it was so difficult to win a big game on the road, that you had to battle both the crowd and the referees, plus fight a home team that felt it had the advantage.

In the other room he could hear Russell joking with singer Johnny Mathis, with whom he had gone to high school. He heard Russell's loud cackle of a laugh, and knew that if you saw Russell in the locker room before a big game, saw him playing poker with Sanders and the Jones Boys, all of them needling each other, you would think Russell was free of tension. The rest of the players knew better. They knew that at some point Russell was going to excuse himself from all the jokes and all the frivolity and go throw up, that Russell had never gone into a big game without vomiting.

A few minutes later the players met in front of Auerbach. There was no pep talk. There were never any pep talks. The Celtics long ago had become too sophisticated for that, had been together too long. They didn't need any "win one for the Gipper" exhortations. They knew what the stakes were.

It was all basic. Auerbach's message was they had to keep Baylor and Rudy LaRusso off the boards. But even those were wasted words. Everyone knew that. There were no surprises. These two teams had gone seven games the year before. Now they were in the sixth game of this series. Words were irrelevant.

There was also an undercurrent running beneath the series' surface, the sense this was supposed to be the changing of the guard, the feeling that the Lakers, with their young stars in Baylor and West, were the future, while the Celtics were the past. It was a theory that had begun in the beginning of the year when the Lakers had gotten off to a great start, and the L.A. papers began referring to them as the uncrowned champions, referring to the Celtics as "Boston's old men."

By February, when the All-Star game was held in Los Angeles, some L.A. sportswriters were calling Los Angeles "the basketball center of the world." Not surprisingly, Auerbach had picked up on it, used it as another motivational tool. Then again, Auerbach was never better than when he felt he was being slighted, when he could portray himself as the embattled underdog.

The Sports Arena was the future. It had a seating capacity of over 15,000, cushion seats, with no poles or steel girders blocking sight lines. It also had Hollywood glamor, complete with Doris Day, America's celluloid sweetheart, always in the front row.

Cousy warmed up, as people from the sidelines called out to him. He didn't respond. He was already somewhere deep within himself.

At the end of the half the Celtics were up 14. By the end of the third quarter it was 10.

Then Cousy got hurt.

At the start of the fourth quarter he fell down while covering Lakers' guard Dick Barnett. Instantaneously, he felt a sharp pain on the left side of his ankle. The pain was so severe that he rolled over to his right side to take weight off it. Trainer Buddy LeRoux came out to look at him. Cousy sat up, holding his ankle, while Loscutoff bent over to get a closer look, and Russell, hands on hips, stood nearby. Minutes later, Cousy hobbled off the court supported by LeRoux and Loscutoff, while Auerbach stood alongside.

He went to the very end of the bench, near the basket the Celtics were shooting at. His back was to the other players, his leg extended in front of him. Is this how it's going to end, he thought? Is it all going to end with him on the bench with the first ankle injury of his career?

Ernie Vandeweghe, a former star with the Knicks in the early days of the NBA, now a doctor in L.A., came over to inspect Cousy's ankle.

"Where do you feel the pain?" Vandeweghe asked.

All of a sudden Cousy didn't feel the pain anymore.

"It's numb," Vandeweghe said. "You've probably got a bad sprain."

LeRoux packed his foot in ice. Then he taped it tight, so tight it felt like a cast. Cousy bounced up and down on it, felt no pain.

The Celtics' lead had dropped to one point.

Cousy started walking toward Auerbach.

Could he play? He wasn't sure. But he felt his presence on the court would be a psychological lift to a team that was sliding, and maybe play into the heads of the Lakers a little bit, too, for he knew the Lakers had gotten the momentum back. He figured that, if nothing else, he could get the ball up the court, bring a degree of normalcy to the Celtics' offense. And if he found out he couldn't run, couldn't play? Then Auerbach could quickly get him out of it.

"How does it feel?" Auerbach asked.

"I think I can go," Cousy said.

Auerbach looked at him again.

"Go in for Havlicek."

There was 4:43 left to play.

Cousy went into the game, but there was no celebration, no

pep talk from his teammates, nothing. This was all business. He was in the game, and because he was in the game, it was assumed he was ready to play. There was no time for sentiment. Almost immediately he got a pass from Heinsohn in transition, dribbled into the middle, and hit a streaking Sanders for a layup. Now the Celtics were leading by five with three and a half minutes to play.

A minute later the lead was four and his ankle was throbbing. Should he take himself out? Could he make it to the end of the game? What should he do? But as these questions were running through his head the play went on, and he went up the court with it, as if jumping into a river and being caught up in the current. Suddenly, the ankle began to feel better again.

With 1:07 left to play the Celtics were clinging to a two-point lead. But Sam Jones, who only had one basket, hit a jumper and now the lead was four with just 45 seconds left. Yet Barnett came back with a three-point play, and once again the lead was down to one point, the Sports Arena crowd in a frenzy.

There were 33 seconds remaining, the Celtics working the ball, when Sam Jones passed the ball to Cousy for an open one-hander. He threw it up softly, as he had done so many times before, in so many games, in so many different arenas. One last shot in what had been a lifetime of shots. He thought it was good. It was not. But Heinsohn got the rebound, was fouled going back up. He made the two free throws, giving the Celtics a three point lead with just 20 clicks of the clock left.

And with just four seconds left on the clock, the Celtics still leading by three points, Cousy got the ball from Sam Jones. He knew it was over. He took three or four big leaping strides up the court and then threw the ball as hard as he could toward the ceiling as the buzzer sounded.

Russell leaped over the bench to retrieve the ball, as Cousy had momentarily forgotten that he wanted the ball as a souvenir. Russell ran up to him holding the ball, and Cousy jumped on his back. Someone else had Russell by the hair, and then there was Auerbach in the mix, too. Soon they were all standing on the court in a celebration as the Lakers players slowly walked off the court, once again having been nosed out by the Celtics in the final seconds.

Cousy went into the locker room, into the middle of another victory celebration, and there was no awareness that never again would he be with these players in the same way, no sense of regret that what had defined his life was now over. That never entered his mind. Not then, anyway. That would come later. Now it was just the exultation of the moment, the incredible sweetness of victory, and the pressure that seemed to leave his body like steam escaping a manhole cover.

Russell gave him the ball.

"You were a tiger tonight, baby," he said.

"You feel like crying again, Bob?" a reporter asked.

"I'd cry for you," Russell said to the reporter, "but I'm too big and ugly to cry."

There was little time for anything, even celebration. The Celtics were due to fly back East, had been told there would be champagne on the plane.

Cousy wanted a beer. It had become one of his postgame rituals, a can of beer, maybe a cigar. But there was not a can of beer to be found, nothing to drink at all.

Before they left the room, though, there were reporters to talk to, interviews to do.

One of the television reporters was Tommy Harmon, the former Heisman Trophy winner from Michigan. Cousy was called to go with him. Still, he wanted something to drink, and asked Celtics' trainer Buddy LeRoux to please find him a can of beer somewhere. He thought he'd never been this thirsty.

"I always wanted to be the best," he said. "It wasn't enough to be good enough. It wasn't enough to be very good. I had to be the best, because that's what it was all about. So I wanted to go out with a good last game for myself. I wanted to go out winning a game, and I wanted to go out with a world championship. God has been good to me. He granted me my final wish."

He walked out on the arena floor. It was mostly empty, just a smattering of people still there. Auerbach and Cousy were on the floor being interviewed by Bob Wolff as photographers knelt in front of them. Cousy was still in his uniform, with a green warmup jacket on and a white towel around his neck.

"I guess Los Angeles isn't the basketball capital of the world yet," Auerbach said, a line Cousy knew he would say, for it was vintage Auerbach.

"We didn't do bad for a bunch of old men," Auerbach continued.

Old feuders never die, Cousy thought to himself, they just crow away. But he didn't mind. Good old Arnold, he thought. Never back down. Never give an inch.

Soon afterward the team left for the airport. As the plane left the ground, circled, and began to head East, Russell said gleefully, "And as the basketball capital of the world sinks slowly into the sunset, we can only say, 'Goodbye, Los Angeles. Goodbye, to the basketball capital of the world.'"

It had been a classic Celtics game, six players ending in double figures, Cousy finishing with 18 points and seven assists.

It was a game that had been televised back East, ending in the wee hours of the early morning. When the Celtics landed at Boston's Logan Airport later in the morning they were met by Boston mayor John Collins and a contingent of people. Cousy's ankle was so stiff he could barely stand, so he let Heinsohn drive them back to Worcester. An hour later, at the bridge over Lake Quinsigamond that leads into Worcester, they were met by a police escort. The city was having a celebration and both Heinsohn's and Cousy's families were there to meet them. The two players were to ride with their families in special cars.

"Watch the weight next year," Cousy said to Heinsohn, before they parted.

"Basketball just isn't going to be the same without the Cooz," Arthur Daley wrote in *The New York Times*.

In the column Daley had referred to him as the Houdini of the Hardwood, a reference to how, once again, Cousy had fans gasping, how he "surreptitiously handed off underneath like a three-card monte artist. He dribbled in and out like a minnow flashing among salmon."

Daley went on to say that watching Cousy brought with it "jumbled emotions, an inescapable feeling of sadness. It was like watching Ted Williams hit his farewell home run, the sense of loss one experiences with the realization that we may never see his like again. Cooz was extra special. He was a little guy in a big man's sport and he inexorably cut the giants down to his size. There is an overwhelming tendency to regard him as the greatest of all basketball players. Maybe he was. At least he was not far from it."

A few days later Cousy was driving to New York. He approached a toll booth on the Mass Pike in his new black Cadillac, the one he'd been given two months before on his farewell day in the Boston Garden, the one with "Celtics-14" on the license plate.

He flipped two dimes and a nickel into the bin, but one of the coins missed. The toll taker poked his head out of the toll booth.

"You're retiring, aren't you?" he said. "Just as well."

Cousy smiled and drove away.

Into a new life.

Chapter Eleven

On the surface, being a basketball coach at Boston College seemed like the perfect job for Bob Cousy in the fall of 1963. It kept him in basketball. He didn't have to move from Worcester, where he was now living in a spacious English Tudor home in the city's toniest section. He could, in theory, anyway, have more of a normal life than he did as a professional basketball player.

He was only making $12,000, appreciably less than the $35,000 he had been making the year before, but he still had his endorsements, still had Camp Graylag, and had paid cash for the new house. He was 34, and about to start, if not a new life, then certainly a new chapter in it.

Boston College was not a big-time basketball school. The team played in a small gym on campus that only sat 3,000. The sport was the third-most-popular on campus, behind football and hockey, and the schedule was a regional one. Still, Cousy had big expectations. He had worked with kids at his summer camp for years, felt comfortable around them, knew he could coach them.

Plus, hadn't he almost functioned as a surrogate coach in the last half of his Celtics' career? He was forever coming into the huddle and telling Heinsohn he had to start working harder on defense, that Heinsohn was making a hero out of the guy he was playing. Or saying to Russell that he couldn't just let his guy take jump shots, that he had to start coming out to play him. This had become part of him, a reflection not only of his competitiveness, but of his endless striving for perfection, too. It was more than the fact that he took his role of captain seriously. He had always seen the game like a coach, knowing what everyone had to do.

He also thought his name could attract some decent recruits, and had a promise from Boston College officials that there would be more of a commitment to the sport. He felt he could be successful.

One kid he attracted, in his first full recruiting year, was Jack Kvancz, a great high-school guard from Warren Harding High School in Bridgeport, Connecticut. At one point, Kvancz and his father visited Cousy at his home in Worcester, at a time when Kvancz was still undecided about where he was going to college.

"Once my father met Cousy there was no question where I was going," Kvancz said. "It was done."

Kvancz soon realized that the majority of the BC players were in awe of Cousy. When he said things it was as though the words came down from Mt. Olympus. They were unquestioned, as if chiseled in stone. Why not? Cousy was "Mr. Basketball."

The best team in New England then was Providence College, a small Dominican school coached by Cousy's old Holy Cross teammate Joe Mullaney. The Friars had won the NIT in both 1961 and 1963, and had come out of virtual obscurity to become a basketball name in the East. In fact, basketball had been such a springboard to increasing the school's name recognition that the school's president had once said, "Two thousand years of Dominican scholarship, but no one ever heard of us until we put five kids on the floor at Madison Square Garden."

This was what Boston College was now after, even if it was never particularly articulated.

The first year was a disappointment, the team finishing with a 10-15 record. Cousy's coaching philosophy was an outgrowth of what he'd believed as a player: push the ball, be aggressive, attack your opponent's spirit. The one quality player was a black kid from Washington, D.C, named John Austin, who essentially had been lured to BC by Auerbach, who knew of him from Washington, and was interested in him as a potential "territorial pick." Cousy had approached the season with his usual single-mindedness and focus. Afterward, he realized he probably had made it too complicated, giving his players too much information. He also realized that 13 years of listening to Auerbach hadn't prepared him in any way whatsoever to be a college basketball coach.

At one point in his second year, BC was playing against Marquette, the game coming down to the closing seconds. There was a timeout, BC had the ball, Cousy and his team were in a huddle, and he was trying to come up with some last-second strategy, some dramatic play, that would enable his team to win.

"Hey coach," John Austin said. "Why don't you just give me the ball."

He did. Austin made a shot. BC won.

Cousy was learning what it took to be a successful coach.

His Eagles were 22-7 in the second year, the school's best finish in over a decade, and were rewarded with an NIT berth. But early the next season, on a bus trip to Hanover, New Hampshire, to play Dartmouth, he had such severe stomach pains he couldn't stand up. He went to the game hobbling like an old man. He was diagnosed with intestinal pain, and it remained periodically for the rest of the season. Once again, he had come to realize he internalized pressure, and now it was worse: Now he had no real outlet for that pressure, nothing he could really do to affect the outcome once the game started. Now he had to sit and watch his players, almost powerless. Throughout his six-year tenure at Boston College he would have stomach pains, chest pains, cold sweats.

It wasn't long before he realized college basketball was all about recruiting, the constant pressure to keep bringing in better players, and the ramifications of that. He didn't enjoy it. He believed that, at its heart, recruiting was a demeaning, dehumanizing process. You had to keep sweet-talking the kid, selling both yourself and the school, almost trying to seduce him, all within the larger context of a college basketball landscape where stories abounded of other schools breaking rules, lowering academic standards, doing almost anything to win basketball games. In short, you had to sell, if not exactly your soul, at least some of your integrity. Then, if you actually got the kid, you had to reestablish a relationship, no easy thing after you had to prostitute yourself to get him in the first place.

Plus, there was no recruiting budget.

Instead, most of the recruiting was done over the phone. Either that or by looking through the "High School Basketball Report," the analysis of high-school players by New York City superscout Howard Garfinkel, who rated prospects from one to five, complete with a paragraph or two about their abilities, usually done in a flowery style, with things like, "He jumps so high he talks to God three times a quarter," or, "The greatest swingman since Benny Goodman." Cousy soon realized that, for all the rhetoric from the good Jesuit fathers at Boston College about wanting to win and having a successful basketball program, everything was done on a shoestring. Or a wing and a prayer. The recruiting base essentially was good students from Catholic high schools in the Northeast.

And the more he recruited, the more distasteful he found it.

One time he was recruiting a kid from New Jersey named Bob Dukiet, then one of the most highly sought after high-school players in the Northeast. The word was Dukiet was starting to be recruited by a school in the Atlantic Coast Conference, a more glamorous basketball school, and an alumnus told Cousy that he had to go see Dukiet again, in an attempt to solidify the deal. So one night, after a home game in Boston, Cousy flew from Boston to New Jersey, met the alumnus, and eventually found himself sitting in Dukiet's living room at 11 o'clock at night listening to him play the organ.

It all seemed like a long way from being "Mr. Basketball."

As did waiting outside a high school in Pennsylvania one afternoon for another high-school hotshot, only to be told by the kid, thanks for coming, coach, but I'm really not talking to coaches anymore.

The more he was in college coaching the more he was seeing things he felt no adult should have to do. To him, it was becoming more and more clear-cut: If you wanted to be a successful college coach, you learned to stretch the rules, bend them, circumvent them. There really was no other way.

It was also his new life, so he poured all his energy and focus into it, for he knew no other way.

"He was a perfectionist," said Kvancz. "That came through right away. There was one way to do things, and that was it. In those days you went to his camp for a week in the summer before you went to school, and often he would play in the games with us. If he passed you the ball on the wing and you passed it back to him he would get all over you. He'd say, 'I gave you the ball, you're supposed to score, not throw it back to me.' He was real serious. There was no fooling around. You'd better have strapped it on when he came out to play."

One who might have known that better than anyone was Gerry Friel. He became Cousy's assistant in 1966, but had known him since 1950 when he had been eight years old and a camper in the first summer Camp Graylag opened. Friel went to Graylag every summer of his childhood and adolescence, becoming very close to Cousy, as though he were the son Cousy never had. Friel, in turn, idolized him. When Cousy played golf Friel was his caddy. They played basketball and tennis together, and Friel knew how competitive Cousy was, how if he lost playing tennis he'd be upset. He also knew how intense Cousy was even in a pickup basketball game. He found that out in a dramatic way.

He was in high school, playing in a camp game with Cousy on his team, when he threw the ball around his back, a pass that went out of bounds.

"He didn't say a thing," Friel said. "We go back down the court, the other team scores, and he took the ball out of bounds—I was about five feet away—and he throws the ball right in my face. 'Don't ever throw the ball around your back again,' he said."

The ball had knocked out a few of Friel's teeth. Friel was so upset he left the camp and went back home to upstate New York. A few days later he received a letter from Cousy, who apologized and said he would never have done that to someone he didn't think could be good, someone he didn't care about.

Shortly after Friel was out of college, Cousy hired him. Friel soon learned little had changed. Cousy was still as driven as he'd always been. When he came out to practice that was it. He liked to coach by showing, and many days he would put his workout gear on and demonstrate. On such occasions, the BC players soon learned they better be ready to play.

"He was extremely organized, extremely prepared," Friel said. "He was very demanding, both with himself and the people who worked for him. He was way ahead of his time, not only as a player, but also as a competitor and someone who could teach you about the basics of life: how to work hard, how to have a good attitude, how to succeed."

Cousy had also come to know in his first year at Boston College that his old life was over, in ways he'd never imagined.

In his first year away from playing he'd become very sensitive about the Celtics, for he kept reading in the papers how they had dedicated the year to "winning without Cousy." That had become the Celtics' new motivation, the team's desire to prove that, yes, Cousy had been the fan favorite and, yes, he was one of the best players in the history of the game, and, yes, he had been there for 13 years, but they didn't need him to be successful.

To Cousy, it was the ultimate betrayal. Hadn't they all been a family? Hadn't that always been the mantra, preached by Auerbach and echoed by all the players? Hadn't it always been one for all, and all for one? Hadn't that been what had made the Celtics so different, so special? So what was all this "winning without Cousy" stuff about?

He went to a few games, but never went to the locker room. Emotionally, he tried to distance himself. But he was hurt, no question about it. He no longer felt a part of it, like some son whose father had banished him from the house. Years later, he would come to understand that, at some level, it had been a motivational tool, something both Auerbach and the players used to get themselves ready for yet another title chase. He also came to understand that maybe some of his teammates had resented some of the attention he'd gotten and he'd simply been too myopic, too self-absorbed at the time, to realize it.

By this time he also knew this was what teams were all about, that at their core they were not only insular, they always operated in the present tense. But it had hurt. The Celtics had been his, for many years, and now they were not. Maybe it was that simple. And if he had known that intellectually when he had retired in 1963, now he knew it emotionally, too.

Boston College began the 1966–67 season winning its first eight games. The Eagles were ranked in the top 20. It was the year of Lew Alcindor at UCLA and Elvin Hayes at Houston, and for Boston College to be even mentioned in the same basketball stratosphere as schools like UCLA and Houston was a testimony to just how far Cousy had brought the Eagles in just three years.

In December, in the Sugar Bowl Tournament in New Orleans, the Eagles lost to Utah State in the first round, making their record 8-1 in the young season. In a team meeting the next day, Cousy was at the blackboard in the front of the room going over preparations for the consolation game to be played that night, when he suddenly broke down, tears running down his face. He punched the blackboard. Unable to continue, he put his face down, sobbing.

Later in the day one of the players came to his room. "Hey coach, we didn't know this game meant this much to you," he said. "Hell, we'll win it."

Afterward, he felt terrible, ashamed. How could he have let his players see him like that? Once again he had put himself in an emotional meat grinder. In a sense, it was like being a player all over again, only worse. The more he won, the more pressure he felt to keep winning. The more success he had, the more pressure there was to maintain that success. And the more pressure he felt, the more he became a prisoner of his emotions.

That year his Eagles lost in the NCAA regional final to a great North Carolina team that included Larry Miller and Bobby Lewis. The Eagles featured Kvancz, Billy Evans, Steve Adelman, Jim Kissane, and Terry Driscoll, the only player who would go on to play in the NBA. But it had been a great college team, one game away from the Final Four, and by all standards of measure Cousy had, in just four short years, built one of the top college basketball programs in the East.

But it gave him little consolation.

"I wanted my team to be perfect," he said. "If my team looked bad I felt personally responsible. Even if we won and didn't play particularly well I was unhappy. My unhappiness came in my search for perfection. I had always been a sore loser. Now I was a sore winner, too."

That was the year Auerbach had come to see him. He was stepping down as coach of the Celtics and wanted Cousy to succeed him, at a salary that would have paid him three to four times what he was making at BC. But Cousy was still under contract. Besides, he didn't want to coach guys he'd played with. Instead, the job went to Bill Russell, who became the player-coach, part of the reason being that Auerbach figured that the only coach who could motivate Russell would be Russell himself.

In the summer of 1967, after Cousy's fourth year of coaching at Boston College, Sandy Smith of *Life* magazine came to Camp Graylag. On the phone Smith had said he was doing a story on college basketball, but when he got there he said it was a story on gambling. During the fifties the rumor had always been that Cousy had been saved from a grand jury indictment because of the intercession of Boston's Cardinal Cushing, as the St. John's players had been spared by Cardinal Spellman's influence in New

York. It was something Cousy had always been candid talking about, spending a lot of time in *Basketball Is My Life* a decade earlier writing about gambling and the scandals.

A month after Smith's visit the article came out. It said the Mob had infiltrated college sports, and that Cousy had been involved with known gamblers. Cousy had been in Hershey, Pennsylvania, at the time, had been told about the article by Sam Cohen, the sports editor of the *Boston Herald*, who had been one of Auerbach's first advocates in Boston. Smith wrote that Cousy's name had been found in the notebook of a gambler. Next to his name was the notation "Skiball," which was the nickname of Francesco Scibelli, an alleged gambler from Springfield, and according to Smith, a friend of Cousy's. Another of his friends, wrote Smith, was Anthony Pradella, also of Springfield, and Scibelli's partner.

The article said that, because they always had such excellent information, the Scibelli-Pradella ring was known as the "Scholar Group." Cousy admitted he knew the two were gamblers and that he often talked to them about pro and college teams and their chances of winning.

"I'd be having dinner with Pradella and Scibelli would come over," said Cousy. "They got together each night to balance the book or something."

Did Cousy realize his friends were using what he told them to fix betting lines and to make smart bets of their own?

"No," he said. "I thought they figured the betting line with mathematics. But it doesn't surprise me. I'm pretty cynical. I think most people who approach me want to use me for something."

At one point, Pradella invited him to a banquet in Hartford that turned out to be a gangster conclave. "Police were watching the place," said Cousy. "The whole Mob was there."

Cousy defended his actions. "In this hypocritical world we live in," he said, "I don't see why I should stop seeing my friends just because they are gamblers. How can I tell Andy when he calls and asks about a team that I won't talk to him about that?"

To Cousy, each paragraph was like "a body blow to the heart." He was devastated.

His friends told him to forget about it, told him that *Life* was in trouble, was just trying to sell magazines. He could not forget about it. He drove back to Boston and called a press conference. He stood in front of some 50 reporters and a battery of television cameras. He was nervous and all but choking with emotion, breaking down several times during the press conference.

He said the so-called gangster conclave was a sports banquet, and that he never said the police were watching and the entire Mob was there. He said Scibelli was an acquaintance, not a friend, that he had met him maybe eight times in 12 years. He said he had known Pradella for 12 years, had first met him when his sons went to Camp Graylag. He said they played golf together a few times a year, and often had dinner afterward. He knew Pradella gambled, "as do most of us.

"He was my friend not because he gambled, but because he was and is a hell of a guy. Whatever I told him I would have told anyone else. From my point of view, I think frankly the worst part about this is I'm not accused of anything and I really can't defend myself. The only thing it seems I've done is establish a continual friendship with a man who gambles."

He called his friends in the media, writers like Al Hirshberg in Boston, Jim Murray in Los Angeles, Arthur Daley and Milton Gross in New York.

"Without equivocation," he said to them, "you have my word that this will not backfire on you."

Nearly all came to his defense with columns, articles, broadcasts.

Life was on the defensive. The magazine said that all the article had said was that Cousy knew a gambler and he admitted to that, then said in an editorial, "the fact that one individual was unwise in his friendship for known gamblers is far less important than the depths of which the Mob is infiltrating spectator sports in America and how much it is using players for its own illegal profit."

One of the people who called Cousy was Howard Cosell, who was on ABC's *Wide World of Sports,* and was in the process of becoming one of the most well-known sports broadcasters in the country. Cousy had first met him years before, back in the fifties when Cosell used to knock on his door at the Paramount Hotel on 46th Street in New York and want to interview him and Sharman. Cosell was no celebrity then, just a guy carrying a tape recorder who did a radio show on an independent station in New York. Cosell wanted Cousy to go on *Wide World of Sports* with Smith.

Cousy declined, believing he would be too emotional. Smith didn't. At one point Cosell mentioned the banquet in Hartford that had been called a "gangster conclave" in the article, one given for a prizefighter who had done youth work in Hartford, where Cousy had been at the head table with boxers Rocky Marciano and Willie Pep. Cosell said he knew all about it, had even been invited to be the master of ceremonies, but at the last minute had gotten an assignment.

"If I had gone to the dinner," he said to Smith, "would that have made me a gangster?"

That was the end of it.

But Cousy had lost a little bit of his innocence, too. A *Boston Globe* editorial said that, like Caesar's wife, people who seek public support must be above suspicion. "Cousy, by his own choice, has not fulfilled this."

He had always gotten along with sportswriters, trusted them. He had spent many years cultivating his image, polishing it, protecting it. It had always been extremely important to him, for not only was it his legacy, but it was also the way he made money, supported his family. What did he have in the marketplace if not his good name?

Before the start of the 1968–69 season he told Boston College officials he was going to leave at the end of the season. He had offered a scholarship to a kid named Bobby Griffin, who had been to his camp for years, only to be told by BC athletic director Bill Flynn that NCAA rules forbade that because Griffin had gone to Cousy's camp, the thinking being that his camp had given Cousy an unfair recruiting advantage with Griffin.

Cousy was incensed, not only because he thought the rule was stupid, but because he had promised Griffin a scholarship and now was going to have to go back on a commitment to Griffin and his family. To Cousy, the situation seemed a microcosm of how shortsighted and intransigent the NCAA was, nitpicking him about something as innocent as this, while turning away from the larger, more serious transgressions that had become as much a part of the college game as sweat and cheerleader pyramids. Cousy wanted Flynn to fight the NCAA on this, but Flynn, who lived in a black-and-white world, declined.

To Cousy, this was the last straw.

He had been happy at Boston College. Every night he had dinner in the school cafeteria with assistant coaches Frank Powers, Jack Magee, and Gerry Friel. Missie and the kids went to all the home games, and afterward they would go to Flynn's house. Years later Missie would say that those were the best years, the ones she remembered the most fondly.

In many ways, though, he'd had it with college coaching, specifically the hypocrisy of recruiting.

He also knew he was fortunate in that his financial situation gave him options other college coaches didn't necessarily have. He was making $40,000 a year for his sneaker endorsement, almost another $15,000 for the Bob Cousy ball. He also thought he could franchise his clinics, something no one else was doing at the time, because every year he was turning away kids.

Besides, he never thought he was going to coach at BC forever.

So now, even though he'd given them a basketball program that no one could have envisioned when he'd been hired in 1963, he wasn't satisfied. And he knew he would never be satisfied unless he could win more and more, and to do that he knew he would have to bend more rules, compromise his principles. BC countered, saying they would take a kid every once in a while who was borderline academically. This only upset Cousy more. If they were so anxious to keep him, why hadn't they done these things before?

At the end of the season George Mikan, then the commissioner of the American Basketball Association, called to ask if Cousy wanted to coach the New York Nets. Shortly afterward, he got an offer to coach the Cincinnati Royals. It was for $100,000 a year for three years, big money for a NBA coach, and he was making enough from his outside interests that he would be able to defer all of it.

"You will never have to worry about money again," one of the owners told him.

To someone who had grown up poor, and had always lived with the secret fear that someday there wasn't going to be enough money, it was exactly the right sales pitch. In the end, Cousy believed it was simply too much money to walk away from. So in the fall of '69, even though his family was against it, Bob Cousy became an NBA coach.

The team was owned by Emprise, a Buffalo-based company that owned arenas all over the world, the Cincinnati Gardens among them. It was run by Max and Jeremy Jacobs, and the word was they were looking to sell the Royals, and figured that would be an easier task if they had a big-name coach. So from the beginning it was a Faustian pact: Cousy essentially went because he couldn't say no to the money; the Jacobses wanted his name.

His older daughter, Marie, was starting college in Boston, so he, Missie, and Ticia, who was in high school, left Worcester for Cincinnati. It was the first time he had ever lived outside of Worcester since he'd been in high school.

Cincinnati was a very conservative city, more southern than midwestern, and in the beginning Cousy had a tough time finding housing for his assistant coach Draff Young, who was black, and who had worked for the company that produced the Bob Cousy sneaker. The two used to do promotions in shopping centers together, Young running contests in the parking lot, Cousy giving away autographed pictures inside. Young, whose brother had played for the Globetrotters, knew many of the black players in the NBA. And since Cousy had never coached a team that was predominantly black before, he figured Young could be a bridge between him and the black players. For the league had changed dramatically in the six years since he had left the Celtics, becoming almost 70 percent black.

The first summer Cousy stayed in Cincinnati, went to every Rotary Club meeting, every chicken dinner, everything on the local circuit. He also announced he'd be coming back as a player, albeit in a limited role. Everything was done to try and rev up interest.

There wasn't a lot.

The team's centerpiece was Oscar Robertson, then in his 10th year. Still one of the great players in the league, Robertson had been the league's MVP in 1964, beating out both Chamberlain and Russell, but he could be moody and petulant. It was two years after many of the nation's inner cities had exploded during the summer of '67, and the country's racial situation was never far from Robertson's thoughts. He had come to believe that if a black player helped his team win a game he was accepted, however gradual, grudging, or even conditional that acceptance might have been. In that sense, Robertson believed, athletes were no different from entertainers.

Cousy found Oscar to be smart and aloof, with a definite chip on his shoulder when it came to the white establishment. He listened carefully, said little, and did what he was supposed to do. He was also said to have a certain friction with Jerry Lucas, the other name player, although Robertson always denied that.

He was also tough on his teammates, and many observers thought Robertson had worn out his welcome in Cincinnati. Certainly, he was no longer a novelty, having been there since the fall of '56 when he first went to the University of Cincinnati. The team averaged about 6,000 a game in a building that could seat twice that, and more and more the city was being regarded as one in which professional basketball was simply never going to be successful.

Max Jacobs, in his early 30s, referred to him and his brother as "peanuts and popcorn salesmen," taking over the business their father had started with one pushcart in Brooklyn. Max Jacobs, who had been a Shakespearean actor, worked 13 hours a day, seven days a week. Every night he would call the various arenas around the country he and his brother owned to check on the day's take. So every night he would call Cousy and ask how many people had been at the game. Not whether or not the Royals had won. How many people had been there.

"How come you never ask if we won?" Cousy asked one night.

"Because I don't really care," Jacobs said.

Robertson's style was to use his body to back defenders down, controlling the ball. Cousy, in turn, wanted the team to run and play more uptempo, the style he had known with the Celtics. In retrospect, it was probably inevitable their philosophies would clash.

The Royals had been 41-41 the year before, but Cousy quickly realized that with the exception of Oscar and Lucas, the only other player on the roster with quality NBA ability was Tom Van Arsdale. On the day of the first home game, against the Knicks, the Royals ran newspaper ads that showed a picture of Cousy in a uniform, under the heading, "Would You Believe?"

Still, fewer than 6,000 turned out as the Royals lost. Cousy did not suit up to play, and afterward he stood in the locker room, chewing on an unlit cigar, as if in some grim parody of Auerbach.

As fate would have it, the Royals' next game was in the Boston Garden, against the Celtics. Cousy got a standing ovation when he walked on to the court, kidded with Auerbach, and posed for pictures with Heinsohn, now the Celtics' coach. In the return of the prodigal son the Royals won by two, and Cousy had his first win as an NBA coach.

But the elation didn't last.

Eventually, he would play a total of 34 minutes in seven games, a comeback that later became simply an asterisk on his career. He had worked out some over the summer, scrimmaging with the players in training camp, and became the oldest player in the league at 41. He never intended to play a significant role, and the only time he was a factor in a game was against the Knicks, who had come into Cincinnati having won 15 straight. With about 90 seconds left, the Royals leading by three, Robertson fouled out. Cousy believed he was the next-best option and could give his team some stability in the last minute and a half. So he put himself in, then quickly made two free throws. But he had a pass intercepted, and then when one of his players threw the ball away again, the Royals had lost.

This was not big news. It soon became apparent to him the team was mediocre, the worst place to be in the NBA. Initially, he deferred to Robertson's demands and felt that they coexisted. There were never any confrontations, but it was never a close relationship, either. He also felt Jerry Lucas didn't care enough, that he would come into the locker room before a game and talk about business opportunities, and that Lucas lacked a true competitive spirit. Eventually, he and general manager Joe Axelson thought they had to transform the team. After Lucas told Cousy he didn't think his sore knees would allow him to play the kind of defense Cousy wanted him to, Lucas was traded to San Francisco for two players who proved forgettable, a trade that would turn out to be a bad one, not in the sense that Lucas was moved, but in that the Royals failed to get adequate value in return.

Trading Robertson ended up being similar, even though the situation was different. Oscar was in the last year of a contract, the word being he was going to want big money in his next one, something Cousy and Axelson were reluctant to give him. Besides, there was also some speculation he was going to jump to the ABA. At first, Cousy tried to trade him to Baltimore for Gus Johnson. Robertson, who had veto power over any trade, said no. Eventually, he was traded to the Milwaukee Bucks for Flynn Robinson and Charlie Paulk. It was another trade that, in retrospect, the Royals did not get good value in return, giving credence to the theory that Cousy had given Robertson away.

Still, he was beginning to shape the team in his own image.

But in the second year the team was no better, and Missie didn't like Cincinnati.

"The only people I know are the butcher and the mailman and I don't like the mailman," she said.

Cousy certainly knew about the stresses and tensions of coaching, but now it was worse. More games. More travel. The sense that he was living and dying with it every day. Maybe more important, he knew he had a mediocre team, and nothing he did was really going to change that. He soon realized that, unlike the aberration of the Celtics and a few of the other elite NBA teams, if you had mediocre talent in the NBA there was really no exit. And to someone as competitive as Cousy, as driven to win, to succeed, this went against his very nature.

"How long do you think it will take to win an NBA title?" he was asked.

"Twenty years," he said.

He wasn't kidding.

It was also the first time he saw the beginning of what would become the new NBA. It happened with Sam Lacey, whom the Royals had selected in the draft when they couldn't get Dave Cowens, who went on to be one of the Celtics' all-time great players. A few years into his career Lacey used to hire a limo to pick him up at the airport when returning from road trips. It was just one of the examples Cousy saw of players who were spoiled and pampered, changed by the recruiting process that began corrupting them before they even got to college, and then by the money of the NBA. It was less than a decade after he'd retired as a player, but already Cousy saw the league as a different universe.

The NBA was changing dramatically racially, too. As it had been with the Celtics, invariably the white players would gravitate to each other, the black players to the other black players. Periodically, Cousy would look out at the start of practice and see the black players warming up at one basket, the white players at another.

"Go integrate that basket," he'd say to a player.

Cousy didn't feel he had problems coaching black players, despite his nonrelationship with Robertson. He dealt with them the way he had once dealt with his Celtics' teammates. They were players. Race had nothing to do with it. One of them, guard Norm Van Lier, even dated his daughter Marie for a while, Cousy saying at the time he thought Van Lier would have made a great son-in-law.

To him, the black players were more hungry. That was something he could relate to, for who had been more hungry than he? It's probably why he saw a little bit of himself in Tiny Archibald, a small guard from New York City by way of the University of Texas at El Paso whom Cousy selected in the second round of the 1970 draft: the New York roots. The ghetto experience. The social dysfunction. The distrust of people. The first time he met Archibald the young player was so shy and withdrawn he had difficulty looking at him.

By his fourth year the Royals were still on some treadmill to nowhere and the team had moved, splitting their home games between Kansas City and Omaha. Hoping to build interest and sell tickets, Cousy turned Archibald loose, giving him complete freedom, and Archibald became the first player in history to lead the league in both scoring and assists. But it wasn't enough. The Royals were still below .500 and Cousy wondered how long he could keep doing this.

In Kansas City it had only gotten worse. Missie kept going back and forth to Worcester, leaving Cousy in another rented apartment, and for him, all the pretense of coaching the team soon left. The team was mediocre, and no matter what he did nothing seemed to change. He began drinking Scotch out of water glasses in his hotel room to fall asleep at night. But when he got up the next morning nothing had changed. Coaching in the NBA had become strictly a job. Could he have done it better? Maybe. But he had become too negative about it. He couldn't escape the fact that his wife was in Worcester, his daughters were in Worcester, his home was in Worcester, his friends were in Worcester, and he was in Kansas City with a bad team.

What were his priorities?

That's what he kept asking himself as he lay in hotel rooms around the country drinking Scotch. His daughters were now 20 and 22, and soon they might be married and off into new chapters of their lives, and what was he going to remember, another night in a hotel room?

He knew he had to get out, and he did on Thanksgiving, 1973.

He had told Axelson he wanted out before the season started, and Axelson had asked him to stay one more year. But on the night before Thanksgiving, after another loss, he was walking across the court heading toward the locker room when he said to himself, that's it, no more. So he announced to the sportswriters covering the game that he was resigning. Missie heard about it on the radio the next day, and said that it was the first spontaneous decision her husband had ever made.

Two years later, in 1975, he published a book called *The Killer Instinct,* written with a New York freelancer named John Devaney.

The book's cover was black, with a close-up of Cousy's face, the intensity stamped all over it. The heading at the top said, "Mr. Basketball thought winning was the only thing—until the hunger to win as a coach drove him to the edge of moral and physical collapse."

There were two blurbs on the back. One was by Larry O'Brien, the commissioner of the NBA. The other was by Howard Cosell, now a celebrity with *Monday Night Football* as his weekly sounding board.

The original idea for the book had been an exposé of college basketball, Cousy speaking out on the hypocrisies of recruiting and the various abuses in the college game, but it evolved into something far more personal. At its core, the book was a rejection of the trait that might have been the biggest reason Bob Cousy became one of the greatest basketball players in the history of the game, the killer instinct that had taken him from the school yards of Queens to the biggest arenas in the country, the killer instinct he'd ridden to overcome all the odds and become one of the most successful athletes in the history of American sport.

Now, though, he was saying there was a downside, that much of the obsession with winning, the need to keep winning, was a distortion of values, a walk through a minefield. He was saying you pay a price for this trait, that it had more ramifications than just cheers in an arena.

He talked about the time he had been coaching a team of college stars in a series of games against a team from the Soviet Union in spring 1973, and at one point he told a player named Ron Behagen to "go in and decapitate" one of the Russian players. So Behagen went into the game, threw a punch, and a brawl broke out. Years later, Cousy couldn't believe he could have told Behagen to do that.

But that wasn't the incident he felt the most guilty about.

That happened one summer at his camp, when he was five or six years removed from playing for the Celtics. He was playing in a camp game when he and one of his counselors, a kid named Bob Duffy, who played for Colgate, went for a loose ball. In the struggle, Duffy inadvertently hit Cousy with an elbow, and as they both went to the ground for the ball Cousy wrestled it away from Duffy, exhibiting more force than he had to, then hit Duffy with an elbow as he started back down the court—either intentionally or not, he wasn't even sure—and continued with the play as Duffy lay on the ground bleeding. Moments afterward, he felt awful, and later sat with Duffy that night, endlessly apologizing.

"I came out of the big-city ghetto chasing the American Dream like millions of young men and women of my generation," he said. "It was all about survival, every man for himself."

It was a dream of success, of winning.

To Cousy, these were stitched into the national fabric along with the stars and stripes. Losing was the American nightmare. A loser was the worst thing you could call anyone. America was all about winning, to the exclusion of everything else, and in Cousy's view, it was this sense of myopia that had gotten the country into the quagmire of Vietnam and the moral bankruptcy of Watergate. It was the mind-set of Charles Colson, who had once said that he'd walk over his grandmother to win an election. To Cousy, it was the dark side of the killer instinct.

"What are we creating with our addiction to winning at any cost?" he asked.

So *The Killer Instinct* became a lament for his past indiscretions, almost a public midlife crisis.

He said he was tempted to ignore not only NCAA rules as a college coach, but "my own sense of right and wrong. It became clear to me that I couldn't win as much as my hunger called for and still keep from compromising. I knew I had to walk away from this situation before this conflict destroyed me."

He knew the personal pound of flesh basketball had exacted from him. He knew that going to Cincinnati had been a mistake, that it had further distanced him from his family. He knew that, in many ways, basketball had narrowed his world, cut him off from other possibilities, limited him. In a sense, he now came to resent it, to resent the person it had made him be.

"I had lived my life without really thinking about slighting my family," he said. "Everything revolved around me and my career. I had put my ambition first. Family and other personal relations came second."

The Killer Instinct is a dark book, almost a mea culpa.

"I had always wanted to be a success in anything I tried," Cousy said. "In any competition I had an almost uncontrollable need to win. That killer instinct had brought me success as a

player, and a coach, but it also had tempted me to run over people, to break rules, to neglect my family, to neglect myself to the
point of exhaustion."

For an America sports icon, someone who had been on the
cover of magazines and heard a country's cheers, it was a startling
admission.

"I am no longer proud of my killer instinct," he said. "It may
be the drive that makes a superstar in sports, sells a product, or
even wins a war. But it can do more than blow away an opponent.
It can kill the moral sense, the happiness of a family, even the
man himself. The killer instinct is not something I can get rid of.
It's something I must live with the best I can."

He was 47.

Chapter Twelve

One morning in the winter of 2003 Cousy was in the basement of his Worcester home overseeing the packing of his memorabilia.

He had decided to sell it. There were 155 pieces in all, with some of the pieces containing 10 different items. Included were his 1957 NBA championship ring, his MVP trophy, a letter from President Eisenhower inviting him to the White House, and a lithograph honoring him as one of the 50 best players in NBA history, signed by 49 of the players. There also was his uniform from the 1952 All-Star game, his 1947 Holy Cross national title plaque, and enough other stuff to stock a small museum. They'd been sitting in the basement for over 40 years now, and the problem had become what to do with it. Most of the winter the memorabilia sat in an empty house. And what was going to happen to it when he and Missie were gone?

Nor was it anything he thought much about. For years it had just sat in boxes, not displayed, an assemblage of plaques, trophies, old game programs, magazine stories, the tangible legacy of his career. He certainly didn't think any of it was worth anything. Eventually, the son of a friend had assembled it, displayed it. Still, it wasn't something he thought much about. Until he was told he might get as much as $500,000 for it. That had gotten his interest, and he signed with SportsCards Plus, a California company that a few months later would auction the memorabilia over the Internet. The plan was to give the money to his two daughters. They were both in their early fifties, schoolteachers, and

Cousy figured the money could help them now, not in some undetermined future.

Was it surprising?

Not to those who knew him.

The regret of his life was that he'd not been there enough for his daughters when they'd been growing up. How it had always been his needs, his desires, his career. Be quiet, your father has to take a nap. We're eating at four in the afternoon because your father has a game. No, your father won't be at your school's open house, he's away.

In many ways, it was a familiar lament, especially of successful men who had come into adulthood in the fifties in America, back when men went off to work and women stayed home and raised the kids and no one questioned it. But if Cousy knew intellectually that he wasn't alone in not spending enough time with his family while his daughters had been young, it didn't comfort him. He knew he hadn't done enough normal "father" things. He knew he'd slighted them. It was something he'd spend the second half of his life trying to atone for.

No matter that neither one of his daughters feels they grew up neglected.

In the summer of 2003 they had both visited Worcester and stayed at their parents' house. Marie is married, lives outside Seattle, and has two children. She is a guidance counselor at a high school in suburban Seattle. Ticia is divorced, lives in Florida, and is a teacher. They are both dark-haired and attractive, Marie looking more like her mother, Ticia her father.

They both remember people stopping to knock on the door of the house at Chamberlain Parkway looking for autographs. They may have been just young kids then, but they knew that wasn't happening at their friends' houses. They both remember going into the Boston Garden for Sunday afternoon games, going to Walter Brown's annual Christmas party at the Garden where the kids would get a chance to skate. They remember Bill Russell's kids, and the children of their father's other teammates. They both played sports as kids, but never basketball.

"I wasn't going to do that to myself," Marie said.

Ticia ended up playing a lot of racquetball.

"But I don't have the killer instinct," she said.

Why should she?

She didn't grow up in a New York ghetto in the tail end of the Depression, didn't grow up in a joyless home she couldn't wait to escape from. She didn't come of age knowing you had to grab and clutch and claw, and even that didn't guarantee that you were going to escape your environment.

Marie remembers the time in high school when she discovered a boy she liked was afraid to call the house, because how can you call Bob Cousy's house? She remembers the time one of the nuns at her school said she must be spoiled because she was Bob Cousy's daughter. She remembers when she was in her early 20s and living in a large house in Boston with a lot of roommates and she was just Marie, no last name. They both remember their father often being away.

Yet, in retrospect, they say their childhood was remarkable for its normalcy, their mother making them the focus of her life. Their father was their father, not the professional athlete on magazine covers.

"We always felt loved, and that made all the difference," Marie said.

Both came to grips with their father's celebrity a long time ago.

Both still use their maiden names, have stories about all the times they have said their name to someone who didn't know them.

"You mean, like the old basketball player?" the reply invariably would be.

"Yeh, like him," they'd say.

In 1994 Cousy was paid $150,000 to be in the movie *Blue Chips*. He went back and forth to the West Coast six times. The movie was filmed both at Paramount and in a small Indiana town. Ron

Shelton, who had written *Bull Durham*, had done the script, and Cousy had thought it was very good, an inside look at the hypocrisy and corruption of big-time college basketball. He originally had six scenes with Nick Nolte. Most made it into the movie, which took six months to make, and was directed by Billy Friedkin, whom he had met in the early seventies when Friedkin had been part of a symposium at Holy Cross, shortly after Friedkin's hit movie *The French Connection*.

They had sat in Cousy's living room for an hour and a half that day, Cousy wanting to talk about Hollywood, Friedkin wanting to talk about basketball. Cousy later introduced Friedkin to Auerbach, and Friedkin used to come to a couple of Celtics games a year.

Cousy played the role of the athletic director in *Blue Chips*, Nolte played the embattled coach. In the original script Nolte had once played for Cousy in college, had been his protégé, thus Nolte's corruption and ultimate fall had been devastating to the character played by Cousy. None of that was in the movie, however, so the relationship between the coach and the athletic director is nowhere near as emotionally loaded. Ah, Hollywood.

His best scene in *Blue Chips*? He and Nolte shoot foul shots in the gym. It took half a day to film. Originally, the script had Nolte and Cousy sitting on a bench talking.

"Let's shoot foul shots," Nolte suggested. "It will get some action into the scene."

So they did.

The idea was for one of them to start shooting, then once one missed the other would shoot. The only problem was Cousy never missed. He made his first, he made his second, and he kept on making them. He could see that Nolte was getting upset.

"Do you want me to miss?" he said to Friedkin. "Nick's getting pissed."

"No," Friedkin said. "Keep going."

Cousy kept shooting, kept making them, as the cameras kept rolling. At one point he had made something like 20 in a row, and the technicians thought they were witnessing a miracle. A few

days earlier Shaquille O'Neal, the most dominant young center in
the game, had been in the same gym filming a similar scene and
had been unable to make two foul shots in a row. Then, just to
prove his point, Cousy took a foul shot lefthanded and made
that, too.

It was just one of the ways Cousy has kept his name in front of
the public, certainly in New England.

He started broadcasting television games for the Celtics in
1974, shortly after he walked away from the Royals. He had gone
to Auerbach. The first year he worked with Dick Stockton, and
was paid $500 a game. He had television experience, having done
color for NBA games on ABC for three years during the time he'd
been coaching at Boston College. They were Sunday afternoon
games, and he was forever flying either Saturday night or Sunday
morning to where the games were, working with Chris Schenkel,
who leaned over to him moments before the first broadcast and
said he knew nothing about basketball.

"I knew I didn't have the TV voice, that the only thing I had to
sell was my candor," he said.

For years he did all the road games, and from the beginning he
was both perceptive and straightforward, all presented with his
distinctive speaking style, the one little kids had used to tease him
about back there in the Yorkville of his childhood.

And why did he put himself back on the road once again?
Why did he put himself back into the NBA lifestyle he had grown
to hate, both as a player and as a coach?

"I do what I have to do" he said. "I had to go on the road to do
the games, so that's what I did."

He did it for nearly 25 years.

The best time was the eighties. It was the Larry Bird era in
Boston, the Celtics and the Lakers the two best teams in basketball. Bird versus Magic. West Coast versus East Coast. Showtime
versus the blue-collar, lunchpail ethic of the Celtics. To Cousy, it
was all great theater, and one more reminder of how emotionally
connected he was to the Celtics. The hurt he had felt the year

after he retired was long gone. So was the estrangement he had felt through the years when he'd been coaching, both at Boston College and with the Royals. He was back with the Celtics, still emotionally involved, almost as if he had never left, and there were moments when his eyes would start to tear up, one more reminder of how much his heart was invested in the Celtics.

At one level, it was a treat going to games knowing he would see great basketball, great theater. He prided himself on telling the truth, so with the Celtics so good there was no reason to spin anything. You could be a cheerleader on the air and it was justified. Not like the years that came later, when the team was down and he went on the road knowing the odds were that the Celtics were going to lose, knowing that you had to do something to keep people watching.

Over the years he worked with broadcasters Dick Stockton, Len Berman, Roger Twibell, and Gil Santos. Later, it was Heinsohn, then Heinsohn and Mike Gorman.

"I always found Bob to be a delight," said Gorman. "He's a very gentle man. And unlike most ex-jocks, who think my business is something anyone can do, he has very little ego as a broadcaster. He's almost egoless. I think he's always been insecure about his television work, so he's always prepared. He'll rehearse an intro two or three times, because he wants it to go well. He does his homework. He never just shows up and tries to wing it, like a lot of guys do."

In the winter of 1987 Cousy and Missie moved to Florida, to a development called Bear Lakes in West Palm Beach. They live on a golf course, close to where Havlicek and Jack Nicklaus live. That's where they spend winters, and Cousy used it as home base for years while he flew around the country doing Celtics road games.

He stopped doing games after the 2000 season, settling into retirement.

But, in a sense, he's never really retired, for being Bob Cousy always has been a full-time job in ways he never could have imagined back when he retired in 1963. The plan then was to use his name to make a living, because he had only been 34, with a lifetime ahead of him. But there was no way then he could ever have imagined being able to do it for so long. Even now, in his mid-70s, he still did two national appearances a year for Jantzen sportswear, still did appearances in the Boston area, was still a presence. In the summer of 2003 he did a card show in Atlantic City, $30,000 for the day. The irony of that was not lost on him, the inescapable fact that it was only $5,000 less than he'd made his last season playing with the Celtics.

One reason Cousy kept doing the Celtics games all those years was to keep him visible, part of the traveling magic show that's the contemporary NBA, even if only on the periphery. Another reason, no doubt, was that he and his teammates have come to represent a better era in professional sports, before all the big money and so much of the excess, back when the game, in many ways, seemed better, cleaner, more team-oriented.

But it was more than that, too.

"He's been exceptional at cultivating and maintaining relationships," says Dan Doyle, the director of the Institute for International Sport.

Doyle, who grew up in Worcester and attended Cousy's camp as a kid, sees Cousy as one of the rare great athletes who have an elevated social conscience. "He was very active in youth basketball in Worcester in the sixties, at a time when he was at the height of his fame," Doyle said. "He and a local priest developed a summer league that became one of the biggest in the country. He's always been very much a part of the Worcester community. His house was part of the unofficial Worcester tour. Your friends came to Worcester and you took them by Cooz's house. It was like a rite of passage."

Doyle went to Camp Graylag in the summer of '66 when he was in high school. Working as counselors were several of Cousy's

BC players—Willie Wolters, Billy Evans, Jim Kissane. The camp director was Buster Sheary, Cousy's old coach at Holy Cross. Often, during a lecture, he would poke fun at Cousy, and it was as if it were light rain rolling off Cousy's back.

"He took an interest in kids, and not just at the camp," Doyle said.

Doyle remembers how in the sixties it was not uncommon to see Cousy at a summer league game in Worcester, or to see one of the Celtics there. For a while there was a "Beat Bob Cousy" foul-shooting contest at Assumption College in Worcester, virtually across Salisbury Street from where Cousy lives, a charity he did for the March of Dimes.

He's been active in various charitable causes locally and has long been a civic presence. And as with everything he does, if he committed to something he poured his energy into it, was never just some figurehead.

"There's a tremendous reservoir of affection for him in Worcester," said Doyle. "He's our Monet. Our artist. Our international figure."

He is in his mid-70s now. Yet there is still a presence about Cousy, a powerful sense of self. Maybe that shouldn't be surprising. He's been a star for nearly 60 years.

In the months they are in Worcester he and Missie go to four o'clock mass on Saturday afternoon, then to early dinner at the Worcester Country Club, usually leaving before the room starts to fill up. He rarely puts himself in situations where a lot of people can approach him, for those situations still make him uncomfortable, even now, after so many years.

"Where do you draw the line when you're a public figure?" he asked rhetorically.

It's a question he'd grappled with his entire adult life. As he grew older he would say that in a perfect world he would have been the Howard Hughes of sports, a recluse, dealing with people only in very small groups. In a sense, it's how he deals with people now. He still gets five or six pieces of mail every day, correspondence he deals with religiously. He still does a handful of games a year for the Celtics, keeping his name out there. He still does an occasional appearance, part of the retinue of former sports greats who float around New England, on the conveyer belt from celebrity golf tournament to corporate outing. He picks his spots.

Earlier in the summer there had been a press conference at the Basketball Hall of Fame in Springfield, Massachusetts, announcing the "Bob Cousy Point Guard Award," to be given to the college player who best exhibits the playmaking qualities Cousy almost put a patent on so many years ago.

There was a sliver of irony in that, too. He once had been very involved in the Hall of Fame, especially working for improved benefits for the NBA players of the early days, the ones who played before 1965, then had a falling-out and had been estranged for roughly 15 years.

Now, that was all ancient history, and to him, this was a way of tidying up the scorecard, making sure there weren't any loose ends left, not just with the Hall of Fame, but in all his relationships. Jokingly, he referred to it as "the legacy," but there's truth in that, too.

A statue of him will eventually be placed in front of the Hart Center at Holy Cross. There will soon be a "Bob Cousy Humanitarian Award," which will be given out every November in a ceremony at the FleetCenter in Boston, honoring people from around the world who have done something in sports that's served humanity.

This was another example that he had grown since leaving basketball, that his view of the world got larger, more encompassing. Then again, he had always believed that jocks grew up late in America and were allowed to be adolescents longer than they should be.

There's little question Missie had helped him in this, for she'd always had a social conscience, marching against the Vietnam War before it became fashionable, always concerned about social justice. Cousy was always kidding her that she was on every "do-gooder" mailing list in the country. Yet social justice always had been part of Cousy's worldview, too, dating back to his senior thesis at Holy Cross and his sensitivity to Chuck Cooper that long ago night in North Carolina, even if it hadn't always been articulated. He never lost the sense that basketball was just a "child's game," something that shouldn't measure a life, even if his life had been so defined by it.

In a sense, that's been the great contradiction in his life, the fact he'd put so much of his time and emotional energy into this child's game.

"Everything I've done is because of basketball," he said. "I pay it due homage. But I'm not addicted to it. Outside of the Celtics I watch very little basketball on TV."

Yet he'd also come to see basketball as an art form, especially when played unselfishly, played well. It's a theme he often expressed when speaking in public, the sense that the Larry Birds and Magic Johnsons of the world, the Jordans and Russells, had been artists in their own way, their art taking us to new places, elevating us, letting us see new ways of expression, new worlds, basketball as a form of exploration.

What was left unsaid was he had been the same.

His new passion was golf. For years it had been both tennis and golf, but after a hip replacement it became solely golf. He attacked it as he had once attacked basketball. He practiced. He hit balls. He kept trying to get better, the way he had once gone to O'Connell Park every day after school to get better at basketball back in the St. Albans of his youth, as if everything had changed, yet in many ways nothing had changed. Three mornings a week he worked out at Holy Cross, often sitting on one of the exercise bikes next to students who had no idea who he was.

On the golf course his unrelenting competitiveness is still there, to the point he long ago became infamous within his circle of golfing friends for the way he took a generic weekend match and seemed to elevate it into an NBA playoff game, urging his partners on, being demanding, seemingly wanting to win as much as he wanted to win in the old Boston Garden in a big play-off game. Afterward, he'd laugh at himself, but it's a testimony to how the juices still boil, even after all the years. As if the killer instinct never really goes away; it just gets rechanneled.

And he finally felt secure financially.

In a sense his obsession with money had been there his entire life, even through all the cheers and all the money he had made. The fear had always been that it was all fragile, that it was only a matter of time before it all disappeared. Maybe that was the Depression's legacy to him. But that insecurity never left him, no matter how many contracts he signed through the years, how many deals were consummated, as if it was never enough to make him feel he could stop worrying about it. So he never bought any-thing he couldn't pay cash for, never got over those painful les-sons from his childhood, when money was simply something you never had enough of.

It was the insecurity he'd used as fuel, the driving force that enabled him to overcome the odds, to come so far from those days in Yorkville when kids used to make fun of him, so far from those first years in St. Albans when he first used basketball as acceptance, then for an identity. It had been such an improbable journey, and he'd never forgotten that. Never forgot the lesson he'd learned in 1966.

He was 37 then, three years removed from that incredible farewell celebration in the Boston Garden. The trip was sponsored by Gillette, and after a press conference in Paris the game plan was to travel around the country, every day a different town, where Cousy would kiss babies, do clinics, whatever he was asked to do. Cousy had a map, could speak French, and he and his fam-ily did 21 towns in 24 days.

At the end of tour he took his own private tour. It was to La Chappelle, a small town in the northeastern part of the country, in the middle of farming country. Cousy knocked on the door of the local church, asked where the Cousy farm was. The local priest gave him directions, and shortly afterward Cousy knocked on the door of a small house that had earthen floors with no electricity, looking like something out of the Middle Ages. This was where his uncles still lived, the farm where they still milked goats and picked potatoes. It was the family homestead, the one his father had left in 1928 to come to America, eventually stepping off a boat at Ellis Island without any money, knowing no English, and with a new wife who was pregnant.

"How's the playboy doing?" one of his uncles said, an obvious reference to his father.

Cousy couldn't believe it. Playboy? His father had been anything but, the absolute antithesis of a playboy. Yet Cousy quickly realized that, to his uncles, stuck here on the family farm, living in what could have been the 19th century, his father had lived a life they had no way of comprehending.

It was one of those moments of epiphany, a moment he would remember always, as if it were freeze-framed. Cousy instantly realized, in ways he never really had before, that if his father hadn't left the farm, hadn't set out to do something that was so incomprehensible to his brothers, his life would never have unfolded the way it did. Realized for the first time that he'd be one of the people out in the fields with the potatoes and the goats.

It was the spring of 2002, the Celtics against the Nets in the Fleet-Center in Boston, the first time the Celtics had been in the playoffs in seven years.

It was a timeout in the fourth quarter, the building rocking with excitement and frenzied cheers, and there on the message board that hangs over midcourt was part of the Celtics' storied history, the images of several icons of the past who were there in the building, the camera having found them in their seats. The first was of Auerbach, the master builder, sitting about 15 rows above half-court. Then there was Russell, the man who had won 11 world championships in his 13 years as a player. There was Heinsohn, now a popular broadcaster.

Then there was Cousy, sitting in the same section as Auerbach.

"Cooz . . . Cooz," roared the crowd, as it saw his face on the message board.

Cousy, now in his mid-70s, looked up and saw his image on the message board. He appeared momentarily startled, almost uncomfortable. Then he held up his thumbs in a victory salute, as if thinking that if he made some gesture the camera would go away.

This was part of the Celtics' living history, the human face of the 16 championship banners that now hang in the rafters of the FleetCenter. And for most of the 1990s those banners had become accusers, as if the greatness of the past had begun to stare down at the sorry present, like some scene out of some grim Cotton Mather tale. In a sense, the Celtics had spent the nineties as a franchise that had become all about the past, a team that couldn't even make the playoffs, never mind seriously contend for another championship banner. The players seemed to be all just passing through, their allegiance to their agents and their contracts, wearing green uniforms by some accident of fate, distanced from the great Celtics players of the past by time and circumstance, playing in Boston as if it were no different from playing in Cleveland.

That had started to change in the spring of 2002.

Part of that was the FleetCenter itself, a new building that was attracting younger, more raucous crowds, more of a party atmosphere, complete with rock music and video images of people dancing in the stands during timeouts, basketball game as event. It was all part of the NBA of the new millennium, a brave new world of nonstop entertainment, the underlying philosophy being that just a basketball game was no longer enough anymore.

Once a basketball game in the old Boston Garden had been almost timeless, as if the players changed, but the atmosphere never did. There were no cheerleaders. There was no piped-in music during timeouts. There were the same trademark black sneakers. The same parquet floor. No frills. Nothing to tell you that it wasn't 1957, save for the fact that the players were overwhelmingly black. But on this afternoon in the spring of 2002 the FleetCenter could have been Dallas, or Denver, or New Jersey, or even Orlando, the place one Boston sportswriter had once called "Hooterville," for its tasteless promotions, its infatuation with being "fan friendly." Now the NBA was all Hooterville, as if all of the league's marketing people had attended the same seminar.

More and more the past seemed to be receding, the inevitable result of a new building, younger fans, and the passage of time. You could see it in the new pregame introductions on the message board, the ones that began when the lights were dimmed. They used to be a paean to the Celtics' past, a montage of memories, complete with Johnny Most's voice, the signature voice to innumerable older fans. Now the past was still there, but it was interspersed with the present, Larry Bird morphing into Antoine Walker, John Havlicek blending into Paul Pierce. As if the Celtics had become one big season, going round and round.

But the past was still there, too, as evidenced by the fact that these faces on the message board still generated loud ovations, even if many of them had played decades before. These were the Celtics of legend, the ones who had once made the Celtics one of the greatest franchises in the history of American sport.

It was curious to watch the crowd cheer Cousy, though, considering that so many of them obviously hadn't been alive when he'd played.

What could they know?

You had to be close to 60 years old to even remember it, had to have come of age with Ike and fallout shelters and the early days of rock 'n' roll, back when Bill Haley and the Comets were on the cutting edge and no one had ever heard of Vietnam. Even then, you would be late to the game, would only have caught the tail end of it, those years in the late fifties and early sixties when the NBA had finally established itself, no longer playing in the old dance halls of its early years, back when its future was as up in the air like a long two-hand set shot.

To many of the people in the FleetCenter that afternoon their sense of the NBA past had started with Bird and Magic in the late seventies. That was their idea of NBA history. Either that or Dr. J. and George Gervin, back there in the really old days, with their Afros and Super Fly threads. Before that it was all some murky swamp, a mental snapshot of old, grainy black-and-white images on the Classic Sports channel, or faded photographs in some musty book. Or just names their fathers had told them about.

Cousy?

They hadn't been born when he was playing, or had been too young to remember. He was just another one of those old guys, just one of the retired numbers that hang in the rafters of the FleetCenter, 21 in all, his no different from all the others. Cousy. Sharman. The Jones Boys. Heinsohn. Sanders. Ramsey. Loscy. Hadn't they all been the same, satellites floating around Russell's solar system?

What did they know?

Earlier that afternoon several of the Celtics' greats had come out and walked across center court, all these icons of the past, as the cheers tumbled down from the upper reaches of the FleetCenter. They were led out of the runway by Auerbach, the old patriarch, now in his mid-80s, walking with a cane, but still crusty and combative, still puffing on one of his ever-present cigars. He was still universally recognized after all these years as the architect of all those banners that hung in the rafters, the one constant through all the years, even if he'd officially retired nearly two decades ago, spending much of his time in Washington.

Cousy felt closer to Auerbach now than he ever had before. He'd come to appreciate him more, to understand that when people talked about the Celtic Mystique it was Auerbach who was the mystique, that it all started and ended with him. He was the one who endured, and if Cousy knew Auerbach had never been a lovable figure, there were times now when he'd go over and pinch

Auerbach's cheeks in a show of affection, not because he thought Auerbach was any more lovable, but because they'd shared so much together.

Then there was Russell, the prodigal son who had returned after a 33-year absence, whose time as a Celtic had always been complicated, all the winning and all the titles marred by the prejudice and discrimination he had always felt. He was now undergoing a certain rebirth, complete with a new book in bookstores called *The Russell Rules,* now being called the greatest winner in the history of American sport. There was the sense, whether rightly or wrongly, that he'd softened somewhat, as if most of the battles had already been fought, his demons exorcised. Now he waved to people, smiled, laughed his big cackle of a laugh, and to those who had known him in the past it all seemed incongruous, as though he was some more friendly twin.

There was Heinsohn, maybe the most visible of all of them now, courtesy of the fact he was the Celtics' analyst on their television broadcasts. He had been doing it for over 20 years, but for some inexplicable reason was now more popular than ever, no longer simply the barrel-voiced ex-player railing against the referees and the Celtics' propensity to walk the ball up the court, but the almost lovable cult figure with his "Tommy Points," his transformation into this generation's version of Johnny Most.

Heinsohn was the most comfortable, smiling, waving, the life of the party. Of all of them he was the one whose celebrity was still in the present tense, now known far more for being a broadcaster than for being either a player or a coach. Of all of the ex-players, he had sustained the life the longest, was still sustaining it 82 nights a year.

And there was Cousy, a little reserved, not totally comfortable, a man who still lived within himself, even after all these years in the public eye.

How many sitting that afternoon in the FleetCenter knew what it had been like to play when he did?

The game is so different now, almost as if it's a different sport in a different universe. The NBA minimum salary is now roughly a half-million dollars a year, with superstars making upwards of $10 million a season. A rookie who is a lottery pick now makes infinitely more from his sneaker contract than Cousy made in his entire 13-year NBA career. NBA superstars have now become almost minicorporations, living in a cocoon of celebrity that was unheard-of in the early days of the NBA. When the "Dream Team," the assemblage of NBA superstars playing in the Olympics for the first time, went to Barcelona, they were treated like rock stars, the ultimate example of how pervasive the NBA and its stars are on the world's sports stage.

When the Celtics traveled now it was on chartered planes to five-star hotels. When they returned to Hanscom Air Force base in suburban Lexington on those cold winter nights, their expensive SUVs were on the tarmac, already started, heaters on full blast, just one of the perks that went with being a Celtics player. How were they ever going to relate to those early days in the NBA when the Celtics played in Rochester, in upstate New York, then afterward took the sleeper train to Fort Wayne, Indiana, getting off in a cornfield at dawn, having to carry their bags a couple of miles to something called the Green Parrot Inn?

How could these players even begin to understand what the NBA had been like in the early days?

It was not something Cousy dwelled on, the difference in two eras, even if he knew that if he played today he would have made more money in his first year than he did in his entire career, even if he had spent virtually his entire adult life worried about money. In fact, it was almost the opposite, the sense of pride he felt being one of the men who had built the league, one of the pioneers who had created the climate that eventually would become the NBA as we've come to know it, the one that so many of today's superstars seem to take for granted.

He was also well aware that his entire career had been marked by a series of unpredictable strokes of good fortune, that he had lived out a script no fiction writer could ever have envisioned,

Horatio Alger in black sneakers. He knew that, in many ways, he had come of age in the right time and place, one that had ultimately given him a fame he never could have envisioned back in the forties in that playground universe of Queens, back when his world seemed bordered by the confines of that asphalt world. Back when all he wanted to do was simply make his high-school team.

He also, at some level, knew the NBA was all out of whack, the money, the glorification of the players, the distorted values, all of it. Hadn't he spoken out against all that in the fifties, for god's sake? Hadn't he said then that one good teacher was worth the whole lot of professional athletes? Yet he also knew his experiences and the ones the current players have are in parallel universes, differences that transcend money, or style of play, or any of the obvious things.

How could they know that, for him, it had been about survival?

That had been the lesson he had taken with him from the ghetto of his childhood, the one that had shaped both him and the generation to which he belonged, the one that had come of age in the Great Depression, and he had carried those scars with him ever since. Why else would he even now occasionally take the soap and shampoo out of hotel bathrooms? Or walk around his house turning off the lights? Why else would he endure endless speaking engagements that he often hated, even when his accountant told him he didn't need the money? Why had he spent so much of his adult life feeling financially insecure, even if all the trappings of his life proved otherwise?

Survival, pure and simple. As if even after all the cheers and all the fame those early instincts had never left him.

He had paid a price for that, too. He knew that. As if he had to surrender a part of himself to get to where he had gotten, some part of his humanity. But he had come to realize that that was the part of himself he'd channeled to become the great player he had been, the inner demons he was somehow able to use to his advantage, the fuel he'd lived on for so long, the unarticulated drive that had defined his life.

He had also come to feel affection for all his old teammates, the ones he sat with in the FleetCenter and the ones who weren't there, the relationships more meaningful now than when he'd actually been playing. As if, after all the years, he now knew they really had been a family after all. Not always without tensions and unresolved feelings, but a family nonetheless. One that knew each other's faults all too well, but long ago had come to accept them, full of affection and memories, ones that seem all the sweeter with the passage of time.

So in that spring of 2002, as he sat in the FleetCenter during that playoff series between the Celtics and the Nets, sat there and saw himself on the message board that hung over center court and heard the crowd chant "Cooz . . . Cooz," the chant that was both a reaffirmation of his past and a tribute to his status as a Celtics legend, there was always a part of him that silently asked the question:

What did they know?

And as he walked through the building on those nights, he was still Bob Cousy after all these years, still as recognizable as he had always been, almost timeless, as if somehow all the years had blended together. And invariably someone would say, in words that cut back through time, in words that were once on the tombstone of his career and now still endure decades later, "We love ya, Cooz."

Notes

The bulk of the book comes from extensive interviews with Bob Cousy, conducted over the summers of 2002 and 2003, and with people close to Cousy. But I also was aided by four books Cousy previously had done—*Basketball Is My Life*, written in 1957 with Al Hirshberg; *The Last Loud Roar*, written with Ed Linn in 1964; *The Killer Instinct*, written with John Devaney in 1975; and *Cousy on the Celtics Mystique*, written with Bob Ryan in 1988.

For the history of the Boston Celtics there are several excellent books that proved immensely helpful: Dan Shaughnessy's *Ever Green*, George Sullivan's *The Picture History of the Boston Celtics*, the *Boston Celtics Encyclopedia* by Peter Bjarkman, and Joe Fitzgerald's *That Championship Feeling*. Throw in Jeff Greenfield's *The World's Greatest Team*, and you have a treasure trove on the Celtics of Cousy's era.

For the overall history of the early days of the NBA I found Leonard Koppett's *24 Seconds to Shoot* of great value, as was Ron Thomas's *They Cleared the Lane*, a history of black players in professional basketball. Charley Rosen's *Scandals of '51* is a detailed look of the scandals of that era.

Bill Russell's three books—*Go Up for Glory, Second Wind*, and *Russell Rules*—as well as *Auerbach: An Autobiography*, written with Joe Fitzgerald, Dan Shaugnessy's *Seeing Red*, and Tom Heinsohn's *Heinsohn Don't You Ever Smile?*, are must-reads for anyone who wants a better understanding of both the era and the people who played in it.

Secondary sources that were used in specific chapters are as follows:

Chapter 1

"Farewell to Bob Cousy," in the March 1963 issue of *Sport*.

Providence Journal, March 8, 1963.

Chapter 2

Basketball Is My Life, by Bob Cousy and Al Hirshberg.

Chapter 3

Background on Worcester comes from *150 Years of Worcester* by Albert B. Southwick.

Background on Doggie Julian comes from newspaper stories in the *Valley News* (Hanover, N.H.) by Bruce Wood.

Background on '47 season comes from *New York Times* story by Jack Cavanaugh and *Worcester Telegram* stories by Bill Doyle and John Gearan.

Eastern Basketball story on '47 Holy Cross team by Dan Wenzel.

Holy Cross Crusader story on Cousy's reminiscences of his Holy Cross career.

Chapter 4

24 Seconds to Shoot, by Leonard Koppett.

Ever Green, by Dan Shaugnessy.

Background on Tony Lavelli comes from January 1949 issue of *Sport*.

Background on Red Auerbach comes from *Red Auerbach: An Autobiography* by Arnold "Red" Auerbach and Joe Fitzgerald, and from *Seeing Red,* by Dan Shaughnessy.

Background on Harlem Globetrotters comes from "Basketball's Greatest Road-Show" in the January 1951 issue of *Sport*.

Background on Ed Macauley comes from Janaury 1949 issue of *Sport*.

Background on Bill Sharman comes from *The World's Greatest Team,* by Jeff Greenfield.

Quotations from Marjorie Brown are from *The Picture History of the Boston Celtics* by George Sullivan.

Seasons to Remember, by Curt Gowdy.

Chapter 5

24 Seconds to Shoot, by Leonard Koppett.

The Scandals of '51, by Charles Rosen.

Tall Tales, by Terry Pluto.

Background on Bob Brannum comes from *The World's Greatest Team* by Jeff Greenfield.

Basketball Is My Life, by Bob Cousy with Al Hirshberg.

Chapter 6

Background information on University of San Francisco team, featuring Bill Russell and K. C. Jones, comes from April 1964 issue of *Sport.*

Background information on Tom Heinsohn comes from *Heinsohn, Don't You Ever Smile?*

Overview of the fifties comes from *The Fifties,* by David Halberstam.

Chapter 7

Boston Globe, April 14, 1963.

Background on Bob Pettit comes from *The Official NBA Encyclopedia.*

Background on Bill Russell comes from *Go Up for Glory* and *Second Wind.*

Seventh-game detail comes from both *The Picture History of the Boston Celtics* by George Sullivan and *Boston Celtics Encyclopedia* by Peter Bjarkman.

Chapter 8

24 Seconds to Shoot, by Leonard Koppett.

Background on Wilt Chamberlain comes from *Wilt, A View from Above,* and *Season of the 76ers* by Wayne Lynch.

Account of first Russell-Chamberlain matchup comes from article by Barry Gottehrer in March 1960 issue of *Sport.*

Background on Russell-Chamberlain relationship comes from *Sports Illustrated: Classic Rivalries.*

Chapter 9

Overview of Boston comes from *Lost Summer,* by Bill Reynolds.

Overview of Red Sox history comes from *Lost Summer,* by Bill Reynolds.

Russell Rules and *Second Wind,* both by Bill Russell, on his relationship
with Celtics teammates in general, and Cousy in particular.

Background on Elgin Baylor comes from "Life with Elgin Baylor" from
the March 1963 issue of *Sport.*

Background on Oscar Robertson comes from *The Big O,* by Oscar Robertson, and *The Greatest Season 1964,* by Ira Berkow.

Anecdote from Earl Strom comes from *Calling the Shots,* by Earl Strom,
with Blaine Johnson.

Anecdote from Lenny Wilkens comes from *Unguarded,* by Lenny
Wilkens.

Chapter 10

Background on John Havlicek comes from *Hondo: Celtics Man in Motion,*
by John Havlicek and Bob Ryan.

Much of the detail of the sixth game between the Celtics and Lakers
comes from *The Last Loud Roar,* by Bob Cousy and Ed Linn.

Chapter 11

The Killer Instinct, by Bob Cousy and John Devaney.

Bibliography

Aquila, Richard. *That Old Time Rock & Roll: A Chronicle of an Era 1954–63*. New York: Schirmer Books. A division of Macmillan, Inc., 1989.

Araton, Harvey, and Filip Bondy. *The Selling of the Green: The Financial Rise and Moral Decline of the Boston Celtics*. New York: HarperCollins, 1997.

Auerbach, Arnold "Red," and Joe Fitzgerald. *Red Auerbach: An Autobiography*. New York: G. P. Putnam's Sons, 1977.

Auerbach, Red, with Ken Dooley. *MBA Management by Auerbach: Management Tips from the Leader of One of America's Most Successful Organizations*. New York: A Wellington Press Book, Macmillan Publishing Company, 1991.

Behrman, S. N. *The Worcester Account*. Worcester: Tatnuck Booksellers Press, 1996.

Berkow, Ira. *Oscar Robertson: The Golden Year 1964*. Englewood Cliffs, N.J.: Prentice-Hall, Inc., 1971.

Bjarkman, Peter C. *Boston Celtics Encyclopedia*. Sports Publishing L.L.C., 2002.

Carey, Mike, with Jamie Most. *High Above Courtside: The Lost Memoirs of Johnny Most*. Chicago: Sports Publishing, 2003.

Chamberlain, Wilt. *A View from Above*. New York: Villard Books, 1991.

Chamberlain, Wilt, with David Shaw. *Wilt: Just Like Any Other 7-Foot Black Millionaire Who Lives Next Door*. New York: Macmillan Publishing Co., 1973.

Cohen, Stanley. *The Game They Played*. New York: Farrar, Straus and Giroux, 1977.

Cousy, Bob, with John Devaney. *The Killer Instinct*. New York: Random House, 1975.

Cousy, Bob, with Al Hirshberg. *Basketball Is My Life*. Englewood Cliffs, N.J.: Prentice-Hall, Inc., 1957.

Cousy, Bob, with Edward Linn. *The Last Loud Roar*. Englewood Cliffs, N.J.: Prentice-Hall, Inc., 1964.

Cousy, Bob, with Bob Ryan. *Cousy on the Celtics' Mystique*. New York: McGraw-Hill, 1988.

Fitzgerald, Joe. *That Championship Feeling: The Story of the Boston Celtics.* New York: Charles Scribner's Sons, 1975.

Gowdy, Curt, with John Powers. *Seasons to Remember: The Way It Was in American Sport from 1954–1961.* New York: HarperCollins, 1993.

Greenfield, Jeff. *The World's Greatest Team: A Portrait of the Boston Celtics. 1957–69.* New York: A Sport Magazine Book, Random House, 1976.

Halberstam, David. *The Fifties.* New York: Fawcett Columbine, 1993.

Havlicek, John, and Bob Ryan. *Hondo: Celtic Man in Motion.* Englewood Cliffs, N.J.: Prentice-Hall, Inc., 1977.

Heinsohn, Tommy, and Joe Fitzgerald. *Give 'Em the Hook.* New York: Prentice-Hall Press, 1988.

Heinsohn, Tommy, with Leonard Lewin. *Heinsohn, Don't You Ever Smile?* Garden City, N.Y.: Doubleday and Company, 1976.

Koppett, Leonard. *24 Seconds to Shoot: The Birth and Improbable Rise of the NBA.* Kingston, N.Y.: Total Sports Illustrated Classics, 1968.

Lynch, Wayne. *Season of the 76ers.* New York: St. Martin's Press, 2002.

Moran, Joseph Declan. *You Can Call Me Al: The Colorful Journey of College Basketball's Original Flower Child, Al McGuire.* Madison, Wis.: Prairie Oak Press, 2000.

The Official NBA Encyclopedia. New York: Doubleday, a division of Random House, 2000.

Pluto, Terry. *Tall Tales: The Glory Years of the NBA, in the Words of the Men Who Coached, and Built Professional Basketball.* New York: Simon & Schuster, 1992.

Robertson, Oscar. *The Big O: My Life, My Times, My Game.* New York: Rodale, 2003.

Rosen, Charles. *Scandals of '51.* New York: Holt, Rinehart, and Winston, 1978.

——— *The Wizard of Odds.* New York: Seven Stories Press, 2001.

Russell, Bill. *Second Wind: The Memoirs of an Opinionated Man.* New York: Simon & Schuster, 1979.

Russell, Bill, as told to William McSweeney. *Go Up for Glory.* New York: Coward-McCann, 1966.

Ryan, Bob, and Dick Raphael. *The Boston Celtics: The History, Legends, and Images of America's Most Celebrated Team.* Reading, Mass.: Addison-Wesley, 1989.

Salzberg, Charles. *From Set Shot to Slam Dunk: The Glory Days of Basketball in the Words of Those Who Played It.* New York: E. P. Dutton, 1987.

Shaughnessy, Dan. *Ever Green: The Boston Celtics.* New York: St. Martin's Press, 1990.

——— *Seeing Red.* New York: Crown Publishers, Inc., 1994.

Southwick, Albert B. *150 Years of Worcester.* Worcester, Mass.: Chandler
     Park Press, 1998.
Strom, Earl, with Blaine Johnson. *Calling the Shots: My Five Decades in the
     NBA.* New York: Simon & Schuster, 1990.
Sullivan, George. *The Picture History of the Boston Celtics.* Indianapolis:
     The Bobbs-Merrill Company, Inc., 1981.
Thomas, Ron. *They Cleared the Lane: The NBA's Black Pioneers.* Lincoln
     and London: University of Nebraska Press, 2002.
Wilkens, Lenny. *Unguarded: My 40 Years Surviving in the NBA.* New York:
     Simon & Schuster, 2000.

Boston Globe, April 14, 1957.
Providence Journal, March 18, 1963.
50th anniversary program of the 1947 Holy Cross national champions.

Sports Illustrated, December 9, 1957.
Sports Ilustrated, January 16, 1961.
Sports Illustrated, December 23, 1968.
Sports Illustrated, August 4, 1969.
Sports Illustrated: Classic Rivalries, 2003.
Sport, January 1949 issue.
Sport, January 1951 issue.
Sport, January 1957 issue.
Sport, March 1960 issue.
Sport, November 1961 issue.
Sport, March 1963 issue.
Sport, April 1964 issue.
Sport, March 1966 issue.
Sport, April 1967 issue.
Sport, August 1967 issue.
Sport, December 1986. "The 40 Who Changed Sports."

Basketball—1950, published by Dell Publishing Co.

Acknowledgments

I am just old enough to remember Cousy in his prime, coming of age in the late fifties when the Celtics were the best team in the world. I was a kid then, in the beginning phases of a lifelong obsession with basketball, and growing up in Rhode Island, with the Celtics only 50 miles away, I have vivid memories of both the team and the era. I long had wanted to write about the NBA of the fifties, but it wasn't until a few years ago that I decided I wanted to use Cousy as the one thread through the era, for the simple reason that I believed that, in many ways, he had been taken for granted, becoming just another one of the ex-Celtic greats, when he once had been so much more than that.

But how to to go about that?

I didn't really know Cousy, and had heard he was both wary of people he didn't know and protective of both his time and his privacy.

So this might not have ever happened, if not for a conversation with Dan Doyle, the head of the Institute for International Sport at the University of Rhode Island in summer 2001. Doyle had grown up in Worcester, Massachusetts, and had attended Cousy's basketball camp as a kid. He was immediately intrigued with the idea and served as the conduit for my first meeting with Cousy about this project.

As did Dee Rowe, who once had coached me at Worcester Academy, and is a longtime friend of Cousy's.

Would this book have happened without their support?

Maybe not.

In retrospect, the genesis for this book also benefited from my longtime friendship with the late Joe Mullaney, the former Providence College basketball coach who had been a teammate of Cousy's at Holy Cross. Joe often told stories of those Holy Cross years, how improbable they had been. Although Mullaney died before I began this book, I heard his voice in my head while writing about Cousy's Holy Cross days, and am grateful to have had the chance to write about a certain time that Mullaney held in such reverence.

David Vigliano, my agent for 17 years now, believed in this from the beginning, and Mike Harriot, at the Vigliano Agency, shepherded this project through the process. Kevin Smith, my editor at Simon & Schuster, was always encouraging, and his suggestions, insight, and knowledge of basketball history shaped the book and made it better.

A book is a long process, and in many ways it's a collaborative one.

I talked with many people along the way, both for their memories and for their insight into both Cousy and the era. They all have my thanks. And I have a special debt to Cousy's wife, Missie, and his daughters, Marie and Ticia.

I also was aided, in a variety of ways, by the following: Larry Napolitano, the sports information director at Holy Cross; Jeff Twiss of the Boston Celtics; John Gearan, the former sports columnist at the *Worcester Telegram,* who might have as much insight into Cousy as anyone; Art Martone, my boss at the *Providence Journal,* who, in the tradition of great point guards, always makes the people around him better; Bill Troberman and Ken Hamwey, two colleagues at the *Journal* who were of great help with this project; Lenny Megliola and Bob Ryan, two talented commentators on the Boston sports scene; and my old Worcester Academy teammate Steve Adelman, who played for Cousy at Boston College.

And, always, to Lizzy, for her encouragement and emotional support.

Index

About the Author

BILL REYNOLDS, a sports columnist for the *Providence Journal,* is the author of several books, including *Fall River Dreams* and the memoir *Glory Days,* and coauthor of Rick Pitino's *Success Is a Choice,* a *New York Times* best-seller.

WITHDRAWN

796.323
Rey

Reynolds: Cousy.

2/05

NEWTOWN PUBLIC LIBRARY
201 BISHOP HOLLOW ROAD
NEWTOWN SQUARE, PA 19073